the great

FACTS ON FILE PUBLICATIONS
460 Park Avenue South
New York, NY 10016

symphonies

Edited by
Clive Unger-Hamilton

Contributors:
Janny de Jong
Clive Unger-Hamilton
Neil Fairbairn
Jan Taat
Derek Walters

Copyright© 1983 by Marix Evans & Chilvers SA/Uniepers bv
1099 Peney-le-Jorat, Switzerland

THIS IS A MARIX EVANS & CHILVERS/UNIEPERS BOOK

From an idea by MARTIN MARIX EVANS and MARINUS VAN RAALTE
Editorial direction: Tim Chilvers and Annelies Bouma
Design and production: Uniepers bv, Amsterdam
Translation: Rollin Cochrane

Illustrations: Fabbri, Milan; Phonogram International Baarn;
A₃-Studio; Michael Evans, London; EMI-records Holland, Heemstede;
Polydor, Hilversum; CBS, Haarlem; RCA, Hilversum; 'Luister',
Amersfoort; AVRO, Hilversum
Werner Neumeister; Bibliothèque Nationale, Paris;
Bildarchiv der Österreichische Nationalbibliothek;
Nationalbibliothek, Berlin; Wiener Stadtbibliothek

Printed and bound in The Netherlands by
Groen IJmuiden bv, IJmuiden; Callenbach bv, Nijkerk

First published in the United States in 1983 by
Facts on File, Inc.
460 Park Avenue South,
New York, N.Y. 10016

Library of Congress Cataloging in Publication Data

Unger-Hamilton, Clive
Great symphonies

Includes index.
1. Symphonies-History and criticism. 2. Symphony.
I. Jong, Janny de. II. Title.

ML1255.U55 1983 785.1'1'09 83-1493
ISBN 0-87196-549-6

Printed in THE NETHERLANDS

Contents

Composers

Conductors

Orchestras

Berlioz conducting characteristically massive forces in the hall of the Cirque - Olympique, Paris.

Introduction

The Great Symphonies, like Caesar's Gaul, is divided into three parts. Its purpose is to help you find out more about the music you know, and to explain and assist understanding of music that is unfamiliar. Its range is the entire symphonic repertoire from the eighteenth century up to our own time, including in-depth analysis of some masterworks along the way. Though it is to be hoped that the information set out is detailed and comprehensive, it has been editorial policy throughout not to presuppose any technical knowledge of music on the part of the reader. Nothing is more boring, and ultimately meaningless, than the kind of prose that attempts to be a substitute for the sound of the music itself. Part One of *The Great Symphonies* describes how symphonic form came into being, how it developed, and how the arts of orchestration and conducting evolved along with it. The symphony is essentially public music, and as such only became common property when concert halls were built for their performance. Accordingly the social history of orchestral performance is also an important part of the symphony's development.

Part Two deals with the composers and their works, divided into chapters. Its aim is to set an examination of all the great symphonies (and a good many of the not-so-great) against a background of the men who wrote them and, where the question can be answered, why they were written.

The last part of *The Great Symphonies* consists of brief biographies of the conductors and orchestras that we can hear today, on record, on radio or in the concert hall. What makes one conductor's interpretation different from another, their styles and repertoires are the most important features here. Following on this is a select and varied discography of the great symphonies, with recommended performances.

Clive Unger-Hamilton

Andre Previn

1

The origins of the symphony

An orchestral concert *c* 1830.

The classical symphony was a product of the mid-eighteenth century, the age of elegance, but its origins extend much further back in time. Two hundred years before then, before the introduction of major and minor keys, a perpetual problem for composers of instrumental music was how to 'go on', how to write an extended work that would not become boring to listen to.

Most of the orchestral music heard today comes from the repertoire of the eighteenth and nineteenth centuries, when a satisfactory system of keys and key relationships was well established – and ever enlarging. Before this structure had evolved, music was generally restricted to staying in one key throughout, with the result that any piece much longer than five minutes' duration could become extremely monotonous to the ear, particularly in instrumental music, which lacks words to help sustain the interest and divert attention from the paucity of modulation (key-changing) available. This is why Elizabethan music, for example, relies heavily on such forms as short pairs of dances, or sets of variations on popular songs such as William Byrd's *The Carman's Whistle* for example.

The paired dances, one slow (Pavane) in duple or quadruple time and one much livelier (Galliard) in triple time, evolved in the seventeenth century into the suite, itself an ancestor of the sonata and the symphony. The suite form is basically two sets of paired dances linked together by a common key: Allemande (moderately slow), Courante (fast), Sarabande (slow) and Gigue (fast). If a suite needed to be longer, extra dance movements such as a Minuet, Gavotte or Bourrée could be interpolated, or there might be a free, rhapsodic Prelude at the beginning. From the suite – generally a keyboard medium – and alongside it, grew orchestral overtures, concertos and sinfonias.

These again would have separate contrasting sections, three or four in number, and more extended as composers discovered how to modulate through other keys and return to close in the original one. In the first half of the eighteenth century, both Bach and Handel (particularly the latter) wrote fairly extended orchestral works this way. Bach's Brandenburg Concertos are probably the best-known examples, though not completely typical since they feature solo instruments in opposition to the body of the orchestra. Orchestral forces in this period, the late Baroque, were fairly small, with rarely more than a dozen string players and such woodwind – a pair of oboes, for example – as was available or necessary. (Woodwind, incidentally, was always popular for performance outdoors, since its sound carried much better than that of the strings.) The ensemble would be supported by a harpsichord, whose function was to keep the players together, cue in the players' entrances and fill out the supporting performances. These 'continuo' harpsichordists fulfilled the role of conductor, and frequently the composer himself would direct performances of his music from the keyboard. But then, as now, the four-part string section (first and second violins, violas and cellos, equivalent to the four parts of a choir: treble, alto, tenor and bass) formed the main body of the orchestra; other, more exotic sounds such as trumpets, trombones or percussion were used for special effects and found their way into the symphony orchestra from their use in the opera house.

As Bach's sons (three of them composers) discovered, little more could be done with the complex intricacies of counterpoint than their father – the supreme master of the art – had achieved. Accordingly they set out to evolve a simpler and more natural approach to composition that relied less on such learned devices as fugue and canon, and used a more straightforward, direct and less elaborate approach.
They and their contemporaries used

instead themes that were readily identifiable and short, contrasted with others and pursuing a relatively constant and predictable series of key progressions that came to be known as 'sonata form' and enabled their music to 'go on', as we said earlier, without tiring the ear.
At this point matters become more complicated, for the term 'sonata form' has two separate meanings: as well as referring to the structure of a movement (particularly the first and most important movement, hence the occasional use of 'first movement form' for this meaning), 'sonata form' also embraces the structure and arrangement of the movements within the entire work. It must also be stressed that, in the Classical era at least, the structure of a symphony, string quartet or sonata is fundamentally the same: a symphony is a sonata for orchestra, and a string quartet is in symphonic form but written for four solo instruments alone.
The first movement is generally the most extended, sometimes with a slow introduction, and most commonly with two contrasted themes or 'subjects'. The second movement is usually the slow one (though it may change places with the third), and is followed by a dance movement. This, in triple time, is a Minuet – later evolved by Beethoven into the scherzo. Designed to let a little air into a listening experience that could become a little overpowering, the Minuet (or scherzo) is in form a dance-within-a-dance. The first dance, in two halves – each repeated – is followed by a Trio. This trio, again in two repeated halves and sometimes given to wind instruments alone, is succeeded by a reprise of the original minuet but this time without the repeats. To listen to, this form (known sometimes as A-B-A) is much less complicated than a description seems on paper. Haydn in particular has a lot of fun in the minuets of his symphonies, trying to throw the listener off balance, as it were, and make him lose count of the familiar one-two-three one-two-three rhythm of the dance.
The last movement is usually the lightest of all. It may be in 'first-movement form', it may be a set of variations (the finale of Beethoven's Eroica symphony, for example), or it may be a rondo. Rondo form, explained in textbooks as A-B-A-C-A-D-A etc, is at its simplest a tune whose repetitions are separated by contrasted episodes in contrasting keys. The last movement of Mozart's Eine Kleine Nachtmusik is a well-known rondo. Other, more elaborate, rondos use two themes

Wagenseil

The early Austrian symphonist Georg Wagenseil (1715–77) worked for nearly all his life as a musician at the imperial Austrian court. He made early successes as a composer of operas in the Italian style, and many of his (about thirty) symphonies were made up of material drawn from the overtures to these works. Though this music shows a ready command of the new musical form, and has often a sophisticated rhythmic propulsion, the melodies tend towards the commonplace and are not helped by rather unimaginative orchestration. But his fame was widespread: it is reported that the six-year-old Mozart, on tour at the Viennese court, asked to see Wagenseil. When the composer was brought before him, the little boy announced 'I am going to play a concerto of yours, you must turn the pages for me'.

Arne and Boyce

In the rarefied native musical climate of the English eighteenth century, there were but two composers of any lasting distinction: Thomas Arne and William Boyce (1710–79). Arne worked primarily in the theatre while Boyce's career was much more synoptic, embracing chuch and instrumental music, masques and stage pieces (from one of which comes his famous song Heart of Oak**), and eight symphonies. These were published in London around 1750 and have a refreshing and vigorous brilliance that has won them a lot of favour with present-day audiences. Perhaps Boyce's most significant work, however, was a large collection he assembled and edited of English cathedral music from the sixteenth and seventeenth centuries.**

with contrasting episodes in between; and since such a shape resembles first-movement form, they are sometimes called 'sonata-rondos'.

The contents and relationships of these four movements are the very essence of musical thought during the period known as the Classical era, and a familiarity with this generalized outline of the structure will give the listener a rough idea of what he may reasonably expect to happen when listening to a symphony, sonata or string quartet by, say, Mozart or Haydn. Next we must look at the sonata form more closely, to see how a typical first movement is made up.

As stated earlier, the form is not one imposed upon the music by composers, but evolved as a convention to enable a piece to be of some substance and length without becoming tiring to the ear. Its origins are to be found in the more truncated binary music of the baroque period, exemplified by the short, one-movement, keyboard 'sonatas' of Domenico Scarlatti (1685–1757) and by the dance movements in the suites and preludes of J.S. Bach (1685–1750). Each of these pieces, though only an average of three minutes' duration, clearly divides into two halves, each repeated, with the first half

The famous Neapolitan opera composer Alessandro Scarlatti (1660-1725) wrote a set of 12 *Sinfonie* as early as 1715.

coming to a close in a different key from its opening and with the second half leading the music back to end in the original key. Sometimes the resemblances to classical first-movement form are even closer, displaying in microcosm the identifiable landmarks of symphonic first-movement shape, which depends on a final, more or less full restatement of all the opening material contained in the first half after a free discussion of some of those themes has taken place at the beginning of part two. This of course unbalances part two, which now has to contain all the weight of the development as well as a restatement of what happened in part one. But discussion of themes can be fairly rudimentary, and doesn't have to make the music much longer: a familiar piece in typical first-movement form is the overture to Mozart's *The Marriage of Figaro,* a mature work from the middle of the Classical period, which lasts in its entirety – as an observer once remarked – for the exact time required to boil an egg.

After an optional slow introduction, which composers sometimes feel necessary to call the listeners' attention to what is about to take place, just as a drum roll at the circus announces that the tamer's head is about to enter the lion's mouth, the movement begins with a theme (its 'first theme', often coldly referred to as 'first subject' in books on musical theory) which will be in the home key (called the 'tonic') of the piece, to fix the music with a tonality and give it somewhere to come back to. The first theme will also be plainly identifiable to the ear, for if it is to be discussed later during the development section, it is essential that we shall be able to recall the speaker's original argument. For this reason too, the theme is often repeated more than once (perhaps, for variety, on different instruments) and is frequently too short to be called a 'tune'.

When statements of the first theme are complete the music moves away to another, closely related, key for its second theme. This, to provide contrast to the usually terse opening material, tends to be of a more lyrical and extended nature and may consist of not just one, but two or even three, linked tunes of generally more whistleable character; and the first half closes in the new key with a series of cadence-figures (the coda) at what musicians know as a 'double bar', which is a sign that they must go back to the beginning and repeat the entire section over again (though omitting the slow introduction, if there has been one).

A portrait of Johann Christian Bach by Thomas Gainsborough, painted during the composer's residence in London. Johann Christian, one of the three great sons of J.S. Bach, was nicknamed the 'London' Bach from his long stay in the capital, which lasted from 1762 until his death twenty years later. His music was an important influence on the young Mozart.

J. C. Bach

Johann Christian Bach (1735–82) was the youngest son of Sebastian's second marriage, to Anna Magdalena. He studied music first with his elder brother, Carl Philipp Emanuel, and later with Martini in Italy. At the age of 27 he moved to England as music master to the wife of King George III, hence his nickname of the 'London' Bach. He remained there for the rest of his life, writing operas, keyboard concertos, chamber music and about fifty symphonies. He is remembered today, however, as a friend of – and a profound influence upon – the boy Mozart during his stay in London, who modelled many of his earliest works upon those of the older master and began himself to write symphonies after he became acquainted with those of Johann Christian.

Sammartini

Giovanni Battista Sammartini (c1700–75) was the younger of two musician-brothers from Milan (where Giovanni remained for virtually all his working life). Though he was employed primarily as an organist, he is remembered now for his early works in symphonic form, which antedate those of Haydn by as much as twenty years. These brought him a lot of attention, though the music today seems rather nugatory and insubstantial; and its relevance rests mainly in the obvious link it provides between the Italian Overture style of Vivaldi and his contemporaries, and the early symphonic style of the young Mozart. Sammartini was an extraordinarily prolific, incidentally, with about 2000 compositions to his credit.

Antonio Stradivari *above* in his workshop at Cremona, famous by the end of the seventeenth century for the skill of its stringed instrument makers. There are many Stradivari instruments still in circulation in the great orchestras of the world; some estimates claim he may have made as many as 3000 during his long life (1644-1737), all prized for their masterly craftsmanship and inimitable tone.

Gossec

In the mid-eighteenth century, Paris was an important centre of symphonic composition, and in the forefront of the new form's apologists was François Joseph Gossec (1734–1829). Born the son of a peasant in what is now Belgium, his musical gifts materialized early, and he was sent to Paris with a letter of introduction to the great Rameau. With such an invaluable master and helper, and with his own outstanding gifts, Gossec's career flourished in a most gratifying way. He succeeded Rameau as leader and conductor of an important Paris orchestra, and established a reputation as an outstanding musical innovator. His thirty symphonies have passages of tenderness and passion that recall the music of Haydn's 'Sturm und Drang' period to mind, particularly in the slow movements. Of all the lesser-known eighteenth-century symphonists, it is perhaps Gossec whose music is most unjustly neglected today.

The 'exposition' having been played twice, to fix its material in the listener's mind, the music is now set to embark on its second (development) section. Here there are no rules: the composer most frequently makes use of his first theme to a substantial degree, perhaps even starting a fugue with it. He may ignore his second theme altogether and introduce fresh material entirely at his fancy. New and distant keys are explored. All we can be sure of is that when the development comes to an end the music will have been led back to the home key, ready for another restatement of the opening section – part three: the 'recapitulation'.

Though there may be a number of differences between this restatement and the original exposition, one is of especial importance. This lies in the preparation of the music now for its second theme(s), so that it takes place not this time in any new key but in the tonic, so that the movement can close in the key that it began. The final coda, too, may be more extended as further proof of the music's imminent end (Beethoven's coda for the first movement of the *Eroica symphony* is 140 bars long). These few facts are quite sufficient for any listener to follow, and identify the landmarks in, a straightforward first movement in sonata form. Though it has been outlined in little more than five hundred words, it will always stubbornly remain more confusing to read about than to hear. One's ear will quite readily pick out certain points of reference along the way.

The double bar at the end of the exposition is usually the easiest to spot – particularly the second time it comes round. Great masters of the form such as Haydn, Mozart and Beethoven found it a marvellously malleable mould for their ideas: about three-quarters of the latter's entire output depends upon just this structural medium for its shape. This is not to say that Beethoven composed mostly first movements and left everything unfinished, for slow movements and finales can just as easily utilize this compact and satisfying ternary shape.

In fact, by the time Beethoven had finished with the form, after nine symphonies, sixteen string quartets and thirty-two piano sonatas, it is hardly surprising that composers after him felt more than a little daunted by his achievements within it. Conformity with a pattern failed to meet the needs of the Romantic age that followed Beethoven, and the formal approach that had governed the construction of symphonic movements became less easy to identify, if indeed it was present at all. But the four-movement structure endured much longer in the works of some musicians, as we shall see.

The Count Unico Willem van Wassenaer *left* may have been another composer of the earliest symphonies, for long wrongly attributed to the young Giovanni Battista Pergolesi (1710-36).

A caricature by Grandville of Berlioz entitled, aptly enough, 'Concert with Cannon'.

F. Chaparier del.   Laurens sculp 1806.

Joseph Hayd'n

Haydn and Mozart

Joseph Haydn

'The Father of the Symphony'. This well-known axiom needs careful qualification, for Haydn was by no means the first composer to write a symphony. That honour belongs to any one of a number of much less well-known composers; either in Italy, such as Galuppi or Sammartini, or else at the court of Mannheim in southern Germany such as Monn, Wagenseil or Stamitz, and the truth is by no means established. But Haydn was the first composer of great symphonies, and he fathered more than one hundred of them. (In addition, incidentally, he wrote eighty-three string quartets, over fifty piano sonatas, more than twenty operas and at least 125 full-length works for baryton, a now obsolete cello-like instrument favoured by his employer, Prince Nicolaus Esterházy. Small wonder that most of his output remains unknown today.) Haydn was beginning to write symphonies when Mozart was born and he was still writing them after Mozart was dead. The magnificence of his works in this genre established the symphony as the leading orchestral form of his day and, indirectly, of all succeeding generations. He was first to see the apparently limitless variety of which the symphony was capable, and he brought to it an entire world of human emotions: from rough, knockabout comedy and the more elegant wit of the drawing-room, through intense passion to profound sorrow. In this sense is Haydn the father of the symphony. He forged its template.

He also brought to it an extra movement, the minuet, not the mincing progressions of an effete nobility across the ballroom floor but a virile country dance that reveals his own peasant origins. He delights in imitating the squawling bagpipes and clodhopping rhythms of the village green, and loves to play tricks upon the listener's ear, throwing the music off beat as if the revellers had lost their way in the steps of the dance. By the time he was in his early twenties, with a few minor successes to his credit, Haydn was beginning to compose chamber music, mostly for string quartet with the occasional addition of horns or oboes, and by applying the styles he had learned from his studies of the younger Bach's keyboard music, evolved his own form of symphonic music – and also the classical string quartet. To begin with, there was little difference between the two, and it is often hard to say whether an early symphony with merely a few instruments is really a divertimento or serenade, or whether a string quartet with a couple of extra wind parts forms a rudimentary symphony. Ultimately, it does not matter. At Esterháza, however, the differences became much more clear cut when Haydn found himself with substantial orchestral forces at his command. Of his string quartet writing, incidentally, the great German poet Goethe remarked that 'One listens to four intelligent people conversing with each other; one expects to gain from their discourse and to learn to know the peculiarities of the instruments'.

Haydn

Joseph Haydn (1732–1809) stands alone among the great composers in being virtually self-taught. His father was an impoverished country wheelwright with twelve children to feed: of his family, incidentally, Joseph's younger brother Michael also became a composer. As a small boy, Joseph's sweet voice and ready ear brought him to the attention of a music-loving relative, and at the age of eight he was placed in the choir-school of St Stephen's cathedral in Vienna. Here, though he learned to play the violin and keyboard and to sing, there was no formal instruction in harmony, counterpoint or composition. Being forced to leave when his voice broke and having no funds to pursue his studies, with borrowed money he bought an old clavichord and rented an attic room where he continued to practise the violin and, more importantly, studied the keyboard sonatas of C.P.E. Bach. Taking the latter's revolutionary, non-contrapuntal style as his model, Haydn set to work to make himself master of the new 'galant' music. He also met the composer Porpora, whose servant he became in exchange for some grudging instruction in composition.

His first appointment, as musician in the house of a wealthy countess, came as the result of an early keyboard sonata he had written, and was soon followed by another job as music director to Count Morzin. This nobleman maintained his own band, which gave Haydn invaluable experience in composing for wind instruments – the opportunity for him in being able to write something for small orchestra and then to have it played through whenever he needed, cannot be over-estimated – and it was soon apparent that he was gaining a unique mastery of the new art of orchestration. Two years later, in 1761, Haydn was taken up by the reigning prince of a great Austrian house, who had been impressed by the quality of the music when on a visit to Count Morzin. The Esterházys were a fabulously wealthy family, and the prince installed the young musician at his immense palace in the remote countryside of north-eastern Austria (now part of Hungary) where he maintained a substantial orchestra, a private theatre, and chorus and soloists to go with it. The next thirty years of the composer's life were spent here, in a happy fever of creativity. The one blot on the horizon was Haydn's wife: in 1760 he had married the elder sister of a girl who had taken holy orders – and with whom he had been deeply in love. His wife seems to have set out to make the composer's life a misery. They had no children, and after some years lived the rest of their lives apart.

It was at Esterháza that nearly all his symphonies were composed and first performed, and as his fame spread through the visits to his employer of royalty and nobility, he became the most prized member of the Prince's household. And there he might have remained, but when in 1790 Prince Nicolaus died, his successor disbanded most of the musical establishment, and Haydn was pensioned off – not without a suitably princely annuity.

Now he was in a position to take up a handsome offer that had been made to him by a London concert promoter called Salomon: namely, to visit England and there conduct six new symphonies he should write for the occasion. The visit, in 1791–92, was so successful that it was repeated two years later with six more symphonies, making up the twelve that are known today as the 'London' set. So magnificent was Haydn's welcome in England that it is conceivable he might have stayed, but the new Prince Esterházy summoned him back with more work to do. He returned to settle at Esterháza for the summer seasons and for the rest lived in Vienna, by now financially independent for the rest of his life.

After this there were no more symphonies. In his final active years Haydn wrote chamber music, his two oratorios The Creation and The Seasons, a wonderful succession of Masses for his patron – and his country's national anthem, the sublime Austrian Hymn, inspired by the impression made upon him by God Save the King on his visits to England. A few days before his death, on 31 May 1809, while the French were bombarding the gates of Vienna, he asked his servants to carry him to the piano where they heard him play this beloved and solemn melody.

The nickname of 'Papa' that was often applied to Haydn was not given to him for his parentage of the symphony: it was a mark of the respect and genuine love that he inspired in those who were privileged to know him. The young Mozart, twenty-four years Haydn's junior, was an especially dear friend although the latter's demanding employer prevented any frequent personal intimacy between the two. Of his confinement in a remote corner of the Austrian Empire, Haydn observed in later years in reply to being asked how he had acquired his unique genius: 'I lived cut off from the world … and I was forced to become original'. For all his fame and fortune he never lost the qualities of honesty, modesty and devotion that endeared him to so many of his peers. It was after a private performance of one of Mozart's string quartets (in which Haydn, Mozart and Mozart's father had taken part) that he made his celebrated remark to Leopold Mozart which seems to sum up his marvellous personality: 'Before God, and as an honest man, I tell you that your son is the greatest composer I have ever heard, or ever heard of'. Even the young Beethoven, to whom Haydn gave some rather unsuccessful lessons between his two visits to London, regarded his master with veneration – though at the time the truculent young genius, nicknamed by Haydn 'The Grand Mogul', had little patience with his teacher's careful methods. Haydn never forgot the good fortune that his genius and his environment had brought him: his manuscripts often ended with the words 'Laus Deo' as if in thanks for his happy and creative life.

He was successful with the opposite sex, as well. Separated from his termagant wife, Haydn captured many hearts, not least in England though already in his sixtieth year on his first visit there. This cannot be due to his appearance, which seems to have been singularly unprepossessing: though formal in manner and fastidious in dress, his plain, good-humoured face was permanently scarred in later life with the legacy of smallpox and by an unsightly growth on his nose, and he habitually referred to himself as an ugly man.

Though his symphonies were taken most enthusiastically to heart by audiences all over Europe and have remained his best-loved works for succeeding generations, Haydn seems to have favoured his operas and other vocal works beyond these, often seeing his purely orchestral compositions as occasional music of greater or less distinction Posterity seems right: each one of his 104 listed symphonies is of a gemlike brilliance, possessed of its own marvels. There will be no room here to analyse every one, and such a lengthy sermon would anyway bring the starry delights of this music down to earth with a bump. Besides, by no means all of them are familiar pieces in recording catalogues today. Posterity has chosen to favour about two dozen of them for regular performance: some half-dozen from the composer's apprentice and middle years, and from his maturity the symphonies he wrote for the 'Concerts spirituels' in Paris and the final twelve composed for Salomon in London.

Accordingly it is these, with one or two additions and subtractions, that are best examined separately, with one written between the Paris and London sets – no. 88 in G major – that it will be illuminating to put under a close lens, see the works behind the face, and watch how he put a symphony together.

Haydn: The Early Symphonies

Haydn wrote his first symphonies for Count Morzin, in the period before he moved to the much larger musical establishment at Esterháza. But, as the lively and invigorating symphony no. 1 shows, from the beginning these were no works of a musical apprentice: Haydn was already an experienced and mature artist.

Though it is now uncertain what the precise specifications of Count Morzin's band were, the forces of Prince Esterházy's orchestra when Haydn moved there in 1761 were much larger. At his command were:

A performance of Haydn's oratorio *The Creation* in Vienna in 1808. Beethoven was present at this performance.

two each of flutes, oboes, bassoons and horns backed up by about fourteen strings, while trumpets and timpani (kettledrums) could also be made available from the Prince's military band. The best known of the early works are nos 6, 7 and 8, which bear the titles of *Le Matin, Le Midi* and *Le Soir*. Though not among Haydn's most daring experiments in symphonic form (in fact they have a decidedly archaic ring in places, reminding one of the old concerto grosso form), these little works have probably retained their popularity thanks to their charming nicknames. It is often hard to know whether Haydn's symphonies become favourites because of their nicknames, or whether it is only the favourite ones that are given them. The next well-known work in the canon is no. 22 in E flat, known as *The Philosopher*, though no-one now knows why. This symphony has an exceptionally beautiful and grave opening movement, and makes use of an unusual instrument, the cor anglais (a sort of tenor oboe). A less often played work is no. 28 in A, dating from 1765, the year after *The Philosopher*. Its buoyant opening movement has a teasing, rhythmically ambiguous main theme with which Haydn has a lot of fun. Also worthy of extra attention in this work is the whirling gypsy dance that forms its minuet. From the same year too is no. 31, whose brassy summons at the beginning (and which also reappears at the symphony's end) has earned it the nickname of the *Hornsignal*.

Sturm und Drang

Much of the music of Haydn's middle years is of a less extrovert cheerfulness than audiences expect of their genial 'Papa', and charged with a high, nervous tension. This has led it to be known as his 'Sturm und Drang' period, after the German literary movement (*Eng*: Storm and Stress) that deals with mighty conflicts between the forces of good and evil. Two works from this period are symphonies nos. 44 in E minor and 45 in F sharp minor, the first of these, subtitled *Trauersymphonie* has hectic, frenzied outer movements that are balanced around a slow movement of the uttermost serenity and loveliness. (At the end of his life, Haydn is said to have asked for this movement to be played at his funeral.) No. 45 is also a marvellously constructed 'Sturm & Drang' work

Boccherini

The paradox of the Italian composer Luigi Boccherini (1743–1805), is that though he must be one of the most prolific composers of all time, with 155 quintets, 102 string quartets, 25 symphonies, 60 trios and a great deal more besides, his fame rests almost exclusively on one trifling minuet from one of the string quintets. Like Domenico Scarlatti

LUIGI BOCCHERINI.
Geb. in Lucca den 14 Jan. 1743
Gest. in Madrid 1806

before him, Boccherini spent much of his mature life in Spain, and his music is often redolent with the haunting and passionate discords of the Iberian folk heritage. Harmonically his music is extremely advanced for its time: the composer was a widely travelled man with a powerful intellect ever alert to new influences. His lyrical themes, subtle orchestration and pointed wit are the hallmarks of a unique musical mind that is too often neglected today in favour of more traditional, mainstream fare.

in a minor key, whose fierce emotions have unfortunately been overshadowed by the story that gave it the name of the *Farewell symphony*. It was time, thought the musicians, that Prince Esterházy should leave his palace for a while and give them a break, so Haydn designed the finale of this work to give his royal highness a hint. One after another the instruments ceased playing, and the performers each blew out the candles that illuminated their music, and left their seats. At the work's close there are just two violins carolling softly (in the extraordinary key of F sharp major): all the rest are gone. It is reported that Prince Nicolaus took the hint.

Perhaps the most tragic symphony Haydn wrote also comes from these years: no. 49 in F minor, *La Passione*. Each of the work's movements is in the minor key, and the first movement is an adagio of surpassing sadness. But it was not in Haydn's nature to remain serious for too long, and he returned to music that was happier, though no less sublime. Symphony no. 60, *Il Distratto*, is a glorious work in C major that features trumpets in addition to the usual line-up, and has six movements. The title comes from a play given at Esterháza for which Haydn wrote the incidental music. It is one of his merriest inspirations, and draws heavily on the folk music that was so dear to the composer. Symphony no. 73 in D has an especially gleeful finale, that has given it its nickname *La Chasse*. This movement was originally the overture to a jolly (but overlong) pastoral that Haydn had written for the opera house the year before in 1780. Unfortunately the other movements seem rather lacklustre beside this gay and spirited ending.

The Paris Symphonies

In 1784 Haydn was commissioned by a music society in Paris to write six symphonies. He was to receive twenty-five 'louis d'or' for each of them, and a further five upon publication of each. This was a lot of money, and the composer must have set about his work with an extra alacrity. What we now know as nos 82–87 were first performed in Paris in the season of 1787, with a much larger orchestra than Haydn had at home. His music, particularly his symphonies, was famous in France, and these concerts were patronized by the royal family.

They are all masterpieces, especially with regard to the beauty and style of their woodwind parts. Haydn is quoted as having said in his old age: 'I have only just learned . . . how to use woodwind instruments, and now I do understand them I must leave the world.' From this set of works it would seem the composer was seriously underestimating the craftsmanship of his late middle years. No. 82, *The Bear*, in C major, probably derives its nickname from the rustic, lumbering finale – just the sort of music to accompany a dancing bear on the village green. This work also has a lovely, simple-sounding set of variations as its slow movement, that hovers between F major and F minor. No. 83 in G minor, *The Hen*, must have been given its subtitle by Parisian audiences when they heard the chuckling second theme of the first movement (played on the violins). The slow movement is a glorious extended melody for strings that is an exquisite miniature of sonata form, complete with repeat of the first half and a development section. No. 85 in B flat was voted her favourite by Queen Marie Antoinette, hence it quickly became dubbed *La Reine*. The high point of its first movement comes at the very end of the development, when the key change that brings the music back to the B flat tonic makes the moment one of Haydn's great surprises.

The well-known set of variations that is the slow movement has as its theme an old French song, *La gentille et jeune Lisette*. Great effect is had here with one of Haydn's favourite devices in his slow movements: the sudden fortissimo outburst by the whole orchestra, as though it were picking up the tune and shaking it – like Alice with her naughty kitten. It is followed by one of the composer's most delightful and undanceable minuets that sandwiches a heartfelt little trio for oboes and horns, and rounded off with a rondo that makes the listener want to dance for joy.

Between writing these brilliant works for Paris and his first visit to London, Haydn composed five more symphonies, two for a rather unscrupulous violinist in the Esterházy orchestra, Johann Tost, to sell in Paris (nos 88 & 89); and three for a German princeling (nos 90–92), which were also sent to the same nobleman in Paris who had commissioned the 'Paris' set on behalf of the concert society.

Symphony no. 88 in G major
This merry and marvellous work was written in 1787, between the six *Paris* symphonies and the composer's first visit to London. It has been suggested that the only reason for this symphony's being less well-known than most of the 'London' set is due to its lack of a catch-penny nickname: it is without doubt one of the golden fruits of Haydn's sunny maturity.
Adagio-Allegro. The work opens, typically, with a slow introduction that serves as a call-to-arms for what is to follow. It is made up of a mere sixteen bars, in 3/4 time, with the jerky rhythm that characterizes the earlier overtures of Handel and his contemporaries. Audiences, as Haydn well knew, were notoriously bad at settling down and lending their noble ears to what was, after all, the paid performance of a band of lackeys. So if (as is the case with this symphony) the work proper was to open with a quietly-stated theme – which here dominates the entire movement – their attention must be grabbed from the very outset, and

Dittersdorf

Karl Ditters von Dittersdorf (1739–99) wrote more symphonies than Joseph Haydn – about 150 in all. He became famous as a violinist in his early twenties, and toured Italy in the company of his friend Gluck. He was befriended by the noble but disgraced bishop of Breslau, and entered into the latter's employment. Much of his music was written for his patron's entertainment; including many operas and singspiele; these made him famous in Vienna, and were also responsible for his employer's elevating him to the nobility.

Apart from their quantity, Dittersdorf's symphonies are unusual in their often descriptive qualities: there is a set of twelve composed 'after the Metamorphoses of Ovid', another one 'in the style of five nations', and a symphony that describes the six humours, for example. Another attractive feature is his use, like Haydn, of folk tunes in his symphonies, though whether these are really traditional melodies or invented by Dittersdorf it is often impossible to say. He was also second violin in an occasional quartet in Vienna that met to play new works by its leader (Haydn) and viola player (Mozart).

The Empress Maria Theresa (in German, Theresia), after whom Haydn's symphony no. 48 was named when it was written for her visit to Prince Esterhàzy in 1773.

this baroque convention fulfilled the composer's needs admirably. Little need be said about the melodic content of the opening adagio: it hovers around the scale of G major and moves purposefully to settle on the chord of D major (known to theorists as the 'dominant', or most nearly related, key to the tonic).

For the allegro of the movement, the tempo changes to a fast two beats in a bar. The jaunty opening theme (and who could not call it a tune?) once over, is immediately repeated forte by the full orchestra, this time with a spirited little ten-note figure accompanying it in the bass that is to become as important in the movement as the theme itself, as the ensuing bars that lead to the second theme well show.

As if to stand convention on its head, it is Haydn's second theme for this movement that is, if anything, terse. Clearly derived from the symphony's first tune, it seems to function only as an establishing of the new, dominant, key of D, in which the music bustles to a noisy close, with the little accompanying figure from the beginning (reminiscent of the opening of Mozart's *Figaro* overture, composed the year before) elbowing its little way into the foreground.

After the repeat of the exposition, it is this same little motif that leads tentative statements of the main tune through a surprising number of remote keys abetted by an irrepressible figure of three repeated notes that are exposed in Haydn's development section for being the husk of the main tune – and of its little accompaniment too. When the first

The elegant lines of the palace of Schönbrunn, on the outskirts of Vienna, reflect the Classical forms of the music that was written for performance there.

Haydn's handwriting, in a letter written from Eisenstadt in his old age.

A concert in the Schönbrunn Palace near Vienna for the Austrian Imperial family (seated in the front row).

Salieri

Antonio Salieri (1750–1825) was a more successful composer in Classical Vienna than his rival, Mozart. He studied music in the Venetian Republic, and followed his teacher to Vienna. There he met the emperor, and probably as the result of a successful comic opera Le Donne Letterate was made court composer – and later Kapellmeister. Most of his compositions (which include two symphonies) are all but forgotten today. Salieri is remembered instead as a famous teacher – of Schubert and Beethoven, most notably – and also Cherubini and Liszt. The rumour that he poisoned Mozart out of jealousy at the younger man's superior powers is almost certainly untrue, though he seems to have suffered much calumny in his time, being suspected as well of poisoning the composer Cimarosa – and of doing away with Gluck too, by pushing him out of a carriage.

An eighteenth-century view of Salzburg, where Mozart was born in 1756.

theme returns for the final, recapitulation, section it is now accompanied in the high treble by some insolent whistling from the flute, and from then on the music chases its own tail through to a rousing finish.

Largo. The only solemn minutes of this symphony are contained in its short and sublime largo. The ardent, hymn-like theme is repeated seven times throughout the movement, with different counterpoints and varied orchestrations. Haydn knew better than anyone that there was no need at all to meddle with such a glorious melody. It is simply a calm, reflective 'time without war' from the hurrying world around it.

Menuetto & Trio: Allegretto. It would be hard to imagine anything further from the concept of a courtly minuet than this lurching waltz that reels through a tipsy fourteen bars before its first repeat. The second part, of thirty bars' duration, incorporates a restatement of the opening after getting lost in some very unlikely keys. The trio has a typical bagpipe-style drone bass supporting an insistent little melodic line that keeps trying to throw itself off the beat, as it were. After the trio, the minuet is played once again da capo – but without the repeats.

Finale: Allegro con spirito. The theme of this blithe and merry rondo is strongly reminiscent of the theme that dominates the symphony's first movement, with its pairs of repeated notes. The theme itself is quite long (with some alarming modulations inside it) and only makes three hilarious appearances in the movement's short duration. After the third time, a general pause in the music is the signal for a headlong, rushing coda that brings the symphony to an end.

No. 92 in G major, the *Oxford*, is likewise one of the composer's finest works. Its nickname derives from the fact that Haydn conducted a performance of it at the Sheldonian Theatre in Oxford when he was awarded an honorary doctorate of Music by the university. It has a wonderfully evocative slow introduction, followed by one of the most unorthodox sonata movements, whose cheeky second theme only comes to the fore at the very end of the piece. The slow movement, in D major, is an adagio set of variations with the familiar fortissimo outburst in the middle and a remarkable passage in the minor. The symphony's wild and unbuttoned minuet is countered by a soothing trio featuring the horns; and the rondo finale presents a glittering series of episodes between a light-hearted but curiously perverse theme. The entire work is Haydn at his most habit-forming.

The London Symphonies

The twelve symphonies that many find to be Haydn's crowning achievement were composed in two sets of six: the first (nos 93–98) for his first visit to London in 1791–92, and nos 99–104 for his second trip there in 1794–95. They were performed at the Hanover Square Rooms, with Haydn himself directing the orchestra from the pianoforte.

No. 93 in D major is a typically delightful work. The second theme of the first movement is the one that predominates in the music's development while the slow movement, a theme and variations, is full of surprises, by turns martial and affectionate. The trio of the minuet has endearing little phrases for woodwind that seem built on to the dance as an afterthought, and the symphony's finale is yet another irrepressible and magical rondo. The last movements of classical symphonies, so often their weakest link, are always with Haydn the moments to cherish and relish. The *Surprise* symphony (no. 94 in G major) must be one of the most famous in the entire symphonic repertoire. Its nickname derives from the loud explosion in the middle of the slow movement's theme, which is said to have been specifically written in by the composer to wake up audiences who always tended to nod off during slow movements. The work begins with a haunting slow introduction that moves eerily through distant keys. The ensuing allegro, in a cheerful, rocking rhythm, can hardly be said to boast a second theme for it is the opening motif that appears to take over most of the movement's fun and games. The andante and variations are too well-known to need much description. Suffice it to say that the composition of such a simple and artless tune is in itself a 'tour de force', a hallmark of genius that only Mozart and Schubert can seem to share with Haydn. Marvellous too is the symphony's finale, a sophisticated rondo whose fearsomely difficult violin writing must have needed lots of rehearsing to point up the music's muscle and wit.

Perhaps the loveliest feature of the next symphony, no. 95 in C minor, is the theme and variations it has for a slow movement, first stated by a solo cello. There is no slow introduction to the first movement, which is also distinguished by dramatic silences that punctuate the music's flow. The blithe, contrapuntal finale is in C major.

No. 96 in D major, is wrongly entitled the *Miracle*. Its name relates to an incident during a performance, when a chandelier fell in the auditorium during the slow movement and, miraculously, no-one was injured. But it seems that this happened during a later symphony, no. 102, on the composer's second London visit. The allegro first movement (hauntingly introduced by a descending little run on the oboe) is typically unorthodox, original, unique and entirely startling. The slow movement (in G major with a minor central section) has a cadenza just before the finish, as if it belonged to a concerto rather than a symphony.

No. 97 in C major is perhaps the least familiar of the twelve London symphonies, though it is difficult to see why. Its first movement is forthright, brilliant and powerful. A rhapsodic adagio contains unusual string sounds, where the performers are instructed to play with their bows much nearer the bridge (sul ponticello) than is customary, producing a thin and distinctive sonority. The trio of the minuet is one of the loveliest moments in the work, and the difficulties of the headlong finale must have given even the virtuoso London orchestra a very hard time.

Symphony no. 98 in B flat has, like the *Miracle* symphony, a cadenza, this time in the finale, and for piano – the autograph of the score is marked 'Haydn solo'. Another endearing feature in the work is the solo bassoon that takes over the trio of the minuet.

In the following work (chronologically the first of Haydn's second visit to England) clarinets make their debut in his orchestral line-up, and remain there for all the remaining symphonies save no. 102. No. 99 in E flat major's most wonderful feature is the central adagio, long and suffused with a sadness that we have not seen perhaps since *La Passione*. The minuet is dominated by the novelty of the clarinets that were, after all, relatively new arrivals on the musical scene, and the work concludes with another sublime and happy rondo.

The *Military symphony* (no. 100 in G major) shows every sign of having been written with English audiences in mind – and they loved it. Its name has come from the clashing percussion of the slow movement that is supposed to have been inspired by a military parade. After a poignant adagio introduction, Haydn opens the symphony proper with what sounds like a toy band: the first theme is played by solo flute and oboes alone. Neither is there any second subject, instead a repetition of the first theme in D (the dominant key). A second theme proper only appears well after the music has found its new key, and even for Haydn this proves to be one of the merriest little tunes ever written. Another theme and variations makes up the allegretto slow movement, full of surprises and at times hilarious when it tries to take itself too seriously. In contrast, the third movement is a fairly orthodox minuet, of an irresistably dancelike character. The finale is in first-movement form, though the tune that starts it leads us to expect a rondo. The latter work vies for pride of place in popularity with no. 101 in D major, known as the *Clock* from the tick-tock accompaniment to the tune of the slow movement. The work was premiered at London's Haymarket Theatre, and lost no time in becoming one of the audience's favourites. An unusual feature of the first movement is the way the

Mozart's wife, Constanze, bore the composer two sons that survived their father.

theme of the movement proper derives from material first presented in the slow introduction. Surprisingly, however, the jaunty first theme plays no part in the movement's development, which is taken over by the more pliable material of the second subject. As we have seen, what you can do with a tune is sometimes more relevant than what it merely sounds like. The well-loved andante of the slow movement is again in first-movement form, and succeeded by a bouncing minuet that contains a trio of matchles serenity. The last movement, marked vivace, is a perfect example of that art which conceals art, for within this rollicking, good-natured paperchase is contained the most complex fugal writing that supports the structure, without the listener ever becoming aware of it.

It is quite a claim to make that the symphony no. 102 (in B flat major) has the best slow movement of all, but it certainly seems like it. Haydn also thought very highly of it, for it was also used as the slow movement of a piano trio. The entire work is relatively short, though in no way deprived of material, and is profoundly dramatic, making a great feature of the timpani. From the hushed largo introduction through to the brilliant finale, the crackling pace and dazzling invention never flag for a moment.

The dramatic opening of no. 103 in E flat major has given it its subtitle of *Drum-roll.* The most surprising feature of the first movement is the recurrence of the slow introduction (complete with drum-roll) as part of the movement's development, a masterstroke that even Haydn had never thought of before. Two contrasting folk tunes, one in the minor, form the basis for a prolonged set of variations in which a solo violin features prominently. After a minuet of pronounced Slavonic flavour, the finale, again long but this time in the highest of spirits, is built entirely from the simplest of themes that is constantly subjected to such a variety of treatment which no-one but Haydn could ever have imagined. The tune itself is fairly simple, but the possibilities within it, never apparent before you hear them, are nothing short of marvellous.

The last symphony, no. 104 in D major, has for some reason won the distinction of being called the *London* symphony. Haydn never again wrote a symphonic work, and the first movement of this one has a gem-hard structure as if he wanted to finish with a firm, enduring masterpiece. The first theme after the introduction is tuneful, fast, but somehow grave, a bit like a speeded-up hymn melody. The development of this movement is constructed with the utmost ingenuity from part of this little theme. The andante slow movement is a heartwarming melody subjected to the customary explosions, and the minuet fairly straightforward – though its trio shifts to the remote key of B flat major. The finale is perhaps the best of all, a sort of rondo with only one theme accompanied by an insistent drone. Notice too the ease and obvious delight with which Haydn handles the woodwind in this last movement.

Muzio Clementi was dismissed as a musical hack by Mozart, who was probably jealous of his rival's international reputation.

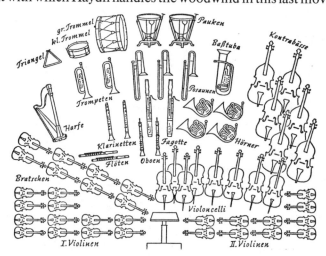

A typical disposition for an orchestra of the late eighteenth century.

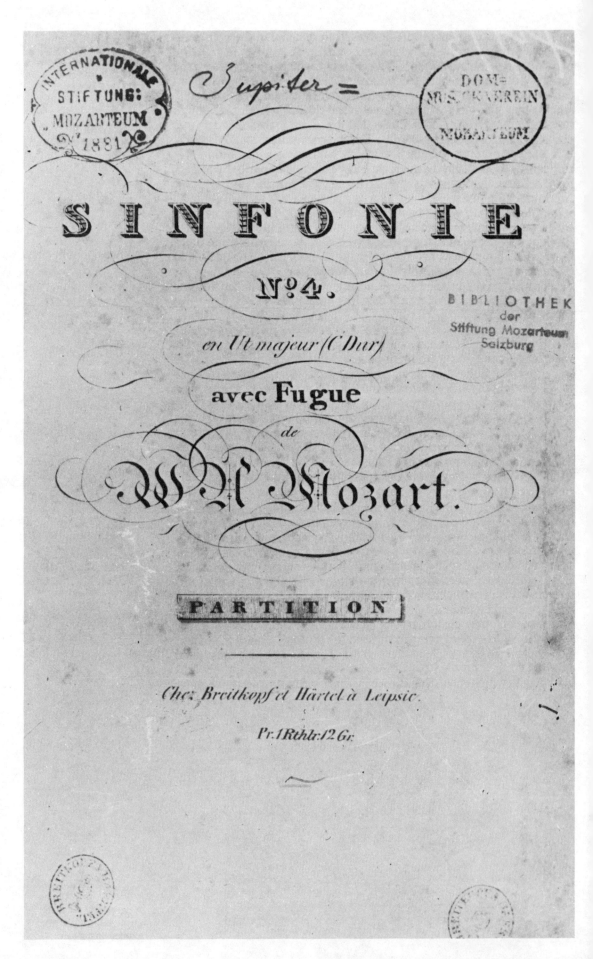

The title-page of Mozart's last symphony shows that the nickname of *Jupiter* was, at any rate, not the choice of its composer. *Facing page:* The conductor Nicolaus Harnoncourt in Salzburg.

Wolfgang Amadeus Mozart

The forty-odd symphonies of Mozart were written over a twenty-five year period of his life, starting in London when he was eight years old and ending in the musically glorious summer of 1788, when he completed his last three works in the form (nos 39–41) in one extraordinary six-week period of white-hot inspiration.

Give or take a few years, then, and we see that this is almost exactly the same period over which Haydn was composing *his* symphonies, though the few years' start that he had over the child Mozart was of crucial importance. When Mozart began, as we said above, he was in London, under the influence of Johann Christian Bach and his partner Carl Friedrich Abel (1723–87) who together ran an on the whole successful series of subscription concerts there. An early symphony that was for a long time accepted as being by Mozart (K.18) we now know to be a copy he made of a work by Abel. As is only to be expected of a young craftsman learning his trade, Mozart's early symphonies are generally derivative, modelled first upon the two worthies just mentioned, then upon such Continental masters as Wagenseil and Monn, and ultimately – and most important – on Joseph Haydn.

Mozart's first symphony (K.16) is a typical such work, in three simple movements, that resembles an opera buffa overture, and bearing all the marks of a youthful experiment. But one year later (1765), the young composer is handling the form with much more familiarity and freedom, as the charming symphony no. 5 (K.22) bears out. Over the next few years of his travels, Mozart continued to develop his control – and therefore by extension his originality – in orchestral writing and the symphonic shape at an alarming rate. By the time he was seventeen, he had absorbed it completely into his own language, as the first example we shall survey shows.

Mozart

Wolfgang Amadeus Mozart was born in Salzburg, Austria, on 27 January 1756. His father, Leopold, must have been a consummate teacher, for the boy was fluent upon the harpsichord before he was five years old. Ever the opportunist, Leopold took the little prodigy (and his elder sister 'Nannerl') on a money-spinning European tour through Brussels, Paris, London, Amsterdam and Zürich that lasted for over two years, and can scarcely have fortified Wolfgang's frail constitution.

When he was thirteen, his father took him twice to Italy where Mozart was quick to absorb the native operatic styles that were to have such a profound effect upon his musical language. He returned from there a fully-fledged professional composer, and picked up several important commissions. Employed, along with his father, by the high-handed and capricious Archbishop of Salzburg, Mozart found the life of a musical lackey intolerable and obtained grudging leave to visit Paris. But the trip was something of a disaster: the opera commissions he was seeking were not forthcoming, and society was much less ready to be won over by a twenty-one year old genius than it had been by a pretty infant prodigy. Mozart's mother, who had accompanied him on this trip, died in Paris and Mozart returned home (via Mannheim) in January 1779. He soon set to work on an important commission for an opera (his twelfth) at Munich, Idomeneo, and moved to settle in Vienna when the Archbishop had him – literally – booted out of his job. Over the next couple of years Mozart continued composing, playing and teaching; he also befriended Haydn, from whom he learned so much about symphonic and quartet writing, and married (much against his father's judgment) Constanze Weber, one of a family of singers he had met in Mannheim. Money was always short, even though the emperor himself was a fan of Mozart's music, and to cope with this difficulty Wolfgang wrote most of his sublime series of piano concertos for benefit concerts, featuring himself as soloist.

In 1784 he became a freemason, and soon after, his operas brought him to the attention of Lorenzo da Ponte, a librettist of genius who obtained the emperor's permission to set (with Mozart's music) Beaumarchais' subversive comedy Le Mariage de Figaro. The work was a great success, though it furthered his career in Vienna not at all. But in Prague the authorities set out straight away to commission another work from the pair, and Don Giovanni was produced there to great applause the following year (1787). On his return to Vienna he continued to compose prolifically, often for little or no money, and his financial situation became desperate. His last three symphonies were written over a six-week period in the summer of 1788. Another opera Così fan tutte had its success checked by the emperor's death early in 1790, and for the remainder of that year Mozart was too exhausted and worried

to write much more. In 1791 he completed his last two operas, La Clemenza di Tito, **and** Die Zauberflöte – **the work he prized above all his other compositions. A Requiem he began as the result of a** commission was destined to remain unfinished: it was as if, he said, he was writing the Requiem for himself. He died in the night of 4–5 December 1791, ill, neglected and impoverished, at the age of thirty-five.

Symphony no. 25 in G minor (K.183)

Aside from the well-known *Great* G minor, this is Mozart's only symphony in the minor mode. It was apparently composed in 1773, when Mozart was seventeen, and we can think of it as his first mature work in the form.

From the very outset (as is frequently the case, he finds no need for the characteristic slow introduction) it is quite clear that this is no apprentice piece. The opening allegro has an urgency and rhythmic drive that gives the work a quite extraordinary power for the music of such a young mind. The texture of the scoring in the piece is richer too, for in addition to the customary pairs of oboes and bassoons, Mozart employs four horns instead of the usual two.

The slow movement is built upon a simple and lovely andante melody in the major, punctuated twice by a little second motif (it is too short to be called a theme) that recalls its composer's preoccupation with operatic melody. The minuet returns to G minor, and to the spirit of urgency that infected the opening; there is nothing gay or dance-like about this minuet. But it is interrupted by a trio in the major, for winds alone, of a touching and heartfelt serenity which points up all the more the starkness of the minuet on its return. The rapid finale resembles the first movement more than a little, with its jerky, dotted rhythms adding an undertone almost of suppressed hysteria to round off this small but perfectly formed masterpiece.

Symphony no. 29 in A major (K.201)

A few months after completing the above work, Mozart wrote this most melodic of his early symphonies. Though orchestrally on a smaller scale than no. 25 (in addition to the strings, it uses only a pair each of oboes and horns), it is the one other heavyweight symphony from this period in the composer's life.

The opening theme of the first movement (marked allegro moderato) climbs gently up the first four notes of the scale, a seemingly ingenuous little melody. We have to wait until the coda to find out how skilfully it can be combined against itself in three-part counterpoint. The slow movement, in sonata form, features a calm, broad melody with muted

A composite silhouette, dated 1785, of Haydn, Gluck, Mozart and Salieri.

Mozart's birthplace in
Salzburg.

strings and is succeeded by a delightful minuet in dotted rhythm, with
'echo' effects for the oboes and horns alone. The last movement, allegro
con spirito, seems to return to the child within the composer in the
innocent fun to be had with such lovely snatches of melody.

Symphony no. 31 in D major (K.297) – Paris Symphony
'You have no idea how they twice scraped and scrambled through it. I
was really in a terrible way and would gladly have rehearsed it again, but
there was no time left. So I had to go to bed with an aching heart and in a
discontented and angry frame of mind.' Thus wrote the twenty-two year
old composer to his father, in a typically chatty and interesting letter.
What he left unsaid is more interesting: as he sat down dutifully to write
home from Paris, his mother lay dead in the next room, a subject that
Mozart seems to have found himself incapable of mentioning.
The performance of the symphony, however, went well, and Mozart was
particularly delighted with the clarinets – the first time he had used them
in a symphony. The work is richly scored in fact, with flutes, trumpets
and drums in addition to the usual line-up. The brilliant first movement
is succeeded by a tender andantino in a rocking 6/8 rhythm. But this
lovely movement failed to impress the director of the Paris concerts, and
Mozart substituted a 3/4 Andante in the same key (G major). Again in
deference to Parisian taste, there is no minuet, so the music passes
straight to its ebullient and frothy finale that contains a particularly witty
passage of fugal development in its second subject.

Symphony no. 34 in C major (K.338)
This work was written in 1780, at the same time as the sublime *Sinfonia
Concertante* for violin and viola, and shortly before Mozart's final move
to Vienna. Like the *Paris* symphony it is on a relatively small scale, and
there is no minuet. The opening movement starts with a joyful flourish
as if for some splendid state occasion, and the feeling is sustained
throughout.
The andante di molto which follows is a graceful and profoundly
touching piece, in a simplified sonata form that lacks any development
section. It is for strings alone, and has almost the character of an aria from

an unwritten opera. The finale is an infectious country dance, with an odd feature near the end when the music comes to a stop as if in anticipation of a cadenza, like a concerto.

Symphony no. 35 in D major (K.385) – Haffner Symphony
While at work on teething troubles of his opera *Die Entführung aus dem Serail,* Mozart received a request from his father that he supply a symphony to celebrate the ennoblement of a prominent Salzburg citizen, Sigmund Haffner. Six years before, he had written the *Haffner Serenade* for a wedding in the same musically discerning family. Mozart complied with his father's wish and sent this symphony, though originally in a slightly different form from the one we now know. It had two extra movements, both of which the composer removed when the work was later given its Viennese première.
The strongly defined first subject of the opening movement, with its two-octave leaps, makes an arresting and festive beginning; and this theme soon reappears as the counterpoint to a busy little second subject in the dominant key. The entire movement needs repeated listening and close attention to uncover all the little miracles Mozart works with this seemingly innocuous opening idea. It is a delight from start to finish, complete with a short visit in the development to the weird and distant key of F sharp major. The andante that follows is a passionate movement with a deceptively calm surface. In the codas to this piece, Mozart delays, as it were, the proper resolution of the chord progressions in a way that makes you feel as though you never want the music to stop. The minuet is bright and pompous, with a happy 'wrong-note' feature in the accompaniment, and a more restful trio which again seems to be extracted from some imaginary opera.
The finale is certainly extracted from an opera, but not imaginary this time. As we said above, Mozart had only just completed *Die Entführung* when he set to work on this symphony, and the theme of this light and fizzy ending is drawn from an aria in that work sung by Osmin, the fat and crafty guardian of the Sultan's harem.

Symphony no. 36 in C major (K.425) – Linz Symphony
In October 1783, on the way back from a visit to Salzburg, Mozart and his wife broke their journey at Linz. He wrote to his father, 'I am giving a concert in the theatre here and, as I haven't a single symphony with me, I am writing a new one at break-neck speed, which must be finished in time.' This marvellous and brilliant work, apparently composed in a matter of days, is unusual in that it opens with a slow introduction that reminds the listener of Haydn – as do other moments in this sunny, extrovert symphony.
The first movement teems with melodic invention. The second subject takes off, unusually, in a minor key before settling down in more orthodox fashion, and the development, though intense, is quite short and to the point. The poco adagio which follows is in a lyrical and gently swinging 6/8, and succeeded by a glittering and martial minuet, whose trio is a gentle rustic dance of the sweetest beauty. The symphony ends with a bustling presto, a seemingly artless movement that is constructed with the greatest craftsmanship and whose pungent wit is timed to perfection.

Symphony no. 38 in D major (K.504) – Prague Symphony
As will be apparent from the gaps between the 'Köchel' (K.) numbers, Mozart's symphonic writing thinned out a lot in his maturity, though the quality continued to climb to the dizziest heights of genius. The *Symphony without a Minuet,* as this work was once rather foolishly known, was written after *The Marriage of Figaro* and before *Don Giovanni.* Mozart had been invited to Prague with a commission to write the latter opera, and took this new work with him, where it was first performed on 19 January 1787.

A charming silhouette of the Mozart family pursuing their customary occupations.

Haydn's studio in Vienna.

Leopold Mozart

Leopold Mozart (1719–87), the father of Wolfgang, was a gifted musician who put a promising career behind him to devote himself to the training of his two children. At the age of twenty he entered the employment of the Canon of Salzburg, but soon moved to the court of the Archbishop, where he was made court composer and, eventually, vice Kapellmeister. (His employer was the same narrow-minded and truculent despot who had the young Wolfgang kicked down the steps of his residence for insubordination.) In the same year that Wolfgang was born (1756), Leopold published his most famous work, a treatise on the art of violin-playing that earned him a wide reputation. He has often received a bad press for the demands he made upon his little son in touring him round Europe like a performing monkey, but just as it was important to make money, it was these travels that exposed Mozart to the influence of the latest and greatest music from all over Europe – giving him a more thorough and eclectic grounding in his art than would otherwise have been possible.

The Graben, the principal street of Vienna, in the eighteenth century. Vienna, as the capital (die Kaiserstadt) of a multi-national empire, attracted musicians from all over the world, including Italy, France, England and Ireland, as well as from its own vast dominions.

The young Mozart with his father, Leopold, and sister Nannerl. A watercolour painted in 1763 by Carmontelle.

Joseph Haydn. He was well aware of his good fortune in having the patronage of the princely Esterházy family, which gave him musical resources in the shape of an orchestra, singers and an opera house – and freedom from financial worry.

Leopold Mozart.

Again there is a slow introduction, infused with a drama that reminds us, and it can be no coincidence, of the music of the Commendatore's ghost in the latter opera. The allegro into which it leads is one of Mozart's greatest musical feats, where seemingly inexhaustible ideas are combined, explored and manipulated to an effect that is simply glorious. There is no space here to examine in any detail the wizardry of this movement's marvellous structure: it seems, however, to be a piece of which the ear can never tire. Melody abounds again in the exquisite andante, whose tunes are sweet but speak of a pathetic sadness. The last movement, a rushing presto, alternates a breathless anxiety tempered with flashes of Mozartean humour and comic relief, in particular from the horns and that traditional clown of the orchestra, the bassoon.

Symphony no. 39 in E flat major (K.543)
Mozart's last three symphonies, written between June and August of 1788, seem to have been composed with reference to a planned (but probably unrealized) series of concerts in Vienna. The scoring for no. 39 is unusual: one flute, two each of clarinets, bassoons, horns, trumpets – drums and strings. After a slow, richly scored introduction, a bright allegro theme in triple time propels this sunlit movement on its way. The musical ideas contained within it are legion, and contrasting phrases succeed each other all the time – though, such is Mozart's mastery of balance, never crowding each other out or jostling for attention.
The ingenuous, dotted theme of the andante which follows, has at first a Haydenesque simplicity about it, though a little later in the movement a repeated-note figure in the minor leads the composer off on some daring harmonic key changes and miraculous contrapuntal flights of fancy. The well-known minuet that succeeds it is, by contrast, simple and straightforward, and Mozart enjoys some delicious play with the clarinets on its trio section. The allegro finale recalls Haydn again, where one little melodic flake of nine notes is made strong enough to carry the weight of almost an entire movement. The piece never for a moment relaxes from being vibrant, joyful, and humming with life.

Symphony no. 40 in G minor (K.550)
Written as they were in an amazingly condensed space of time, Mozart's last three symphonies show an astonishing disparity of moods, and that of no. 40 is the hardest to pinpoint. It has been called 'tragic'; but a molto allegro opening, particularly with such a skipping rhythm (that it shares, by the way, with Cherubino's aria *Non so più* from *Figaro*) must give the lie to those kind of adjectives. Yet on the other hand it is assuredly not gay or frisky, and to call it neurotic or hysterical would be seriously to undervalue its powerful logic and structure. But there is a pathos in the affecting (major) second subject that temporarily checks the restless quaver flow of the movement.
It is followed by a lovely andante in E flat major. The calm of this movement, however, is never allowed to settle into complacency, being repeatedly disturbed by chromatic 'wrong' notes that show off what has been called Mozart's ability to 'poison' a musical phrase. And there is no emotional let-up in the minuet either: its grim, stern dissonances are only relieved by a wistful and soothing trio in G major. The finale, allegro assai, returns once more to the urgency of the opening movement. It also is in sonata form, and has a marvellous, classically pathetic second subject that lends a dignity and poise to the movement's demonic energy.

Symphony no. 41 in C major (K.551) – Jupiter
It was Haydn's impresario, Salomon, who gave this mighty work its nickname. More perhaps than any of the other symphonies discussed here, its strength lies in its development. In the first movement, allegro vivace, the opening flourish is rounded off by a tiny, climbing cadence and both are soon combined with a third

The Austrian scholar Ludwig Köchel (1800-77) lived in Salzburg for thirteen years, and while there compiled his catalogue of Mozart's works.

A portrait of the boy
Mozart hangs above the
composer's piano in his
birthplace at Salzburg.

figure whose most prominent feature is a staccato descending scale. All
this is quite easy to pick out, and occurs within the first minute of the
music. It soon gives way to a second – and third – subject, and the
development after the beautiful little coda makes a virtuoso display of
combining these several motives in magical and psychically satisfying
fashion, before the final recapitulation.

The strings are muted in the tranquil andante cantabile, which
resembles a soft, operatic aria whose peace is only ruffled by some
momentary syncopations that throw the music off its delicate but
insistent triple tread. The orchestration that underlies the melodic line in
this movement is particulary rich and fulfilling.

For a work in the often brilliant key of C major, the minuet is restrained,
though the downward chromatic slips in the little piece lend the music a
gorgeous feeling of quiet ecstasy.

All too often in the classical symphony, it is the finale which is its weakest
point, but in the *Jupiter* it is perhaps the concluding allegro molto that is
its crowning glory. Five themes are stated more or less consecutively and
then combined in the most dazzling fugal work-out.

One motif is made up simply of four long semibreves, as if from some
ancient chorale; another, complete with trill, seems like a snatch of
birdsong; and a very insistent little figure is scarcely more than a bustling,
self-important downward scale. These, and the other motifs, are all
readily and separately identifiable to the ear, but it takes close
concentration to follow and pick out all the interweaving, canonic
imitation, inverting and combining that Mozart can do with these simple
tools. It is as if we are being shown a complete catalogue of all that can
happen to these tiny elements. But this is no text-book display: all the
composer's ineffable artistry is directed towards achieving a consistent
and unified whole that sounds in our ears and our hearts with a sublime
and incomparable happiness.

The last portrait of Mozart
drawn from life:
A silverpoint made by
Doris Stock in 1789.

2

Beethoven

At half past six on 2 April 1800, the citizens of Vienna were invited to a concert at the Royal Imperial Court Theatre. The long programme concluded with 'a new grand symphony composed by Herr Ludwig van Beethoven'. No one in the audience could have foreseen that this engaging but modest work was the prelude to a towering achievement of European culture.

Beethoven wrote nine symphonies, not a great number for a composer of his generation, but these cover an emotional and stylistic range that few artists have ever equalled. He approached the symphonic form with a concentration that was unusual even by his own formidable standards. Piano variations or chamber music he might dash off and later live to regret (he despised his own tuneful and popular septet), but a symphony was a work to be taken seriously. He was twenty-nine when the first symphony, a work he had long intended to write, was performed, and his musical sketchbooks indicate fruitful gestation periods for several of the others. It was in his mind to write music for Schiller's *Ode to Joy* as early as 1793, for example. This idea only materialized in 1824 as the choral finale of the ninth symphony.

As a symphonist Beethoven was aided by a general improvement in the standard of orchestral playing (especially among the winds) and by the sheer number of professional musicians at hand. From the time of his first symphony, orchestras with sufficient strings and two each of flutes, oboes, clarinets, bassoons, horns, trumpets and timpani were available to him. He added another horn for the third symphony (the *Eroica*); the fifth included piccolo, contra-bassoon and three trombones. He dropped contra-bassoon and one of the trombones for the sixth and was content to revert to the smaller requirements of the first two (the so-called 'Beethoven orchestra') for the seventh and eighth, but for the ninth he assembled all his forces, doubling the horn section and adding triangle, cymbal and bass drum to the percussion.

Beethoven used the wind section as an equal partner of the strings. 'The only flaw was that the wind instruments were used too much,' wrote a critic at the première of the first symphony. A plaintive oboe cadenza in the first movement of the fifth symphony and stirring use of trombones in the last: the bizarre rattle of contra-bassoon in the finale of the ninth; and a daring confidence in the abilities of his French horns in the trio of the *Eroica* all mark Beethoven as an innovator in orchestration. He was also largely responsible for taming the kettledrums and for liberating the cellos and double-basses, drudges of an eighteenth-century orchestra, from their rôle as mere time-keepers. It has often been pointed out that Beethoven's symphonies fall into two broad categories: the cheerful and emotionally restrained even-numbered works contrast with the bold and passionate odd-numbered ones (excluding the first, which is taken as the exception that proves the

Beethoven

As Beethoven lay dying, a fierce hail-storm broke over Vienna and a great clap of thunder roused the composer for the last time. He opened his eyes and shook his clenched fist. Then, in the midst of the tumult, he died. This romantic account of Beethoven's death is generally unchallenged by even the most meticulous of scholars. It seems only appropriate that the greatest musical genius of his age should have died as passionately as he lived.

Beethoven was born in Bonn in December 1770. His grandfather, Ludwig, was Kapellmeister (musical director) at the court of the Elector, and his father, Johann, was a tenor in the same service. Johann was a severe, intemperate man, who saw the spark of genius in his son and compelled him to practise long hours at the pianoforte and organ. The boy gave his first public recital when he was eight (though the programme boasted that he was only six). At fourteen, his formal education behind him,

Beethoven became assistant organist at the court chapel. 'A second Wolfgang Amadeus Mozart,' predicted his master, the principal organist C.G. Neefe. Mozart, it is believed, was of the same opinion after hearing the youth play for him in Vienna in 1787.

His mother's death and his father's increasing incompetence and alcoholism forced Beethoven to take responsibility for his two younger brothers while still in his teens. For some years he supported the family by teaching and by playing viola in the court orchestra, but the desire to seek recognition as a composer and virtuoso pianist was too great to be ignored. In 1792 Beethoven moved to Vienna, where he remained for the rest of his life.

He arrived in Vienna with glowing recommendations and soon found devoted and influential friends. Haydn, who briefly taught him composition, thought him prodigiously talented, if personally rather difficult; Salieri, the popular rival of Mozart, taught him free of charge. As a performer he had no peers. His piano rule). There is some truth in this generalization. Robert Schumann called the fourth symphony 'a slender Grecian maiden between two giants'. The cheerful sixth (the *Pastoral*) is a conspicuous oasis of joy between the turbulent emotions of the fifth and seventh. The eighth, a favourite of Beethoven, is a concise and meticulous masterpiece, an unlikely forerunner to the sprawling ninth symphony that appeared ten years later.

These swings in symphonic mood are largely a manifestation of Beethoven's genius; they are also a product of the age in which he lived. Rebellion and the rights of man were the political keynotes of Beethoven's generation. Schooled in the formal traditions of the eighteenth century, he could, and frequently did, write as correct a counterpoint or as rigid a sonata as the most conservative of his elders. He was also a child of his times, full of hope, anger and frustration, emotions that found their way into his compositions.

Beethoven's symphonies, even his most ambitious ones, were generally well received. The *Eroica*, it is true, provoked growls of 'lawless' and 'wild' from the critics and, from an unidentified man in the audience at the first performance, the despairing remark, 'I'll give another Kreutzer if the thing will but stop.' At the tumultuous première of the seventh, however, the public demanded to hear the second movement repeated. A similarly joyful exhibition interrupted the first performance of the ninth. By then Beethoven was totally deaf and could hear neither the music nor the ovation.

The title-page of Beethoven's manuscript of the *Eroica* symphony, clearly showing where the composer obliterated the dedication to Napoleon on hearing that the latter had declared himself Emperor.

In the silence and sickness of his last years Beethoven continued to plan future compositions. On 18 March 1827 he wrote with characteristic confidence of a tenth symphony 'which lies already sketched in my desk'. Eight days later he was dead.

Symphony no. 1 in C major, opus 21
The orchestra at the première of Beethoven's first symphony (Vienna, 1800) was sloppy and spiritless, but behind this lacklustre performance one critic discovered 'considerable art, novelty and a wealth of ideas'. Since then the piece has continued to charm audiences, though it irritates those critics who think of Beethoven as a thunderous prophet and wince to see him on the dance floor in such an amiable mood.
Adagio molto – allegro con brio. Sustained chords in the woodwinds and ambiguous wanderings by the strings clear like morning mist as the adagio introduction resolves into C major and a sunny allegro. The bright, ascending first subject is played by the violins. Oboe and flute emerge as soloists in the graceful second subject, which concludes with a plaintive duet between cellos and woodwinds.
The development section seizes upon the rising dotted rhythm of the first subject, drawing it through a number of keys before descending to the recapitulation. Twenty-one bars of rousing C major dispel any final doubts about the home key.
Andante cantabile con moto. The second violins introduce this elegant movement with a tune which Haydn would have been proud to have written. Stately and sure-footed, it moves with the confidence of a courtly dance. Beethoven's voice is clearly audible across the ballroom, however, bringing the timpani quietly into play during a troubled middle section. Order is discreetly restored, and the initial tune, with delightful counterpoint, brings the movement to a close.
Menuetto – allegro molto e vivace. Here is a 'minuet' that is totally undanceable, the first of these movements that Beethoven was later to label scherzo. The violins rush in with an urgent ascending scale, creating an air of suppressed tension that finally breaks loose in the second section. Calm is suddenly imposed by the woodwinds in a magical trio. The violins hover impatiently while the imperturbable winds repeat their pulsing chords. In true 'minuet' style, the movement ends as it began, with excitement and speed.
Adagio – allegro molto e vivace. 'This is not Beethoven,' complained Hector Berlioz of the cheerful finale. It is not Beethoven of the *Eroica*, he should have said, but it is Beethoven the student of Haydn. The movement begins with a joke and continues in unflagging good humour. A C major scale hesitantly ascends during the introductory adagio section and after several false starts finally gathers courage and races into the allegro. A dance-like second subject enriches the musical material. It is tempting (though rather more picturesque than true) to interpret such wit and high spirits as Beethoven's symphonic farewell to the eighteenth century.

Symphony no. 2 in D major, opus 36
Having fulfilled his audience's expectations with the first symphony, Beethoven went on to surprise them with the second. A critic at the première (Vienna, 1803) was disappointed by what he called this 'striving for the new', and it is said that the violinist Rodolphe Kreutzer ran out of one performance with his hands to his ears. The good humour of this symphony soon proved irresistible, however, especially when compared to the monumental innovations of its successors.
Adagio molto – allegro con brio. An adagio introduction, with suggestions of melancholy and high drama, does not prepare the listener for the bustling first subject of the allegro. An equally cheerful second subject, like the chorus of a drinking song, is taken by the woodwinds. But Beethoven knew that there was more to a tune than meets the ear. With the four semiquavers of the first subject as his principal motif, he

improvisations at private gatherings frequently moved the audience to tears. His compositions, dedicated to those willing to pay for the privilege, were equally well received. These early works, products of what is often called his 'first period', included piano sonatas, chamber music and two concertos for piano and orchestra. The success of his compositions, supplemented by the generosity of wealthy admirers, provided Beethoven with an adequate, if never abundant, income. In 1800, at his first benefit concert, Beethoven conducted the C major symphony. Three years later a second symphony had its première. This ebullient and popular

work is a mystery to those who attempt to match a man's life with his music, for at the time of its composition Beethoven was in a state of profound depression, struggling to admit to himself that the deafness which had irritated him sporadically for some years was progressive and incurable. 'I must live like an outcast,' he wrote in a moment of anguish. 'O Providence – do but grant me one day of pure joy.' The deterioration of his hearing gradually forced Beethoven to abandon the concert platform and to work single-mindedly as a composer. The music of his so-called middle period (1803–12) reflects an increased dedication to

Beethoven's birthplace in Bonn is a popular place of pilgrimage for music-lovers from all over the world.

composition.
Milestones of this fertile decade include the third, fourth and fifth piano concertos, the Appassionata Sonata, **the Violin Concerto, the opera** Fidelio **and the symphonies nos. three to eight.
Throughout these years Beethoven was passionately moved by the philosophical issues of his day. Political liberty and human dignity inspired him to write some of his greatest works, including** Fidelio **and the** Ode to Joy **finale of the ninth symphony. (A belated discovery that Napoleon was not a champion of egalitarianism led him to destroy the original dedication of the third symphony.) The powerful emotions apparent in these works heralded the beginning of a Romantic movement in music. Form was giving way to feeling. The elegant citadel of classical music, so carefully erected in the eighteenth century, began to crumble under the thunderous blows of Beethoven. For all his democratic ideals, Beethoven delighted in mixing with the privileged and powerful. When he first arrived in Vienna, his intense eyes, broad pockmarked face and mane of black hair, made him a striking, but never a handsome, man. In his later years, physical decay and personal neglect reduced him to a wildly eccentric figure. (On one of his country rambles he was detained by the police as a suspected tramp.) Yet he exerted a magnetism that absolved him from the petty obligations of Viennese society. He might dress like a peasant, roar with insulting laughter at a roomful of high-born ladies, throw eggs at**

A twentieth-century sketch of Beethoven, by Leonid Pasternak.

leads this rather banal material up to an unexpectedly emotional peak.
Larghetto. As if to prove that he could write as good a tune as anyone, Beethoven begins this movement with a melting 'Schubertian' melody (Schubert was, at the time, five years old). While any other composer might have been content to write variations on this beautiful theme, and so end the movement, Beethoven adds a second and then a third subject, bringing the whole to a powerful climax before returning to the original theme. The romantic Hector Berlioz, entranced by this long movement, described it as 'the delineation of innocent happiness hardly clouded by a few accents of melancholy'.
Scherzo – allegro. The word scherzo means joke, and here Beethoven took the title literally, passing his boisterous three-note motif from strings to horns to oboes. The woodwinds attempt to introduce a note of quiet seriousness in the trio section, but the strings will have none of this and interrupt noisily to take the movement back to the beginning.
Allegro molto. The comedy of the scherzo continues in this light-hearted and eccentric finale. The principal theme is an explosive two-bar passage, a sort of musical sneeze that seems to catch Beethoven unaware whenever he threatens to become too earnest. A languorous second subject gives the woodwinds, especially the bassoon, a brief chance to float above the scurrying strings. And a mysterious pizzicato passage in the coda offers the glimpse of another world, before the jeering first subject brings the symphony to a happy close.

Symphony no. 3 in E flat major, opus 55 – Eroica

Beethoven's third symphony did not break completely with the past: within the first movement are the bones of a sonata form, and the scherzo could be described as a frenetic eighteenth-century minuet. But in size and emotional breadth the *Eroica* is revolutionary and truly heroic. Beethoven once remarked that if he understood the art of war as well as he knew the art of music he could conquer Napoleon. With this great symphony (first performed 1805) alone he could have gone confidently to battle.

Allegro con brio. Two massive E flat major chords assert this symphony's heroic intentions. The cellos then enter with the legato first subject, but they have already lost their grasp of it in the seventh bar, when an intrusive C sharp gives an early indication of ensuing conflict. It would be vain to attempt a coherent description of this huge movement in such a brief space, but the following are significant points of reference: a serene and organ-like second subject (though an abundance of themes and rhythmic motifs make conventional analysis difficult); massive syncopated chords at the end of the exposition and again (sounding as much like Stravinsky as Beethoven) in the development; a distant and dissonant solo horn introducing the recapitulation; bold, verging on the brutal, modulation at the beginning of the coda; and a cheerful contrapuntal passage, the horn again playing the simple first subject and leading the movement to an optimistic conclusion.

Marcia funebre – adagio assai. Simulated 'drum rolls' by the double basses accompany the slow tread of a solemn march. But this is no mere funeral procession. Hector Berlioz described it as 'a drama in itself', referring to the glowing C major interlude and a tempestuous fugue in F minor. Perhaps these are no more than fleeting impressions in the minds of the mourners, for in the end, the sombre theme returns, now with long cruel silences, as if drawing near the grave.

Scherzo – allegro vivace. Excited scurrying among the strings is aggravated by their apparent difficulty in finding the key of E flat. Their joyous arrival at the tonic is short-lived, however, as three French horns now begin the trio section with a triumphant fanfare. This exultant tune becomes a pensive hymn before the scherzo returns. Beethoven temporarily shatters the rhythm with four bars in duple time, but three-in-a-bar order is quickly restored. Horns and strings unite to conclude the movement on a resolute fortissimo.

Finale: allegro molto – poco andante – presto. As if trying to capture all the moods of the preceding three movements, Beethoven chose to write variations for this unconventional finale. At first he reveals only the bass line, introduced by pizzicato strings in a manner both mysterious and strangely comical. The theme itself is a light-hearted melody that lends itself to joyous, even playful, variations and fugues. Then suddenly it becomes the solemn vehicle for a beautiful andante chorale, one of the most moving passages Beethoven ever wrote. A concluding presto passage, the horns in full cry, recalls the heroic confidence of the very first two bars of the symphony.

Symphony no. 4 in B flat major, opus 60

In the summer of 1806 Beethoven stopped work on his C minor symphony (later to be known as the fifth) in order to compose this comparatively neglected masterpiece. It is an astonishing aspect of his genius that he could turn his attention with such apparent ease from an intense and stormy composition to one that so overflows with wit and good cheer.

Adagio – allegro vivace. The violins tiptoe mysteriously through a number of unexpected keys before coming triumphantly to rest on F major at the end of the adagio introduction. This chord is then, as it were, wound up until it springs into B flat major and one of the happiest first movements Beethoven ever wrote. The woodwinds contribute a robust and bucolic second subject, and such is the abundance of melodic

his cook, come to blows with his brothers in the street, accuse his loyallest friends of treachery – but be forgiven and remain beloved. His intense relationships with a succession of women, many of whom were married or his social superiors, give some suggestion of his compelling attractions.

Despite a longing to share his domestic life, Beethoven never married. This unfulfilled desire for a family led to the disastrous years of legal battle over the guardianship of his nephew Karl. Beethoven finally won his case, but the emotional toll was immense, and Karl's abortive suicide attempt in 1826 may have hastened his uncle to the grave.

For a few years after the completion of his eighth symphony (1812), Beethoven's output dwindled, but his energy and inspiration returned during the last decade. The Missa Solemnis (1822), the Diabelli Variations for piano (1823), the ninth symphony (1824) and five profound string quartets (which include the last music he ever wrote) are the works not just of prodigious genius but of a priest-like

devotion to Art. Though never a conventionally religious man, Beethoven gratefully received the last sacraments of the Catholic Church on his death-bed, and surrendered himself to the God he had so often addressed in his diaries and in his music. Some 10,000 people jammed the streets of Vienna at his funeral (1827). 'Thus he was,' wrote the poet Franz Grillparzer, author of Beethoven's funeral oration, 'thus he died, thus he will live to the end of time.'

material that the development section begins to digress with a theme of its own. Then, while the timpani roll apprehensively, the violins are allowed a rare moment to catch their breath before rushing back to the country dance with a joyful and boisterous recapitulation.

Adagio. Critics who seek biographical information from a composer's music see this voluptuous adagio as clear evidence that Beethoven was blissfully in love, with a dotted accompanying rhythm, for all the world like a lover's heart-beat. The movement is dominated by two beautiful melodies, the first introduced by the violins, the second by the clarinet – each characterized by sighing, descending slurs. These are repeated, the first with shimmering ornamentation, before a final 'heart-beat' from the timpani brings this lovely adagio to a close.

Allegro vivace; trio – un poco meno allegro. Between the raptures of an adagio and the excitement of a finale Beethoven was determined to prevent his audience from falling asleep. Here he mocks the complacent three-four rhythm of the minuet in a short movement of unsettling syncopation and unconventional harmony. The woodwinds establish a rustic interlude in the trio section, but the tipsy opening, with its sliding unisons returns to restore disorder.

Allegro ma non troppo. This bubbling finale gives the strings little respite. The ebullient semi-quavers of the opening bar continue relentlessly with only a brief pause when the winds play their relaxed second subject. Eleven bars from the end the tempo suddenly unwinds and the whole symphony grinds to a halt, only to pluck up courage again in a mad dash for the final double bar.

Symphony no. 5 in C minor, opus 67

Historical musical events are not always impressive at the time. Beethoven's fifth and sixth symphonies received first performances on the same evening (1808), but the only accounts of that remarkable concert tell how the *Choral Fantasy* (also receiving its première) came to an embarrassing halt. As if to make up for the ignominy of its birth, the fifth has become the most popular of all Beethoven's symphonies.

Allegro con brio. The four most famous notes in symphonic music – the familiar dot-dot-dot-dash 'victory' motif – establish a rhythmic pattern that persists throughout the movement. The fortissimo courage of these opening bars, however, does not continue. After this initial burst of confidence, the strings introduce a melancholy first subject, charged with a nervous energy that infuses the whole movement. Likewise, the horns boldly introduce a graceful second subject, which is quickly absorbed into the compelling rhythm of the opening. This tension between despair and courage is most evident at the end of the development section, where strings and winds exchange a series of panting, repetitive chords, to be fiercely revived by the opening theme, now played by the full orchestra. In a defiant coda Beethoven reasserts the determination of his first five bars.

Andante con moto. Resignation and triumph alternate in this stately slow movement. The opening theme in A flat major (a dotted rhythm that one critic has described as 'sadly suave') is introduced by the cellos and violas. It solemnly proceeds with a number of variations, but its progress is impeded by a triumphal procession in C major, with a band that includes trumpets, horns, oboes and timpani. A royal funeral and coronation have taken place on the same day.

Allegro. Cellos and basses slide almost imperceptibly into the first few bars of this extraordinary movement. Their mysterious reverie is shattered by the horns playing a fortissimo four-note motif – a distorted version of the opening bars of the symphony. The 'trio' section involves lower strings again, this time in an aggressive and grotesque fugue ('the gambols of a delighted elephant,' said Berlioz, possibly mistaking the technical struggles of the bass section for deliberate comedy). The timpani, echoing the horns' four-note rhythm, finally summon the entire orchestra without a pause to the finale.

Allegro – Presto. An ascending C major triad dispels all the doubt and darkness of the previous three movements. Reinforced by the piccolo, contra-bassoon and three trombones, the orchestra marches confidently through an exposition and development section, only to be recalled abruptly by a ghostly reminiscence of the four-note phrase that haunted the third movement. This disturbing presence is purged by the full orchestra in a triumphant recapitulation. Untroubled by any subsequent musical memories, the symphony comes to an emphatic and noisy close.

Symphony no. 6 in F major, opus 68 – Pastoral
Beethoven delighted in the country, drawing inspiration from the peace and beauty of his surroundings. 'My unhappy ears do not torment me here,' he wrote. 'It seems as if in the country every tree said to me Holy! Holy!' Although it could be argued that many of Beethoven's great compositions have their origins in the Austrian countryside, it was only in the sixth symphony (the *Pastoral*) that he chose to be explicit.
Allegro ma non troppo. 'The cheerful feelings excited by arriving in the country' was Beethoven's own subtitle for this movement. He achieves a sense of untroubled well-being by repeating the tumbling second bar of his first subject until it becomes a pulse for the whole movement. This repetitive two-beat unit (a quaver, two semi-quavers and two more quavers) provides no precise image. The listener must 'see' for himself the wind in the leaves or water falling over smooth stones. Because of its descriptive nature, it is easy to forget that this movement is written in strict sonata form: exposition, development and recapitulation are all in their 'correct' places.
Andante molto mosso. 'By the stream'. This is a broad and peaceful stream, its gentle murmur coming from the lower strings which 'flow' steadily throughout most of the movement. Above them a number of liquid melodies float among the violins and the winds, obscuring the fact that this movement, like the first, is written in traditional sonata form. A nightingale (flute), a quail (oboe) and a cuckoo (clarinet) emerge at nightfall in a delightful coda.
Allegro. 'A happy gathering of the peasants'. The peasants do not have long to celebrate, but they fit in a noisy and drunken dance before the impending storm scatters them. Their little wind band includes an oboist who plays consistently off the beat, a flamboyant clarinettist and a sleepy bassoonist who can manage only three notes. This scherzo modulates suddenly to the sombre key of F minor, and proceeds without pause to the next movement.
Allegro. 'Storm'. 'Listen to those rain-charged squalls of wind,' exhorted Hector Berlioz, referring to the turbulent opening of this movement. The staccato violins are quickly joined by an ominous growling from basses and cellos. The woodwinds shriek, the timpani rumble, and eventually trombones enter on a fortissimo that had the impressionable Berlioz trembling with fear and admiration. 'It is no longer merely rain and wind, but an awful cataclysm,' he wrote. The storm passes, and amid distant thunder the oboe and flute herald a serene sunrise.
Allegretto. 'Shepherds' song. Joy and thanksgiving after the storm'. Again there is no break between movements, as calls by solo clarinet and horn arise from distant mountainsides. The violins then enter with a gracious melody, the shepherds' hymn of thanksgiving. This is taken up by the full orchestra and remains, with exquisite variations, the central theme of the final movement. A muted horn, repeating the call of the first bars, brings the symphony to a tranquil close.

Symphony no. 7 in A major, opus 92
The première of the seventh symphony in 1813 marked a high point in Beethoven's popularity. Sad to say, the merits of this great work were partially eclipsed by another of that evening's first performances: *Wellington's Victory* (also known as the *Battle Symphony*), a noisy money-

A caricature of Beethoven walking in the streets of Vienna.

Ries

Ferndinand Ries (1784–1838) was born into a family of court musicians in Bonn. Although precociously talented on both the violin and piano, his own musical future appeared in doubt after the French invasion of Germany. His fortunes changed in 1801 when he arrived in Vienna and knocked on the door of Ludwig van Beethoven. Delighted to be of assistance to the son of his old teacher and benefactor Franz Anton Ries, Beethoven took the young man on as his first official piano pupil, showering him with musical encouragement and financial aid. Later in life, Ries repaid Beethoven's generosity by acting as his agent in London. To the world of Beethoven scholarship he is remembered for his valuable and affectionate portrait (written with F.G. Wegeler), *Biografische Notizen über Ludwig van Beethoven*. Ries became an eminent solo pianist and composer, distinguished (according to the London *Harmonicon*) for the 'Romantic wildness' of his playing. His compositions owed everything to Beethoven – except their inspiration. Eight symphonies, twenty-six string quartets, twenty-eight violin sonatas and a myriad of pieces for solo piano are among his many works.

The interior of Beethoven's birthplace in Bonn, with one of the composer's pianofortes.

The title-page of Beethoven's eighth symphony.

Maelzel

Johann Nepomuk Maelzel (1772–1838). Although a talented pianist, Maelzel's true genius lay in inventing 'musical instruments', mechanical novelties that intrigued the audiences of Europe and America. Even Beethoven was beguiled by the Panharmonicon, a huge music box which, with the aid of weights, cylinders and massive bellows, imitated all the instruments of the orchestra. For this monstrous toy, at Maelzel's instigation, Beethoven wrote his monstrous Battle Symphony, also known as Wellington's Victory. **Their relationship soured when the two fell out over the rights to an orchestral version of this enormously** successful gewgaw. Maelzel was, according to the irate Beethoven, a 'rude fellow wholly without education or breeding'. A simpler but more significant invention was the metronome. Maelzel, in fact, borrowed the idea for this classic machine, but with his flair for showmanship and sharp practice was soon regarded as its sole creator. 'Every village schoolmaster ought to use the metronome', wrote Beethoven in 1818, when the two had patched up their quarrel. Perhaps this fulsome endorsement owed something to the efforts Maelzel had expended in developing an ear trumpet for the deaf composer. Maelzel died on board an American ship, while seeking new markets for his eccentric genius.

spinner that Beethoven had turned out with Maelzel, inventor of the metronome and manufacturer of the composer's ear-trumpets.

Poco sostenuto – vivace. Here Beethoven returns to a practice he had seemingly abandoned: a slow introduction to the first movement of a symphony. This long and dignified passage, almost as much an overture as an introduction, leads to the key of E major (the dominant of A), where it begins a bouncing 6/8 rhythm that is to continue throughout the movement. A flute quietly introduces the first subject of the vivace, taking up the light-hearted rhythm. This bouncing single beat (dotted quaver, semi quaver, quaver) is clothed, but never fully disguised, in a splendid variety of dynamics and keys. As if trying to break its relentless grasp, Beethoven brings the music to a complete halt. After a stunned silence the orchestra recovers its balance and proceeds irrepressibly to the end.

Allegretto. Allegretto is a disconcerting direction for this most beautiful and mournful of movements. Beethoven presumably feared that a more conventional andante would encourage it to plod. The key is A minor; the rhythm a resigned and constant two-bar unit (crotchet, quaver, quaver; crotchet, crotchet). The lower strings lead this sombre, simple march. A plangent obbligato joins the procession, and twice the steady footfalls pause in deference to a melting tune in A major. The movement ends as it began, on a weary and unresolved A minor chord.

Presto – assai meno presto. Beethoven's mastery of the scherzo form was by now awesome. In the first few bars of this presto he skips playfully up an F major arpeggio; twenty bars later he lightly descends in the key of A major. The wonders of such harmonic sleights-of-hand are matched by the remarkable 'trio' section. The key abruptly changes to D major and the mood from impish gaiety to a serene pilgrims' hymn, one long suspended A suggesting that the pilgrims' organ is not entirely air-tight.

Allegro con brio. Two jarring and fortissimo E major chords introduce this exuberant finale. The whirling rhythm of the first subject (in A major), with its huge hammer blows on the second beat, dominate the movement. A dance-like second subject finds little time to expand before its massive companion comes thundering back. This great tune lurches forward with convulsive upward slurs and stumbling breaks in rhythm. The effect is both grotesque and unforeseeably sublime.

Weber

Writing about his youth in 1811, Carl Maria von Weber (1786–1826) painted a characteristically Romantic picture. 'I have no happy childish days to look back upon,' he complained, 'no free open boyhood.' He was thinking of the restless years when his musical education was governed by the wanderings of his father's theatrical company. His greatest promise as a pianist and composer became evident in these early days, but his gifts did not fully mature until much later. Indeed, the young man's future did not look promising in 1810 when, employed by the dissolute Duke Ludwig at Stuttgart, he was accused of corruption and thrown into prison.

After this unfortunate episode he 'settled matters' with himself (as he put it) and rededicated his life to the performance and composition of music. In 1813 he was appointed director of the Prague Opera, where he proved himself a first-rate conductor and astonished his colleagues with theatrical expertise in all fields, from prompting to scene-painting. Among his hand-picked cast in Prague he found his future wife, Caroline Brandt.

Weber spent the last nine years of his life as director of the Dresden Court Opera. By this time he had already composed some of his greatest instrumental works, among them concertos for the piano, clarinet, horn and bassoon. These revealed his gift for ravishing melody and mastery of orchestration. At Dresden he composed the one work that established the direction German opera would take for the remainder of the century. From its first performance in 1821, Der Freischütz was an astonishing success. Weber's music perfectly captured the menace and magic of the opera's Romantic plot. 'I tremble to think of the future, for it is scarcely possible to rise higher than this,' Weber wrote after conducting a performance in 1822. These words were prophetic. Neither Euryanthe (1823) nor Oberon (1826) surpassed Der Freischütz as works of art.

Weber died of consumption in London after the successful première of Oberon. .Eighteen years later his remains were returned to Germany, where his funeral oration was read by his great successor, Richard Wagner.

Beethoven's ninth symphony was first performed in 1824 at the Kärntnertor Theatre in Vienna.

An engraving of
Beethoven in 1814

Symphony no. 8 in F major, opus 93
Beethoven was fond of his eighth symphony. He called it the 'little one', and when it was pointed out to him that this new work had not received the same applause as the seventh he replied sharply, 'Because it is much better'.

Notwithstanding the composer's approval, the eighth has remained a puzzle and, for some, a disappointment. To begin with, it is very short; only the first symphony takes less time to perform. Those who value a work by its sheer length will be bound to see this symphony – dwarfed by the sixth, seventh and ninth – as an inferior creation.

And then there is the problem of style. How can the man who wrestled with angels in the third and fifth symphonies suddenly turn his attention to clockwork soldiers? The eighth seems to be a conventional symphony in form, and yet it is full of wrong turns, surprises and deliberate jolts to the audience. What is it all about? The answer is partly in the question. Those who can only think of Beethoven as a marble bust, a noble figure staring at some distant mountain range, will for ever be disappointed with the earthy, witty and sometimes petulant craftsman of the eighth symphony. Yet here is Beethoven, a man of the world (or at least of Vienna), at the height of his powers. The jokes and anger of the first movement, the affectionate games of the second, the grace of the minuet and the fierce wit of the finale are as much a portrait of the composer as anything that remains on canvas or stone.

Allegro vivace e con brio. Without a note of introduction, the full orchestra bursts in with a cheerful first subject. This is a twelve-bar passage – four bars of determined forte and then, as if to compensate for such bravado, a dolce piano answer by the winds before the orchestra recovers its energy and completes the tune. An exuberant tutti seems to be leading to the second subject when the music suddenly develops a limp, coming down heavily and unexpectedly on the third (last) beat of

Clementi

The symphonic works of Muzio Clementi (1752–1832) are perhaps the least important part of this extraordinary man's output, which was mainly of piano music, but his works are important in the way they developed sonata form from the early Rococo period, right through the Classical era into the Romantic age. Imported to England while still a boy by a wealthy patron (a cousin of the eccentric pederast William Beckford), Clementi made his home and his fortune in that country. As well as composing about 100 piano sonatas and the famous Gradus ad Parnassum studies, he was also music publisher and founder of a piano factory (where he employed the young John Field as demonstrator of the instruments) in Soho, London. Almost the only symphonic work to be heard today of his, for he failed to publish most of his orchestral music, is the extraordinary Great National Symphony, which boasts an elaborate contrapuntal treatment of God Save the King.

the bar. It finally hobbles to a halt. There is a bar of complete silence before the strings and solo bassoon, now soft and staccato, persuade the second subject to begin. This turns out to be a beautiful legato melody but in the 'wrong' key – not the anticipated C major (the dominant of F) but the harmonically distant D. The winds salvage the situation by repeating the passage in C, but even they are unable to bring it to a satisfactory cadence. It remains a tune without a proper ending.

In the development section Beethoven takes the opening (a crotchet and four quavers) and plays with it furiously, as a tiger would a mouse. He drags it through key after key – C, B flat, A, D minor. And in the climactic recapitulation only the bassoons, cellos and basses are allowed to continue with this ill-fated first subject. The rest of the orchestra rages at triple forte, a dynamic Beethoven used very rarely. Good humour returns for the second subject, but the excitement erupts again (and again in triple forte) during the long coda. As if deliberately calming himself, Beethoven stops the music for a complete bar and then, very softly, brings the movement to a delicate close.

Allegretto scherzando. This is the shortest symphonic movement that Beethoven wrote, lasting only about three minutes. It is said to have been inspired one boisterous evening in 1812 by the chronometer, an early form of metronome. Imitating its monotonous ta-ta-ta-ta, Beethoven wrote a simple canon in honour of the inventor, his friend Maelzel. This tune introduces the surprising allegretto scherzando. The chronometer, represented by woodwinds and horns playing pianissimo and staccato, accompanies a delicate first subject picked out by the violins. Characteristically, Beethoven does not let his audience drowse off to this hypnotic ticking. After only four bars of the second subject he shatters his fragile structure with a savage fortissimo from the strings and, two bars later, by another. The orchestra quietly picks itself up and finds its way back to the initial theme, whereupon the whole opening section is repeated with only minor variations.

As if impatient with his clockwork conceit, Beethoven ends the movement with a noisy and deliberately trite coda, mocking at once both his music and the expectations of his audience.

Tempo di menuetto. One of Beethoven's great achievements as a symphonist was to transform the traditional minuet and trio (the third movement) into an exuberant and passionate scherzo. Here, however,

As the autograph shows, Beethoven dedicated his ninth symphony to Friedrich Wilhelm III.

A mill at Grinzing, outside Vienna. Beethoven lived for a time nearby, and was influenced by the peaceful countryside to compose the Pastoral symphony.

The wedding of Napoleon and Marie Louise of Austria. Napoleon was at first hailed as a liberator by many countries seeking feedom from feudal traditions, and Beethoven too was fired by this enthusiasm. But Napoleon's dictatorship and dynastic ideas soon turned the tide of liberal thought against him.

A catalogue in the *Allgemeine Musikaliche Zeitung*, advertising the latest publications for sale, including Beethoven's cello sonata, opus 69, and an arrangement of his fifth symphony for piano duet.

At Beethoven's funeral on 29 March 1827, 20,000 people filled the square in front of the Schwarzspanierhaus. Schubert (who was to follow him to the grave one year later) was one of the torchbearers, and the poet Grillparzer composed the funeral oration.

INTELLIGENZ-BLATT
zur Allgemeinen Musikalischen Zeitung.

October.   No. I.   1809.

Anzeige.

Schillers Lied von der Glocke, durch Andreas Romberg in Musik gesetzt, schon öfters in Hamburger Concerten mit dem grössten Beyfall aufgeführt, ist bey N. Simrok in Bonn verlegt und in allen guten Musikhandlungen zu haben. Die Partitur zu 16 Franken, der Klavierauszug zu 6 Fr. und die Orchesterstimmen zu 9 Franken. Der Klavierauszug kann auch bey der Aufführung als ausgeschriebene Singstimme benutzt werden, und so kann dies schöne Meisterwerk sogleich aufgeführet werden. Zur Verständlichkeit der Zuhörer ist der Text, nach der Behandlung in der Musik, besonders abgedruckt, und wird für 2 Gr. verkauft.

Dies Werk ist bey Breitkopf und Härtel zu haben
in Partitur für   4 Thlr. Sächs. Courant.
in Stimmen für   2 Thlr. 6 Gr.
im Klavierauszug   1 Thlr. 12 Gr.

Neue Musikalien, welche im Verlag der Breitkopf- und Härtelschen Musikhandlung in Leipzig erschienen sind.

Beethoven, L. v. Sinfonie à grand Orchestre. No 5. (C moll)   4 Thlr. 12 Gr.
— Sinfonie pastorale à gr. Orchestre. No 6. (F dur)   4 Thlr. 12 Gr.
Pär, F. Ouverture de l'Opéra: les Mines de Pologne, à gr. Orch.   1 Thlr.
— Ouverture de l'Opéra: Numa Pompilius, à gr. Orchestre   1 Thlr.

Für das Pianoforte.

Beethoven, L. v. grande Sonate av. Violoncelle. Op. 69.   1 Thlr. 12 Gr.
— 2 Trios p. Pianoforte, Violon et Violoncelle. Op. 70. No 1.   1 Thlr. 12 Gr.
— do   do   — 2.   2 Thlr.
— 5me Sinfonie, arrangée à 4 mains   2 Thlr. 12 Gr.
Beethoven, L. v. 8 Variations sur le Trio: (Tändeln und Scherzen) del' Op: Soliman, No. 10.   16 Gr.
Dussek, J. L. 3 Sonates progressives à 4 mains Op. 67.   1 Thlr. 8 Gr.
— Notturno p. Pianoforte et Violon, avec un Cor ad libitum. Op. 68.   1 Thlr.
Fischer, M. G. Sonate à 4 mains. Op. 12.   1 Thlr. 12 Gr.
Gyrowez, A. Ouverture de l'Op. Agnes Sorel.   8 Gr.
Nözel, C. F. Sammlung v. Schottischen Anglaisen, Walzern u. Anglaisen f. d. Klavier.   14 Gr.
— Sammlung von 6 Montferino's, Quadrillen, Ecossaisen, Walzern und Massurischen Tänzen f. d. Pforte mit Begleit. einer Flöte und Violine.   16 Gr.
Righini, V. Ouverture de Tigranes.   8 Gr.
Steibelt, D. 6 Sonates doigtées d'une difficulté graduée. Liv. 1.   1 Thlr.
— do   do   — 2.   1 Thlr. 12 Gr.
— grande Sonate p. le Pianoforte av. accomp. de Violon obligé. Op. 79.   12 Gr.
— grande Sonate av. Violon obligé. Op. 80.   16 Gr.
— grande Sonate av. Violon obligé. Op. 81.   1 Thlr.
— Fantaisie av. 9 Variations sur une Walse Russe.   16 Gr.
— Methode de Piano, ou l'art d'enseigner cet Instrument. (Französisch und Deutsch).   2 Thlr. 12 Gr.

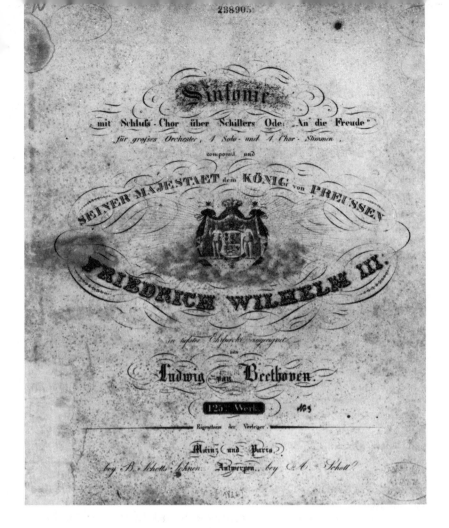

9th Symphony
The title-page of
Beethoven's symphony
no. 9, the *Choral*.

he deliberately returns to the elegance of pre-revolutionary Europe, as if to apologize for his previous irreverence. The one-two-three rhythm is boldly established for two bars by strings and bassoons before the violins enter with a smooth descending line that is both graceful and, for once, danceable. Beethoven cannot resist the temptation to throw the dancers off their beat in the second strain of the minuet, but the bassoonist quickly finds his place and restores order.

Two French horns and solo clarinet, accompanied by an athletic cello, introduce a ravishing trio section, 'this most charming of all idylls', as Richard Wagner called it. The violins, who next take up the tune, fail to improve upon this opening, and the music passes back to winds and lower strings before returning to the stately minuet.

Allegro vivace. With the first few lively bars of this finale Beethoven seems determined to remain in the eighteenth century, among the untroubled tunes of Haydn. Only when his skittish opening is rocked by a discordant C#, does it become clear that Beethoven the practical joker is waiting in ambush. Time and again throughout the movement he surprises his audience wiith sudden changes in dynamics, startling silences, abrupt key changes and bizarre orchestral effects. Again, as in the first movement, a lyrical second subject enters in the 'wrong' key, and again the conscientious woodwinds put it right. A short development section attempts to introduce a note of seriousness which ends in burlesque when bassoon and timpani go bouncing off on their own for an extended solo. Beethoven was never more full of fun or of invention. In the lengthy coda he begins a stately march, forces it to quicken its pace and finally to jog into the distance, once again with the bassoon and kettledrums. Then, just as the cheerful first subject reappears, it is compelled to enter the jarring key of F# minor. Having hijacked his own tune (his weapon being the sudden C# heard earlier in the movement), Beethoven finally brings the symphony to a jolting and noisy close. His own laughter is almost audible above the crashing F major chords.

Diabelli

Today Anton Diabelli (1781–1858) is not generally remembered for his accomplished songs, Masses and piano music, nor for the successful Viennese music publishing company that bore his name. He is known instead for the simple waltz tune upon which Beethoven based his thirty-three 'Diabaelli' Variations, one of the great monuments of the solo piano repertory Diabelli had not expected to unleash a masterpiece of these dimensions. His original plan had been to commission fifty variations, each by a different composer (including Schubert and the young Franz Liszt). Beethoven, it seems, got carried away with the enthusiasm for the project.
Diabelli made a more deliberate contribution to the history of music in recognizing the genius of Franz Schubert and, with the song Erlkönig (opus 1), becoming his first publisher.

Symphony no. 9 in D minor, opus 125

None of Beethoven's symphonies have caused so much controversy as his ninth. This is the result of its great length ('at least twice as long as it should be', complained the *Harmonica* after the English première in 1825), its enormous difficulty to perform and the unprecedented choral finale, a setting of Friedrich Schiller's 'An die Freude' (Ode to Joy). For some these difficulties remain, but most now share the farsighted opinion of Robert Schumann: 'In this work the great man has given us of his greatest'.

Allegro, ma non troppo, un poco maestoso. The symphony opens with ten bars of shimmering suspense, while the violins hesitantly pick out sparse descending notes. Then, as if a dam has broken, the full orchestra bursts out with the fierce theme that dominates this movement. The woodwinds exercise a calming influence in their legato second subject, but this is only a false peace, soon disturbed by the unsettling beat of the kettledrums. Likewise, a fugue in the development section, suggesting stern resignation, is shattered by the angry return of the opening theme. In the long coda the winds finally accept the prevailing passion and, to a growling repetitive bass, begin a funeral march that leads to the defiant conclusion.

Molto vivace - presto. This ebullient 'scherzo' is a perfect antidote to the emotional rigors of the preceding movement. Strings, timpani and then full orchestra pounce on the audience in eight introductory bars. Then begins a buoyant fugue that gradually builds in intensity until it has become a wild dance, its joy bordering on frenzy. As if alarmed at losing his good humour, Beethoven now takes the music into a major key and a pastoral mood for the trio section (marked presto). The movement concludes as it began, both playful and violent, like a kitten with its claws extended.

Adagio molto e cantabile - andante moderato. In profound stillness the strings introduce the beautiful adagio. Each phrase is echoed by a choir of winds, their organ-like tones enhancing the religious tranquillity. The tempo now changes to andante and the key from B flat to D major, with violins and violas playing a yearning, restless melody. This wistful andante emerges once more, but the remainder of the movement consists of exquisite variations on the adagio theme. The serenity is briefly challenged by the brass, but peace descends once more and the movement ends as calmly as it began.

Presto - allegro ma non troppo - allegro assai - presto - allegro assai vivace - alla marcia - andante maestoso - adagio ma non troppo, ma divoto - allegro energico, sempre ben marcato - allegro ma non tanto - prestissimo - maestoso - prestissimo. A violent chord from the full orchestra introduces a long declamatory recitative by cellos and basses. As if uncertain where to proceed, the orchestra next plays snatches from each of the three preceding movements before discovering the beautiful anthem that is the subject of this finale. The bass soloist now enters, resuming the recitative heard earlier and then putting words (from Schiller's Ode to Joy) to the majestic tune. He is followed by full chorus and then solo quartet. The rest of the movement consists of five sections, each of which is an extended variation on the Ode to Joy theme. Briefly these are a spirited 'Turkish' march with tenor and men's chorus; a devout choral episode; a boisterous and brassy exhibition piece for chorus; a variation for combined forces, concluding with a solemn adagio; and a tearaway prestissimo which is reigned back for a prayerful section before the tumultuous final bars.

The young Beethoven, at the height of his powers as a lion of the keyboard.

Beethoven's tomb in
Vienna.

Below: Napoleon's forces
marching into Vienna.
When the French were
bombarding the city,
Beethoven was forced to
seek refuge in a cellar.

3

Schubert

Schubert

Schubert (1797–1828) was born in Liechtental, on 31 January. His father was the parish schoolmaster, and the family lived in genteel poverty. The household was a musical one: Franz learned the violin and piano at home, before being sent away to the imperial 'Convict' seminary in Vienna where he had won a choral scholarship. His most important teacher there was Salieri, but such was the boy's precocious talent that even the grand old pedagogue (who had given Beethoven lessons) found he could teach Schubert very little. He was obliged to leave there when his voice broke, attended teacher training college, and in 1814 became an assistant teacher in his father's school – a job he detested. That same year, at the age of just seventeen, he wrote his great song (to words from Goethe's Faust), 'Gretchen at the Spinning-wheel'. Four years later he decided to give up teaching and support himself through his compositions, an especially difficult situation since Schubert was no virtuoso pianist or conductor and could not earn his living through performances. But he continued to compose at an astonishing rate, despite poverty, lack of recognition, and serious illness. He remained almost always cheerful and optimistic, and knew at least the comfort of a devoted circle of friends who believed in his music and loved him as a brother. Only at the end of his short life were there signs that he was going to become successful. Till then, his fortunes had been at a perpetually low ebb, allowing himself to be bilked by unscrupulous publishers. Paradoxically the year of his greatest creative output was 1828, the year of his death. It was as if he was hurrying to complete his life's work. That year produced a succession of masterpieces: the Great C major symphony, the wonderful C major quintet, the three last piano sonatas, twenty songs, church music, and the miraculous F minor Fantasy for piano duet. Weakened by syphilis, he contracted typhoid fever in October and died in the arms of his brother Ferdinand the following month. It took the musical

On the strength of a single work, the symphony no. 8 in B minor (known as the 'Unfinished'), Schubert has become one of the most popular and best loved orchestral composers in the world. But anything even approaching such acclaim was totally unknown to the composer during his lifetime: his genius was recognized and appreciated by only a small circle of friends, who occasionally met at 'Schubertiads' to perform his songs, piano pieces and chamber music in a genial atmosphere of conviviality. But such a lack of recognition was no great cause of distress to Schubert: he died at the age of only thirty-one, young enough to be still buoyed up with optimism, and on the edge of yet greater discoveries. The tragedy is ours, not his.

But it remains a remarkable fact that such a relatively large part of his (admittedly copious) output remains little-known and unperformed – much more than is the case with Mozart, say, or Beethoven – and this curious state of affairs is well exemplified in his symphonies. In some respects, the neglect is understandable. In an output of more than 600 *Lieder,* even if we ignore the difficult and subjective problem of variation in quality, there would still remain the practical impossibility of more than a fraction of these pieces achieving any broad popularity; and on the whole posterity has opted to favour the most tuneful among them, such as 'The Trout', *An die Musik* (which has even been successfully transformed into an instrumental rock number), and perhaps a couple of dozen more. Schubert's fifteen operas too are almost entirely neglected, for while they contain much music of outstanding beauty, their plots unfortunately are so trumpery and two-dimensional as to render them virtually unperformable to all but the composer's most ardent apologists.

The symphonies fall into two groups: nos 1–6, which are predominantly works of the composer's youth, and nos 8 & 9 (the *Unfinished* and the *Great* C major), both masterpieces of Schubert's maturity. There is no seventh symphony: this was originally the number given to the ninth, mentioned above, and (to add to the confusion) sometimes to an incomplete and unpublished work in E minor. In addition to these, there is strong evidence for a lost symphony written in 1825, known as the *Gmunden-Gastein* symphony after the places where it was composed. (The musicologist Otto Erich Deutsch, compiler of the chronological catalogue of all Schubert's works, has even given it a 'Deutsch' number: D 849.) Some Schubert scholars also believe that the marvellous Grand Duo for piano duet is an arrangement for four hands of a symphony, and there are piano sketches too for a projected symphony in D (D 615).

As mentioned above, not all of these works are familiar to audiences. Several of the works from the composer's apprentice years have much in them that is juvenile and obviously derivative (particularly of Haydn). But they have nevertheless a noticeable personality of their own, and anyone concerned to understand the development of Schubert's ineffable genius will find much food for thought in the early symphonies, as well as rich delights. Even in the first symphony, written while the composer was still at school, there are moments we can already hear to be 'typically Schubertian', such as the sudden switches from major to minor, the long-spanned and seemingly spontaneous melodies, and the fondness for rocking triplet rhythms.

The orchestration is, on the whole, unadventurous. The forces used are typical of the period, and display a frequent preference for the woodwind section. The scoring in all of the symphonies is not yet what we think of as 'Romantic': Schubert had studied the art at first hand, playing symphonies of the earlier classical period in the school orchestra, and this background is obviously reflected in the early works. It must be remembered as well that the young man hoped and intended that these works would be performed. Their only opportunity, of course, would be amateur performance, so conformity in instrumentation was additionally important.

Symphony no. 1 in D major, D 82

Franz Schubert put his first symphony on paper while still a schoolboy, at the age of sixteen. No sketches of it remain, nor of the following two. We know only when and how it happened from recollections by fellow-students and letters Schubert himself wrote to his parents. The first performance took place within the closed circle of the school orchestra

world many years before they knew what a mighty genius they had lost. Only those close to the composer realized the true scale of the tragedy. 'Schubert is dead,' wrote his friend Moritz von Schwind, 'and with him all that we had of the brightest and fairest.' At his own wish, he was interred next to the grave of his hero, Beethoven.

A Romantic and imaginary conception of Schubert at work.

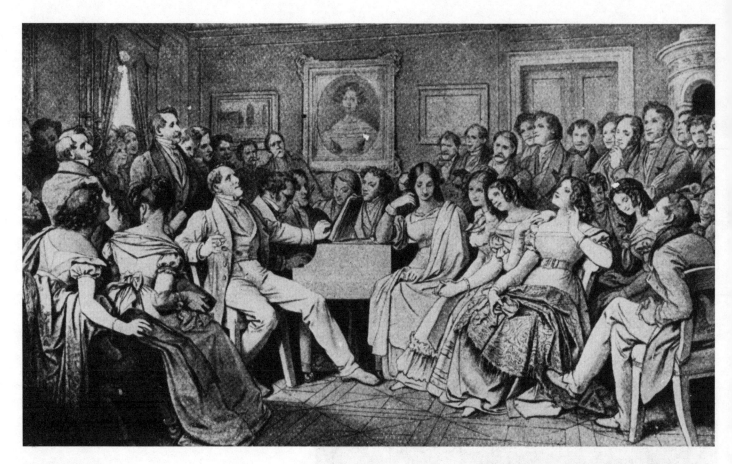

An impression of a
Schubertiad, with the
composer at the piano
accompanying the great
singer Joseph Vogl at his
side.

in which Schubert played, but little more than this is known. The genesis
of the first three symphonies remains largely undocumented. They may
also have been put before the amateur orchestra of which Schubert's
father was a member. Schubert completed the work on 28 October 1813.
For a sixteen-year-old he shows an exceptional grasp of form. He was
well-acquainted with Haydn and Mozart, and no doubt Beethoven as
well. But aside from these he can have had few other examples to follow,
as his familiarity with the repertoire was slight.

The first symphony begins with a slow introduction, leading to the first
allegro vivace. In this movement Schubert is not yet recognizable as the
lyrical master he was to become. The first and principal theme is nothing
more than a scale; but the second theme is more melodic, introduced by
the violins with subsequent support by the woodwinds.

The second movement, an andante, is extremely simple and lyrical. It
could just as well have been written for string quartet, for all the
important melodic and harmonic elements are given to the strings.

After the andante comes a minuet which makes a resolute and purposeful impression. The rhythm is sturdy and pointed, the trio, a dance-like
melody for violins and bassoons.

The finale, allegro vivo, is an almost naive, ingenuous movement. Here
again the strings take precedence, with a rhythmic melody in the first
violins, a staccato accompaniment in the second violins and melodic
ornamentation in the winds.

The first symphony suffers from a typical 'Schubertian' defect: excessive
prolongation of material containing only a few ideas. But Schubert is not
the only one who sometimes seems unable to cut his music short. It was
Schumann who referred to its 'heavenly length'.

Symphony no. 2 in B flat major, D 125
Between 1813 – the year of the first symphony – and 1815, Schubert
devoted himself intensively to the creation of compositions other than
symphonies. A number of string quartets, an unsuccessful opera and his

first religious work, the Mass in F major, were written during these two years. But above all, this period saw a milestone in the history of the *Lied, Grettchen am Spinnrade.* Schubert managed instinctively to set the essentials of Goethe's poem in *Faust* to music, with a rhythmic piano accompaniment imitating the whirr of the spinning-wheel and above this, a simple but eloquently expressive melody for the voice. The genius of this song and the seeming ripeness of the Mass in F major find a surprising counterweight in the youthful immaturity of the second symphony.

Schubert follows the customary path: a slow largo introduction to the first movement's allegro vivace. The main theme is a spiritedly accented melody built of scale figures. The second theme is of a more lyrical character, though the concluding triplet provides a suggestion of restlessness. The second movement, andante, presents a theme, both lovely and simple, in the violins. Schubert's preoccupation with smaller forms is clearly evident; the melody could easily have served as a theme for one of his *Moments musicaux* for piano. Five variations follow the theme, the only instance of Schubert's use of the variation form in orchestral music. The third movement a minuet has more the character of a scherzo. A forceful melody, played loudly in 3/4 time, forms the movement's principal material, interrupted by a trio section consisting of an airy oboe melody. The finale, presto vivace, offers a combination of witty and lively themes cast in a somewhat unusual form midway between a rondo and a sonata.

Symphony no. 3 in D major, D 200

The third symphony was composed in the summer of 1815, and though a lovely piece and full of invention, must pale beside important progressions that Schubert made that year in his songwriting: *Der Erlkönig* and *Die junge Nonne.*

Notable is the first movement's introductory clarinet theme, given to this instrument rather than to the strings which Schubert normally favoured. We know from letters that he made a first attempt at writing a theme for horns and oboes, then another for strings, finally opting for a simple clarinet melody. This adagio maestoso introduction is short and its melodic material is of no further importance in the rest of the movement. The second movement is not the traditional slow movement, but an allegretto in the middle of which the clarinet again assumes prominence. The third movement is a scherzo-like minuet with a trio reminiscent of a Viennese waltz. Here Schubert's partiality for the woodwinds can be clearly heard. The last movement, presto vivace, has its principal theme a rhythmic melody in 6/8 time. The movement in its entirety strongly recalls that well-known Italian dance, the tarantella.

Symphony no. 4 in C minor, D 417 – Tragic

The name *Tragic* was given to the symphony by Schubert himself, though just why is not clear. Possibly by using this suggestive nickname he wished to awaken the interest of the public, for in the years of early Romanticism symphonies were not widely popular. Opera was held in high regard, but since Beethoven the symphonic repertory had fallen into a certain neglect. C minor is the key of Beethoven's fifth symphony, though this is the only occasion on which Schubert used it in his orchestral works. Another explanation for the nickname *Tragic* is that Schubert simply wrote it above the score as a joke, perhaps thinking of the continual monetary difficulties which obliged him to earn a living in what was for him a highly unsympathetic way: teaching.

It is true that in the period previous to this fourth symphony Schubert was occupied setting to music texts of a more or less tragic nature, having to do with melancholy, death, nostalgia, love and longing. Typical Romantic concerns in a nutshell: *Der König in Thule, Lodas Gespenst, Das Grab, Des Mädchens Klage, Lied der Mignon* ('Nur wer die Sehnsucht kennt'). But the origin of this utterly inappropriate sub-title

Rossini

–Gioacchino Rossini (1792–1868) **Rossini was born in the Italian town of Pesaro and received musical instruction in Bologna, but soon left all academic learning behind. He wanted simply to write music and to avoid being crushed under a burden of theoretical ideas. His first one-act opera,** La cambiale di matrimonio, **presented in 1810, was a great success with both public and press alike. As of the second performance of Il** barbiere di Siviglia **(the première itself was not** successful), Rossini's name was definitively established. He wrote one opera after another, usually on commission, and always in a remarkably short time. At the age of thirty-seven he turned his back on opera composition to produce only salon pieces and two larger devotional choral works. He wrote in a romantic** bel canto **style. Extremely melodic arias with lively orchestral accompaniments, 'catchy tunes' which nearly always proved instantly memorable, were the chief ingredients of his success. Rossini travelled widely throughout Europe, eventually taking up permanent residence, along with his second wife, in Paris in 1855. He was by now extremely wealthy, and lived and entertained on a lavish scale. There he was visited by many musicians, among them Arthur Sullivan and Richard Wagner, and at his death left a fortune worth more than one million pounds.**

remains a mystery. In the entire work there is not one trace of sadness or melancholy, of 'dark thoughts' or drama. On the contrary, the music manifests only a natural, lively and melodic beauty. Without preliminary sketches or other preparatory work, Schubert wrote the symphony directly in score.

Again the first movement, allegro vivace, begins with a slow introduction, adagio molto. A robust opening chord is followed by a lyrical melody of almost solemn magnificence, played by the violins with a lovely recapitulation by the cellos. If this introduction gives a somewhat sombre impression, this is immediately dissipated by the beginning of the allegro whose first theme sparkles as if glittering in sunlight. The second theme is lyrical, but as both themes are developed Schubert concentrates mainly on the first lively material with its many small rhythmic ideas.

The second movement, andante, displays a similarity with the famous *Impromptu no. 6, D 935* for piano. The theme is in the same key and distils the same atmosphere. The graceful theme is unfolded by the strings as if by a string quartet. The second theme is distinguished by the continual repetition of the same note in the accompaniment. The first theme eventually returns, as befits the rondo form, and both combine to bring the andante to its conclusion.

The following minuet has nothing in common with the traditional minuet, but is actually a lively scherzo in which the theme is immediately proclaimed by fortissimo winds and strings. The trio is short, dance-like and airy. If there were a 'tragic' element in the symphony, it certainly would not be found here.

The finale, allegro, consists of short motivic themes which seem to some extent to get in one another's way and as a result are not truly developed, but rather undergo a long series of repetitions. In this movement a number of unusual harmonic progressions can be heard. The movement leads to a festive conclusion in C major.

Symphony no. 5 in B flat major, D 485
This symphony is one of easily accessible charm and melodic richness. To express what he here has to say, Schubert needs only a small orchestra: strings, one flute, two oboes, two horns and two bassoons. As

The great German writer Wolfgang van Goethe was a friend of Beethoven, though he had no time for Schubert's miraculous settings of his poetry.

Schubert's birthplace
at Liechtental, a
working-class suburb
of Vienna.

Overleaf:
Above In 1818 Schubert
lived at the Schloss
Zseliz as music master
tot the Esterházy
family. His own room
is at the left of the
illustration. It was at
Zseliz that he wrote his
sixth symphony.

Overleaf: Below Dancing
in the garden at
Atzenbrugg, by
Schubert's friend, the
Romantic painter
Moritz van Schwind. It
was a favourite place
for merrymaking of
Schubert and his
friends; he once wrote
a set of Atzenbrugger
dances.

Overleaf: Facing page
The Romantic movement
in Russian music arrived
with Glinka's opera *A life
for the Tsar*, containing
this lively chorus.

SCHLOSS ZELIZ

a consequence the symphony has come to be known as 'the symphony without trumpets and timpani', but just as remarkable for Schubert is the absence of clarinets. The work dates from the last half of 1816 when Schubert was nineteen years old.

Though the music still bears traces of Haydn's influence, and is suffused with a Mozartean delicacy, it is at the same time replete with so many of those unmistakeable Schubertian fingerprints that the listener loves to identify. There is no need here for any portentous slow introduction: the bright, gauzy allegro springs to life with the help of a vivacious little violin figure, from which the more reflective second theme also seems to derive. The entire, life-enhancing movement is all too soon at an end, and the ensuing andante con moto takes itself much more seriously. This is just such a movement as Haydn might have written, with a lovely melody 'so simple that one feels one has always known it' accompanied and embellished with the utmost tenderness, and a beautiful excursion into the minor.

The third movement, Menuetto: allegro molto is in the minor, balanced by a warm and bucolic country-dance as its trio section (in G major). This movement is altogether more of a traditional minuet than the racy third movements in the previous symphonies, perhaps in order to give the ear enough time to hear the chromatic notes in the theme; and its setting in another key than the home B flat of the symphony is a typically wayward trick of the composer's musical thought.

In the last movement, marked allegro vivace, there are again many Haydnesque touches. The irrepressible gaiety of the (often repeated) first theme buoys the entire movement along, and is counterbalanced by another melody which, this time, could belong to no-one else than Schubert. To convey the impression of apparent spontaneity within the carefully-wrought framework of an orchestral score as Schubert does here, not withstanding the wit and good humour of the movement, is a masterstroke of craftsmanship.

Symphony no. 6 in C major, D 589

With the first of Schubert's C major symphonies, we come to the end of his first period of symphonic composition. It was completed in February

Romanticism

The word 'Romantic' signifies something different for everyone, its intensity varying from individual to individual. The most common definition implies a highly personal and emotional manner of expression. Another refers to a more or less defined period in the nineteenth century. The word itself is of French origin – literature written no longer in Latin but in Old French was given the name of 'lingua romana'. From this derived the word 'romance', a short poem of epic-lyric character. This lyricism in turn gave rise to the use of the word 'Romantic' to indicate anything which is considered free, individual, spontaneous, imaginative, emotional, heroic or fantastic. The word became fixed in common usage when in 1813 E.T.A.

Hoffmann employed it in an article concerning individual expression in Beethoven's instrumental music. The specific period of Romanticism spans nearly 100 years, from about 1800 until the century's end. The beginning of this era must be seen as a reaction against the previous period of rationalism, in which the emphasis was upon man as a rational, intellectual being fully capable of expressing his thoughts and feelings in clear language and of solving problems in a sane and intelligent way. Romanticism rebelled against this cerebral approach to existence. 'Feeling' assumed a place of central importance. A need for greater space was felt in order to allow external influences to penetrate to the fullest. A love of nature and the beauties of the countryside gained ascendancy. An early outstanding example is Beethoven's sixth

symphony, the Pastoral.

Another hallmark of the Romantic period is the consciousness of national or individual identity. Subjective sentiments sought liberation from dominating rules and laws, leading to revolutions in Europe in the wake of the French revolution and the subsequent Napoleonic empire. This observation by Jean-Jacques Rousseau is characteristic of the period: 'I am distinct from all others. I may be no better, but at least I am different.' These new ideas and ideals inspired a search for innovation and renewal in the arts. The dramatic musical form par excellence, opera, developed rapidly, encompassing all the elements of Romanticism, from the supernatural, as in Weber's Der Freischütz, through nationalism, as in Glinka's A Life for the Tsar, to the summit of operatic history, Wagner's mythology-based 'Total art work', The Ring.

Purely instrumental music also underwent changes. The symphony as an abstract musical phenomenon became less popular. Composers endeavoured to link their works to nature, literature, painting. 'Programme music' came into being: Liszt with his Faust and Dante symphonies, Mendelssohn with his Hebrides Overture, Smetana with his symphonic cycle My Fatherland, Richard Strauss with his Tod und Verklärung and Also sprach Zarathustra, to mention only a few. These last are examples of the symphonic poem, usually a one-movement work based on extra-musical particulars.

Two paths presented themselves: one, the inclusion of innovative Romantic ideas in a renewed symphonic form, the other, avoidance of new currents in favour of continued development of the traditional symphony, as was the case with Brahms and Bruckner. A clear Somewhere in the middle were the composers who were subjected to influences from both sides, such as Tchaikovsky, who eschewed programme music but could not entirely avoid it, and Dvořák, who avidly embraced whatever was new and used what appealed to him. Romanticism also seemed particularly appropriate to the development of smaller musical forms. The Lied underwent a rapid evolution, from Schubert to Hugo Wolf and Richard Strauss. Short pieces, mostly for piano, became widely current and were given titles such as 'Impromptus', 'Nocturnes', 'Fantasiestücke', 'Mazurkas' 'Preludes', 'Waltzes', etc. Hundreds of examples can be found in the piano music of Chopin, Schubert, Schumann and Brahms. Compositional techniques were also considerably revolutionized. The old rules of harmony, based on the hierarchy of the notes of the scale, were overthrown and, in principle at least, any succession of keys became possible. The search for additional means of musical expression resulted in the expansion of the size of the orchestra and the use of more and varied instruments. The music of Wagner, Mahler and Berlioz (particularly in his Messe des Morts) offer obvious examples.

1818, and shows many echoes of Rossini, whose operas were coming very much into vogue in Vienna at that time. Coincidental with its composition was Schubert's decision to abandon school-teaching as a means of earning his living and make his compositions support him: this may be why he adopted such a frankly popular approach to symphonic writing in this work.

After an introductory adagio, the cheerful first movement weaves a merry and predictable way through some delightful modulations.

The central andante is a Romantic 'song without words', enhanced by a strongly rhythmic central section and some delightful, quasi-operatic part-writing for the woodwind.

The third movement, for the first time, is a scherzo and not a minuet. There are possible comparisons with Beethoven's seventh symphony to be drawn here, not least in the relationship of the trio's key to that of the scherzo proper (E major to C; and in Beethoven, A major to F).

The finale is again operatic in much of what it has to say. Melodic ideas abound – indeed Schubert, of all composers, was never short of them – but there is little attempt at reasoned development. Nevertheless, the movement provides a bright and happy *envoi* to this lesser-known group of early works.

Symphony no. 8 in B minor, D 759 – Unfinished
Why Schubert never finished this symphony will always remain a mystery, unless, as some suggest, the manuscript was subsequently lost by his friend Hüttenbrenner. Only the first two movements exist in their entirety, plus a few bars of the third. The finale is missing altogether.

Overleaf: A contemporary silhouette of Schubert at the piano.

The score, complete or just these two movements, was passed to Hüttenbrenner and thence to Johann Herbeck, conductor of the orchestra of the *Gesellschaft der Musikfreunde* in Vienna. In any event, the two existing movements awaken a desire for more. The first movement, allegro moderato, begins with a dark, eight-bar motif in the basses succeeded by the first theme proper on oboe and clarinet, an anguished expression of great longing. But the best-known theme is the second subject, an extended melody for cellos. The development, however, depends on the material used at the very opening of the work rather than on either of the subjects as such.

The second movement, andante con moto, is unhappily all-too-often played so slowly that it drags. Its subject-matter is poetical in the extreme: if ever any orchestral work can be considered the harbinger of Romanticism, this must be it. Repeated listening to the heavenly and serene themes of the movement, and their reappearances within it makes one aware of the marvellously constructed balance of the piece, which is perhaps its most perfect and satisfying element. It is pitched in the unlikely key of E major, which again seems to set an ethereal mood, enhanced by some of Schubert's most magical key changes.

The title page of Schubert's *Heidenröslein*, to a romantic verse by Goethe.

Frédéric Chopin, one of
the leading figures of the
Romantic movement.

Symphony no. 9 in C major, D 944 – Great

This and the *Unfinished* are Schubert's most important symphonies.
The work dates from February or March, 1828. In November of the same
year Schubert died. His request to the *Gesellschaft der Musikfreunde* in
Vienna to perform the symphony was denied by reason of the work's
great length and difficulty, thus Schubert himself never heard it
performed. After Schubert's death, his brother Ferdinand took an
interest in the composer's unpublished works and thanks to a visit paid
him by Robert Schumann, the symphony was finally performed in 1839
by the Gewandhaus orchestra of Leipzig under the direction of
Mendelssohn, albeit in a shortened version.

The opening andante can not be considered a mere introduction to the
allegro ma non troppo. It is a slow lengthy section on its own terms, cast
in a rondo form. The opening melody for the horns is extremely
beautiful. The *allegro*'s principal theme is strongly rhythmic. The
second theme is short with a characteristic triplet motif. In developing
these two short themes Schubert was unfortunately unable to avoid
rather too many repetitions of the themes themselves or of elements
drawn from them.

The second movement, andante con moto, contains a very lovely
principal theme, played by the oboe and recurring many times. Before
one of the repetitions there occurs a passage which is often referred to as
the most beautiful in all Schubert's symphonic œuvre. Robert
Schumann described it in these terms: 'There is a passage ... in which the
horn sounds from afar, as if coming from another world'. A small
rhythmic motif taken from the principal theme turns up again and again
throughout the entire movement.

The scherzo which follows manifests a scintillating vitality, its main
subject a waltz-like theme. The trio, ushered in by the horns, unfolds a
broad flowing melody. The finale is built upon three themes, but suffers
from the 'Schubertian defect' mentioned earlier: the too frequent
repetition of material of relatively minimal interest.

4

Schumann and Mendelssohn

Mendelssohn

Felix Mendelssohn (1809–47) was born in Hamburg but grew up in Berlin, where his family moved when he was three. His father Abraham was a wealthy banker, who oversaw the education of his children with a severe affection. Young Felix and his older sister Fanny began their day at 5 a.m., a discipline that encouraged their precociousness in music. At the age of nine, Felix made his first public appearance as a pianist. By then he had already begun to study composition, and at sixteen he confirmed his genius with the Octet for strings, one of the century's great chamber works. 'Ce garçon est riche,' pronounced the crusty old composer Cherubini (without the hint of a 'double entendre').

Mendelssohn's adult life is a bewildering series of travels and musical triumphs. Leipzig, where he conducted the Gewandhaus orchestra and founded the Conservatory in 1842, became his spiritual home, but London had an almost equally strong claim. His first trip to Britain, when he was twenty, inspired two of his finest works, the Scottish symphony (No. 3) and the Hebrides overture. By his tenth visit, in the year of his death, he was a friend of Queen Victoria and Prince Albert, and the undisputed idol of English musical society. This public figure was in sharp contrast to Mendelssohn the family man, a devoted husband and the father of five children. Mendelssohn's influence extended far beyond his own compositions. When only twenty he conducted Bach's St Matthew Passion in Berlin, the first

The symphony is a slow, conservative beast. When the first fireworks of Romanticism exploded behind its back, it did not leap up and charge into the new century. Instead it merely ambled forward, forcing composers to drag their heels alongside or to run ahead after the more excitable songs, operas and caprices.

Beethoven and his great predecessors Haydn and Mozart were largely responsible for creating this monster. These three geniuses devoted much of their lives to writing symphonic masterpieces. By the time Beethoven had finished his monumental ninth symphony, there appeared to be little more that could be said. Yet the challenge was still there, and few Romantic composers could resist the temptation of trying to urge that mammoth creature to move at their own bidding.

Two men who succeeded in impressing the symphony with their own particular stamp of genius were Felix Mendelssohn and Robert Schumann. In education and temperament these two were quite dissimilar. Mendelssohn was a wealthy, highly trained and intensely self-disciplined musician – a well-established composer by his twenty-first birthday. Schumann was emotionally volatile (in later life mentally ill) and largely self-taught; he had composed next to nothing when he was twenty-one. Despite their differences, both Mendelssohn and Schumann approached the symphony in the same manner, revealing caution and respect that is not popularly associated with the Romantic movement. Neither man fundamentally challenged the division of the symphony into four movements, or even the form these movements took; there was still the opening allegro in traditional sonata form, still the light-hearted scherzo or minuet, still the eloquent adagio and the rousing finale. What then distinguishes these 'Romantic' symphonies from their classical ancestors? To begin with, there is a modest but insistent attempt at description. Pure form was not always enough; music could be improved upon with an idea or an image behind it. Mendelssohn may not have had a precise picture in mind when he wrote the first movement of his *Scottish* symphony, but he was clearly trying to describe in music the grey and rugged 'feel' of Scotland. There is also a Romantic reverence for the distant past, beautifully captured by Schumann, for example, in the fourth movement of his *Rhenish* symphony, a musical tribute to the Gothic splendour of Cologne Cathedral. An interest in folk music, which was later to become a school of composition in itself, is evident in Mendelssohn's ebullient *saltarello* (symphony no. 4) or Schumann's *ländler* (the second movement of symphony no. 3). Perhaps the most significant innovation was the effort by both men to unify their symphonies internally with common musical themes and thus to invest a traditional, formal structure with a modern life of its own.

Other men did their best to lead the classical symphony into the Romantic age. The Frenchman Hector Berlioz hauled it off the beaten track on an extraordinary diversion that few could follow. Niels Gade in Denmark, Johannes Verhulst in Holland and the durable old campaigner Ludwig Spohr each made worthy, but generally forgettable, contributions. It remained to Mendelssohn and Schumann, with their old-fashioned minds and modern sensibilities, to forge a permanent link between the nineteenth century's two greatest symphonists, Beethoven and Brahms.

The symphonies of Mendelssohn

For young Felix Mendelssohn there was no escaping the symphony. He was more than just a teenage prodigy, an able pianist and a precocious composer. He clearly possessed genius as well, and was thus the unfortunate heir-apparent to Beethoven, whose symphonies cast an

performance of that work since the composer's death. Throughout his life he tirelessly championed the music of Bach. He also conducted the first performance of Schubert's C major symphony, which his friend Robert Schumann had discovered in manuscript on a visit to Vienna. Mendelssohn composed with obsessive energy throughout his life. Some of his more superficial works are justly neglected but much remains to be rediscovered and reappraised. His status declined in the late nineteenth and early twentieth centuries, when the charm and skill of his music was mistaken for mere facility, his conservatism for timidity. But certain masterpieces have survived the sternest critical scrutiny: the Italian symphony (no. 4), the violin concerto, the overture and incidental music to A Midsummer Night's Dream (written when he was seventeen and thirty-four respectively) and several of the Songs Without Words for solo piano.

Weakened by years of overwork, Mendelssohn was unable to recover from his shock at the death of his beloved sister Fanny. He died at thirty-eight, the most celebrated symphonic composer of his day.

Facing page: By the age of twelve, Mendelssohn was already an accomplished composer. *Left:* A sketch by the composer of the garden-house at the family home in Berlin.

Mendelssohn's beloved
sister Fanny, little more
than three years older
than her brother, wrote
several songs and some
chamber music. Her
death in May 1847
shocked Felix terribly and
hastened his own end,
less than six months later.

intimidating shadow across the path of his successors. Mendelssohn
began confidently enough. No one denies that his first symphony was a
remarkably mature work for a fifteen year-old composer. But his later
efforts did not fare so well. Poor Mendelssohn has been at times judged
trite, cautious, academic, over-sentimental and passionless. Above all,
he has been rebuked for what he lacked. He was not, like Beethoven,
engrossed in the struggles between suffering and joy; he was not, like his
contemporary Berlioz, an outrageous bohemian, intent upon sensation.
Mendelssohn was not, in fact, a natural symphonist. His talent was for
the miniature, whereas the age clamoured for another Beethoven. Yet in
spite of this hostile environment, which has existed to some extent since
his death, the third and fourth symphonies are recognized as masterpieces because of what Mendelssohn possessed. Meticulous craftsmanship, boundless energy and an abundance of enchanting tunes create
more than mere charm. They invest these works with enduring genius.

Mendelssohn: the early string symphonies

Sunday morning was a time for informal music-making in the
Mendelssohn household. This was the ideal opportunity for young Felix
to hear the compositions he had been working on during the week. Piano
sonatas, chamber music, even chamber operas had their premières at
these get-togethers. Among the more ambitious works were twelve
symphonies for strings, written between 1821 and 1823, before the boy's
fifteenth birthday. These are no masterpieces, but they do reveal
Mendelssohn's uncanny ability to imitate his great predecessors. Here is
a fugue by Bach, an overture by Handel, an allegro by Haydn or a rondo
by the young Mozart. Mendelssohn goes through his paces, generally
content to remain in the shadow of his masters, but every so often a spark
of irresistible originality brightens these student compositions. It is as if
the schoolboy, having correctly recited Latin verses all day, now bursts
out of doors and turns cartwheels in the playground.

Symphony no. 1 in C minor, opus 11

Mendelssohn wrote his first symphony for full orchestra (first
performed in 1827) when he was fifteen years old. It is a work of
originality and technical maturity, far greater than the apprentice piece of
a precocious adolescent.

'A searing fire pours out of this first allegro,' wrote his friend Adolf Marx
at the first private performance. The second movement, andante, makes
up in warmth what it lacks in fire, and reveals the teenage composer's
astonishing mastery of orchestration. In the third movement, a robust
menuetto (allegro molto) contrasts movingly with an ethereal trio
section. The symphony ends with an allegro con fuoco. This finale is
more vigorous than truly passionate, but an interlude for solo clarinet
and pizzicato strings adds a charming and novel touch.

Symphony no. 2 in B flat major, opus 52 – Hymn of Praise

Mendelssohn's second symphony (first performed 1840) is neither his
second, nor a symphony in the conventional sense. It consists of three
movements for orchestra, followed by an oratorio for two soprano
soloists, tenor, chorus and orchestra. Mendelssohn was very fond of the
work; so, at first, was the public. But the novelty of its structure has not
been able to sustain a general lack of musical fibre. The first movement
(maestoso con moto – allegro) begins with a gusty solo for trombones, a
tune that unfortunately reappears sporadically throughout the work.
The second movement (allegretto un poco agitato) is a charming
Italianate melody with some striking touches of writing for the
woodwinds. The symphonic section ends with an adagio religioso, after
which the orchestra subsides into accompaniment. The remainder of
the work, nearly two-thirds of its length, is for chorus and soloists.

In 1835 Mendelssohn became the director of the Leipzig Gewandhaus orchestra, and eight years later founded the famous Conservatory there. His sister Fanny painted this watercolour of his living-room in Leipzig.

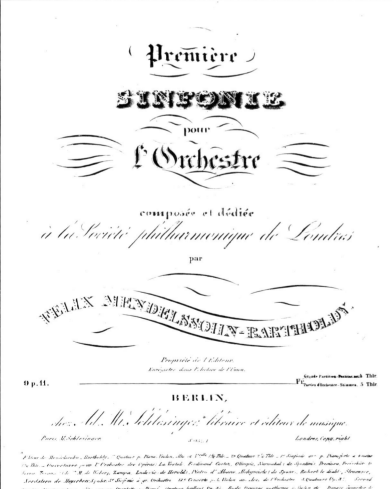

The title-page of the first edition of Mendelssohn's symphony no. 1.

Spohr

In his own day, Ludwig (or Louis) Spohr (1784–1859) was ranked alongside Beethoven and Mendelssohn as a composer of genius. He was born and educated in Brunswick, and first achieved fame as a virtuoso violinist. His many compositions include four oratorios, eleven operas, thirty-three string quartets and nine symphonies. Among these latter works, written between 1811 (when Mendelssohn was two years old) and 1849 (when he was two years dead) are several interesting experiments. In the sixth symphony each movement imitates a different style, from the Baroque to the 'modern'; the seventh is written for two orchestras; the ninth depicts the seasons.

Felix Mendelssohn in
1844.

The pianist Clara Wieck
(1819-96), painted in
1840, the year of her
marriage to Robert
Schumann.

1844

AU THEATRE MICHEL.

Vendredi, 17. Mars,

MADAME CLARA SCHUMANN,
NÉE WIECK,
première pianiste de S. M. l'Empereur d'Autriche,

aura l'honneur de donner un

DERNIER
CONCERT,

AVANT SON DÉPART,

dans lequel elle jouera plusieurs fois avec accompagnement d'orchestre.

Première partie.

1. Ouverture.
2. Concerto, en Sol mineur pour le piano avec accompagnement d'orchestre . . . . F. MENDELSSOHN-
   BARTHOLDY.
   exécuté par Mme Clara Schumann.
3. Air, chanté par Mr Versing. . . MOZART.
4. a) Scherzo . . . . CLARA SCHUMANN.
   b) «Gretchen am Spinnrad» Lied de
   Schubert, transcrit pour piano par F. LISZT.
   c) Etude en La mineur . . . F. CHOPIN,
   exécutées par Mme Clara Schumann.
   Seconde partie.
5. Ouverture.
6. a) «Lied ohne Worte» . . . MENDELSSOHN-
   BARTHOLDY,
   b) Etude «wenn ich ein Vöglein wär» A. HENSELT.
   c) Prélude et Fugue . . S. BACH (demandée),
   exécutées par Mme Clara Schumann.
7. Lieder, chantées par Mr Versing.
8. Concertstück pour piano, avec accompagnement d'orchestre . . . C. M. v. WEBER.
   exécuté par Mme Clara Schumann.

ON COMMENCERA A 8 HEURES DU SOIR.

Symphony no. 3 in A minor, opus 56 – Scottish

Inspired by the ruined chapel at Holyrood Palace in Edinburgh, the twenty year-old Mendelssohn conceived an idea for his *Scottish* symphony. Thirteen years later this composition was finally completed and performed in 1842. It is an exciting and picturesque work in which the occasional glimpse of Scotland is dwarfed by a magnificent panorama of Romantic Germany.

A melancholy introduction (andante con moto) establishes the Scotland of Mendelssohn's Romantic imagination, a world of twilit ruins and brooding skies. This opening passage also provides the first theme of the allegro un poco agitato. Scotland now becomes stormy and dangerous. The unquiet rhythm and restless swells in volume are, in fact, more reminiscent of the ocean than of the mountainous Highlands. Marine images become inescapable in the long coda, when several massive chromatic waves come rolling out of the string section. The last bars return to the theme of the opening andante as if Mendelssohn (who was very prone to sea-sickness) had gratefully stepped ashore.

For all his love of Scotland, Mendelssohn could not bring himself to write an orchestral imitation of the bagpipe. He came closest to meeting this challenge in the vivace non troppo (a 'scherzo', though it is written in strict sonata form). Here the clarinet introduces a spirited 'Scottish' dance. But this is a pipe without a bag, for Mendelssohn wisely omitted reproducing the overpowering drone.

Any visions of Scotland vanish into the mist during the beautiful third movement, an extended adagio. It is as if the composer here stands up to reassure his audience that he is still the sentimental German traveller they all love.

Mendelssohn originally called his finale allegro guerriero (warlike), which says more about the fierce enthusiasm of its opening theme than the conventional allegro vivacissimo that remains. The second subject extracts from the storm-tossed first movement a prayer for victory. This, it seems, is granted, for in the coda (allegro maestoso assai) all the sullen thoughts and clouds of Mendelssohn's Scotland are transformed into a major key and a triumphant hymn of praise.

Symphony no. 4 in A major, opus 90 – Italian

'I can continue to enjoy nature and the blue sky without thinking of anything else,' wrote Mendelssohn from southern Italy in 1831. This was not entirely true, for he had already begun to work on a symphony, now known as the *Italian* (first performed in 1833). Surprisingly, Mendelssohn went through agonies composing this most sunny work. In the end he was dissatisfied with the results, and the symphony remained unpublished during his lifetime.

From the first bar of the allegro vivace the winds establish an air of quivering excitement with rapidly repeated chords. Out of this shimmering accompaniment the violins spring with joyful energy. The upward leaps of this delightful opening melody and of the second subject that bounds along after it are irresistibly optimistic. It is difficult to bear in mind that Mendelssohn struggled in writing this spirited movement. The first movement shows us little of Italy except sunshine. The second, andante con moto, is said to portray a religious procession that Mendelssohn encountered in Naples. Cellos and basses describe the devout tread of the marchers with a steady pizzicato. Above this, violas, oboe and bassoon (an unusual and particularly effective combination) play the hymn-like tune, a perfect blend of piety and suppressed joy. Curiously, any sadness here comes not from the D minor melody itself but from a sighing tune in A major, introduced by the clarinet midway through the movement.

The third movement, con moto moderato, is a gracious and flowing

Van Bree

The music of Beethoven, Schumann and Mendelssohn found a versatile Dutch champion in Van Bree (1801–57). He began his career as a solo violinist but by the 1830s had turned his attentions to conducting. His Caecilia Orchestra tirelessly played music of contemporary German masters to sceptical Amsterdam audiences. From 1849, as leader of his own string quartet, he continued to preach the same gospel in the field of chamber music. In 1853 he became director of the new Amsterdam school of the Society for the Promotion of Music.

Van Bree was also the leading Dutch composer of his generation. His music includes two symphonies, five violin concertos, several Masses, operas and choral works.

Facing page: Clara Schumann, at this period in her life much more famous than her husband, used to promote her husband's works by performing them in public on tour. On this occasion in St Petersburg, however, she included one of her own works instead.

Mendelssohn by Aubrey
Beardsley, a more
restrained and respectful
caricature than many of
the artists' other
impressions.

FELIX
MENDELSSOHN
BARTHOLDY.

dance, troubled only by a mysterious summons from the French horns
in the trio section.

Dancing continues in the finale, called saltarello after the vigorous
Italian dance of that name. This movement remains in A minor
throughout, a highly unusual way to end a symphony that started so
brightly in a major key. The opening is both airy and earthbound, as if
danced by rustic gnomes rather than ethereal sprites. This gives way to a
second dance, a quietly intense tarantella, whose reckless triplets have
proved too much for many an unwary string section. The movement
ends with a wistful farewell to the opening theme of the symphony, now
strangely transformed by the minor key.

Symphony no. 5 in D minor, opus 107 – Reformation
Mendelssohn loathed his *Reformation* symphony. Of all his compositions, he claimed, this was the one he would choose to burn. So it
comes as a pleasant surprise to find that it is a work of power and often
great beauty. The number five is misleading. Mendelssohn completed
this symphony when he was twenty-one, but it was published and
numbered posthumously. It was written on commission to celebrate the
300th anniversary (1832) of Lutheranism.

A religious atmosphere is established in the opening andante, which ends with a devout cadence known as the 'Dresden Amen'. The muscular allegro con fuoco that follows is more the Church Militant than the Church Penitent, but this bold posturing is unexpectedly interrupted by the Dresden Amen, and when the allegro resumes it is soft and subdued, as if chastened by a divine rebuke.

The second movement, allegro vivace, is a delightful scherzo that seems to have escaped from Mendelssohn's music to *A Midsummer Night's Dream*. The trio section is a lilting serenade, more the stuff of Italian piazzas than Lutheran cathedrals. There follows the beautiful andante, a brief interlude of sheer peace and reflection before the struggles of the finale (andante con moto – allegro maestoso). This is introduced by solo flute playing Martin Luther's famous chorale, *Ein feste Burg ist unser Gott*. Mendelssohn's own contributions are frail compared to Luther's majestic anthem, and in the last thunderous bars the full orchestra returns to this chorale before a final mighty amen.

Gade

Niels Gade (1817–90) won fame as a violin virtuoso in his native Copenhagen but achieved wider recognition when he became Mendelssohn's assistant conductor in Leipzig. In 1848, shortly after Mendelssohn's death, he returned to Copenhagen, where he spent the rest of his life. His compositions, which include eight symphonies, bear witness to the overpowering influence of his early friendship with Mendelssohn and Schumann.

The symphonies of Robert Schumann

'Sometimes I would like to smash my piano,' wrote Schumann in 1839, 'it has become too narrow for my thoughts.' The orchestra, he confessed, was the medium for which he longed to write. Two years later his wish came true. In 1841 he completed his first two symphonies and a three movement work, a near-symphony called Overture, scherzo and finale. Schumann was thrilled with this new venture. 'I wish you knew my symphony,' he wrote of the first to a friend, 'How I enjoyed hearing it performed.' But critics have not always shared his enthusiasm. They point out, and Schumann would have agreed, that his knowledge of orchestral writing was slight. As a result, his beautiful melodies sometimes lack clarity, thickened by too many instruments playing the same line. Rejection of Schumann's orchestration reached such a point that at the end of the century Gustav Mahler rescored all four symphonies in order to reveal what he called the 'latent treasures … which the composer's imagination but dimly perceived'.

Today Schumann is treated with greater respect. Although no one claims that he used the orchestra as inventively as Berlioz or Mahler, his symphonies abound in passion, energy and ravishing melodies. The flaws in works of such genius are best left untouched.

Symphony no. 1 in B flat major, opus 38 – Spring

Schumann began writing his *Spring* symphony in mid-winter, 1841. By the end of February it was complete, and on the 31 March, on the brink of the season it celebrates, Felix Mendelssohn conducted the première in Leipzig. The symphony was inspired by a poem, and at one point Schumann considered giving each of the movements titles: *Spring's Awakening, Evening, Merry Playmates* and *Spring's Farewell*. These name-tags he wisely discarded – only the first may help describe a story behind the music. A work as confident as this needs no supporting text to evoke the vigour and freshness of spring.

'I should like the trumpets to sound as if from on high, like a call to awaken,' Schumann wrote of the andante un poco maestoso, the introduction to the first movement. The grip of winter is not immediately broken, but the liquid strains of a flute gradually soften the frozen earth, and with the allegro molto vivace Spring arrives bubbling and tumbling like a mountain torrent. This boisterous weather subsides in the coda when a beautiful hymn-like melody briefly suggests the warmth of June. Gusty, exuberant April then blows back to bring the movement to a close.

The second movement, larghetto, is a tender, wordless love song played first by violins, then cellos, and finally by oboe and horn. A chill creeps into this idyllic scene in the last few bars when trombones quietly draw the key from E flat major to G minor and prepare us for the unsettled emotions of the scherzo.

In addition to being a composer of great genius, Schumann was also a music critic of rare wit, sympathy and perception.

Marked molto vivace, the third movement is a tug-of-war between its sombre first theme and the gayer tunes that attempt to displace it. If spring is still in the air, then this is a squally day of black clouds and grey sky, which ends, as a spring day will, with an unexpectedly tranquil sunset.

The spirit of the first movement returns with the playful and robust finale – allegro animato e grazioso. A soulful horn call, followed by the trilling cadenza of a lonely flute, suggests that there is still sadness in this bright world. But the rest of the orchestra has no time for clouds or contemplation, and dances on to the sunny conclusion.

Symphony no. 2 in C major, opus 61

Schumann suffered a mental and physical breakdown in 1844 and was still feeling its effects when he composed this symphony two years later. He described it as a struggle between the spirit and the body, and admitted that only in the finale did he begin to feel himself again. Although traditionally his 'second' symphony, this was the third such work he had completed. A dark and passionate masterpiece, it is the least played of Schumann's four symphonies.

In a slow introduction, sostenuto assai, trumpets, horn and trombone promise to break through the dark murmurings of the strings. But instead of the glorious sunrise we had anticipated, this day dawns in wind and rain. The turbulent allegro ma non troppo establishes a feverish mood, its double-dotted rhythms lashing out restlessly. At the end of this long storm the brasses attempt, again fruitlessly, to shine through the ragged clouds.

This nervous energy persists in the second movement: scherzo – allegro vivace. Violins scurry desperately with incessant semiquavers before subsiding, as if into an uneasy sleep, during the first trio. A second trio establishes some welcome calm, if not contentment. But the unhappy semiquavers wake up and bring us back to the restless opening.

Like a pool that interrupts the tumult of a noisy stream, the adagio espressivo affords a moment of peace. This is peace of the body and not of the mind, for a minor key and great sighing leaps in the melody allow the spirit little rest. Here Schumann confounds those critics who find fault with his orchestration. Woodwind solos are beautifully handled and give the movement a simplicity and purity that his music sometimes lacks.

Felix Mendelssohn, who conducted the first performance of this symphony, must have been surprised to discover a similarity between the opening bars of the allegro molto vivace and the first movement of

Schumann

Robert Schumann (1810–56) spent his early years in Zwickau, Saxony, where his father, August, was a prosperous bookseller and publisher. The boy began piano lessons when he was seven and soon revealed a precocious ability at improvisation. All encouragement he received from his family in this field, however, died with his father in 1826. Robert, then sixteen years old, reluctantly took the advice of his mother and guardian to pursue a respectable career in law. Shortly after his twentieth birthday he had persuaded the law faculty at both Leipzig and Heidelberg Universities (and,

finally, his mother) that his was not a legal genius. The rest of his life he devoted single-mindedly to music.

Schumann's early compositions were for the piano, works of great imagination and descriptive power, including the exuberant Carnaval, three sonatas, Kinderscenen and the Études Symphoniques. A permanent injury to his right hand in 1832 forced him to give up any ambition of becoming a virtuoso pianist, but he found a more valuable outlet for his abilities in criticism. As founder, chief contributor and, until 1844, editor of the Neue Zeitschrift für Musik, he became a perceptive champion of what was worthwhile in modern music, being the first his own *Italian Symphony*. The resolute good cheer of this finale, however, does not survive, and Schumann's unquiet spirit returns in the development section. Then, as if determined to recover his tranquillity, he brings the music to a complete halt and introduces a new tune, a quiet, flowing melody that carries him to the end of the movement. Drums and brass contribute noisily to the final bars, as if Schumann needed all their support to sustain his newfound confidence.

Symphony no. 3 in E flat major – Rhenish

Robert and Clara Schumann moved to Düsseldorf in 1850, where he became conductor of the city's flourishing orchestra and chorus. This was a disastrous step. Schumann had never studied conducting and in the previous few years had become increasingly subject to fits of physical and mental depression. (So withdrawn and emotionally unsuited for this work was he that on one awful occasion, the entire chorus stopped in confusion without Schumann noticing anything wrong.) Yet his genius, though fitful, had not deserted him. In the first three months of his residence at Düsseldorf he completed this confident and melodious work. He called it his *Rhenish* symphony, in celebration of the River Rhine and the country surrounding his new home. It is his last symphony (the fourth was actually written in 1841, nearly ten years earlier) and one of his last indisputably great compositions before madness ended his creative life.

Lebhaft (lively). The symphony opens with a joyous and powerful theme, as if Schumann had succeeded in shaking off the demon of depression that had clung to him for so long. The time signature is 3/4, a metre commonly used for dance music, but here Schumann employs syncopation to give his tune a march-like quality, as if to portray the confident strides of a hero. Suddenly the mood changes and the 3/4 rhythm asserts itself in a quiet and yearning dance (the second subject) introduced by the oboes. This is at first no more than a wistful interlude, but it re-emerges throughout the movement like a sad memory. At one point it would seem that Schumann is succumbing to its melancholy, but he calls upon his brass section to drive away these unwelcome thoughts. The French horns now take up the noble opening theme and urge the full orchestra back to its original optimism. Trumpets and drums finally gallop upon the scene, like an army of reinforcements arriving in the nick of time, to bring the first movement of a triumphant conclusion.

Scherzo – sehr massig (moderate). Schumann called this movement a scherzo, but it lacks the fierce wit of a scherzo by Beethoven. Instead it sounds like an old-fashioned minuet in peasant garb. The rhythm is a slow but good-humoured one-two-three, and the tune is sedately introduced by lower strings and bassoon. This gives way to the livelier rhythm of a new dance that begins competing with the first. The horns enter with a solemn chorale and the dancing ceases, as if a black cloud threatened to send the revellers inside. This interlude is short-lived. The original theme returns, now strengthened by full orchestra. Two mighty horn calls finally signal that the dancing is at an end, and the music winds down to perfect stillness.

Nicht schnell (not fast). The dancers have departed and night has fallen. The human bustle and simple good spirits of the scherzo give way to this lyrical slow movement and its world of melancholy reminiscence. Clarinets and bassoons introduce the first theme, a melody heavy with the perfumed night air, and followed by a mournful second theme for bassoon and strings. Lest too much slowness and sweetness should begin to resemble syrup, Schumann recalls his original theme and concludes this brief and nostalgic excursion into the realm of sentiment.

Feierlich (solemn). Shortly after settling in Düsseldorf, Robert and Clara Schumann made a brief excursion up the Rhine to Cologne. There, in the magnificent Gothic cathedral, they attended the ceremony that inspired this solemn movement. In his slow and measured music, Schumann evokes not only the formal occasion but the antiquity and

to publicly acknowledge the brilliance of his contemporary Chopin and, years later, of the much younger Brahms. In 1840 Schumann married Clara Wieck, who at twenty years old was already a distinguished concert pianist. For years this match had been bitterly opposed by Clara's father, Schumann's former piano teacher Friedrich Wieck. In the exultation of his love, Schumann sought words for his music and composed in that one year nearly 150 songs, including the great cycles Liederkreis and Dichterliebe. 'I should like to sing myself to death, like a nightingale,' he wrote to Clara. In the year following their marriage he turned with equal passion to the orchestra, completing the first two of his four symphonies (now, confusingly, numbers one and four). In 1842 he wrote almost exclusively for chamber ensembles. Three string quartets and the famous quintet for piano and strings date from this year.

Schumann's health, undermined by syphilis, now began to fail. He and his family moved to Dresden, seeking a peaceful life, but he was not a moderate man and continued to overwork. The great A minor piano concerto and two more symphonies are among the best works from his last decade In 1850, his creative powers dwindling, he began an unfortunate period as director of music at Düsseldorf. Madness finally descended in 1854. After attempting to drown himself in the Rhine, he was taken to a private asylum near Bonn, where he remained until his death two years later.

The house in Inselstrasse,
Leipzig, where Robert
and Clara Schumann lived
from 1840 to 1845.

strength of the building itself. The trombones (heard here for the first time) introduce a stately procession that remains the principal theme throughout the movement. In its deliberate pace, resonant orchestration and austere counterpoint the music recreates the atmosphere of an earlier age. The excitement mounts as restless semiquavers on the strings suggest a great crowd of people pressing into the cathedral. There is a moment of holy silence, and then the brass section plays two magnificent fanfares which seem to reverberate in the great dome high above the heads of the congregation. The strings and woodwinds respond in awe, and the movement ends with hushed and reverent chords.

Lebhaft (lively). Scarcely have the last organ chords died away than the finale begins a joyful dance. With gusts of contagious glee, it blows away the last remnants of solemn devotion. A slower second subject is compelled to hobble along after the dancers, wheezing with laughter. The grave processional of the preceding movement now reappears transformed, as if the Cardinal himself had buckled on his dancing shoes and joined the celebration. Only near the end of the movement do the revellers pause, silenced by a moving cry of thanksgiving from the brass section. The dance then bounds onwards to the final tumultuous bars. So near his own unhappy end, Schumann had created one of the happiest endings in symphonic literature.

Symphony no. 4 in D minor, opus 120
In 1841, with characteristic enthusiasm and speed, Schumann wrote his first two symphonies. The *Spring* symphony was an immediate success; the second, in D minor, was less popular and remained neglected for ten years. Schumann finally returned to it in 1851, when a revised version was published, misleadingly described as symphony no. 4. This work is a rich source of pleasure for musicologists, who find in its opening bars ideas that link all four movements. Ignorance of such complexity detracts in no way from our joy in this symphony's energy and beauty.

A sombre introduction, marked ziemlich langsam (rather slow), leads directly into the main section of the first movement, the dramatic lebhaft (lively). Violins introduce the principal subject, a fiery wave of semi-

Kalliwoda

One of the most admired and industrious contemporaries of Schumann and Mendelssohn was the Bohemian composer and violinist Johann Wenzel Kalliwoda (1801-66). He was born and educated in Prague but spent most of his life in Germany as conductor of the court orchestra at Donaueschingen. There he attracted some of the greatest soloists of the day: Liszt, Clara Schumann and Sigismond Thalberg.
His compositions were treated respectfully by contemporary critics. Robert Schumann admired the fifth symphony (there were seven in all). About Kalliwoda's eighteen concert overtures, however, he was less enthusiastic. They were pleasant enough, he complained, but all sounded the same. The subsequent neglect of Kalliwoda's music has confirmed Schumann's judgement.

quavers, that at first threatens to overwhelm all other musical ideas. This aggressive theme eventually encounters stiff competition from a resolute three-chord motif. Then, as if from nowhere, emerges the majestic melody that carries the movement to its end.

A slow and plaintive melody, played by oboe and cellos, introduces the romanze. Although Schumann wrote few more lovely tunes than this, he drops it immediately for the unsettled quavers that introduced the first movement. A solo violin, playing delicate triplets above the rest of the orchestra, suddenly emerges from the gloom and spans the movement like a rainbow. At its end there is a pot of gold – a final glimpse of the tune that began this enchanting romance.

The third movement – another lebhaft – starts life as a footstamping country dance. This is transformed by the airy trio section, in which the same rainbow as in the preceding movement appears in the sky. The music continues without a pause into the solemn introduction to the finale, marked langsam (slow). Violins quietly recall their semiquaver passage in the first movement and crescendo to the main section, the mirthful lebhaft. This is based on the three dramatic chords originally encountered in the first movement. A light-hearted second subject appears to complete the musical material. But upon reaching his logical conclusion, Schumann strikes a rich new seam of ideas with which, like a conjuror, he dazzles us in the exciting coda.

Verhulst

Johannes Verhulst (1816–91) was born in The Hague where, at seventeen, he became a violinist in the court chapel. His real musical education began in 1838, however, when he settled in Leipzig as conductor of the Euterpe orchestra. There he became a friend and admirer of both Mendelssohn and Schumann. As a member of the Davidsbund, a society dedicated to overthrowing musical philistinism, he fell particularly under the influence of Schumann, to whom he submitted many of his compositions. Schumann was an indulgent critic, comparing the nationalism of Verhulst (in one flattering critical essay) to that of Chopin. He later stood as godfather to Robert, Verhulst's first son. In 1842 Verhulst returned to Holland, where he embarked upon a long and influential conducting career in Rotterdam, The Hague and Amsterdam. As a composer he was an ardent disciple of German Romanticism, and his varied output reflects Schumann's encouragement to him: 'You are quite right to cultivate every style'. Among his compositions are choral works, songs, overtures, two string quartets and a much-admired symphony in E minor.

A cartoon of the Leipzig Gewandhaus Orchestra, drawn in 1850 by the cellist Carl Reiners. Conducting the band is Julius Rietz,

5

Brahms and Bruckner

Classical Romanticism

The second half of the nineteenth century marked turbulent years in the history of the symphony. The great genius of symphonic form, Beethoven, had brought the classical symphony to a point of perfection which could scarcely be surpassed. High Romanticism, giving more importance to individual and personal expression, made its appearance. The form best suited for such expression gave rise to a clear-cut divergence of opinion. Liszt, Wagner and Richard Strauss elected to abandon traditional form and seek new pathways for saying what they had to say musically. 'Programme music' came into being, music with a story, based on literary particulars or personal experiences. Wagner turned his back on the orchestral form as a self-sufficient means of expression and created the *Gesamtkunstwerk*, the total blending of all the arts. The 'invention' of the symphonic poem is credited to Franz Liszt. Brahms and Bruckner clothed their Romantic ideals in classical dress, employing traditional compositional techniques in matters of form, melody and harmony, although Bruckner made frequent harmonic detours under the influence of Wagner.

In France during this period relatively little importance was assigned to the symphony as a compositional form. Hector Berlioz wrote symphonic poems, including the *Symphonie fantastique*, despite his calling it himself a symphony. Charles Gounod wrote three authentic symphonies, Georges Bizet wrote one at the age of seventeen, Saint-Saëns, three, among them the celebrated 'Organ' Symphony, and César Franck composed one. Wagner's influence had indeed seeped into France, but the French symphonies were nonetheless cast in orthodox moulds. Of these, only the works of Berlioz, Saint-Saëns's third symphony and that of Franck have remained in the standard repertory. Both Bruckner and Brahms sought a synthesis of the classical and Romantic traditions. Brahms's approach was to fit Romantic ideas into concise, intellectual forms, based on those of his predecessors. Bruckner sought to link himself to the innovators, Wagner in particular. He developed one specific style and in the main held to it without deviating. This accounts for the well-known aphorism that Bruckner did not compose nine symphonies, but one symphony nine times. He was, and still is, criticized for saying the same thing in each of his symphonies, whereas Brahms, in each of his, expresses himself in a totally different manner. For Bruckner, the Church and a deep 'God-consciousness' were of extreme significance; for Brahms, not at all. Lines can be traced from both these composers back to Johann Sebastian Bach, the similarities being for Brahms an intensive use of counterpoint, for Bruckner, his frequent use of sequences, repetitions. As mentioned, Bruckner admired Wagner greatly, while Brahms rejected him.

The young Brahms (seated), with his friend the violinist Joachim.

Wagner's Festival
theatre at Bayreuth in
1876, the year of its
completion.

Anton Bruckner in
1893, by Anton Miksch.

Brahms

Johannes Brahms (1833–97) was born in Hamburg on 7 May. His father played the double-bass, and according to report, none too well. But he did give his son music lessons at a very early age. From his seventh year Brahms received piano lessons from an official teacher and gave signs of possessing an extraordinary talent for the instrument. Three years later he went to the celebrated teacher Eduard Marxsen, who also instructed him in theory and composition. At this time Brahms earned money by playing the piano in bars in the red-light harbour district of Hamburg, and learned early on to accept life as it is, lost all belief in God and armed himself against his own sensitivity behind a mask of indifference.

On 21 September 1848 in Hamburg, he gave his first public piano recital. By 1853 the way to fame lay open. Robert Schumann helped greatly in this regard by writing enthusiastically about Brahms in his Neue Zeitschrift für Musik. Brahms became friends with Schumann and his wife Clara, an acclaimed concert pianist. In 1857 he received a permanent appointment to the court of Lippe-Detmold, giving music lessons to Princess Friederike and working as choral director. With only a few short interruptions, he remained there until 1860. During one of these, he founded the Hamburg Women's Chorus, composing for them and giving many concerts. In 1863 he accepted an invitation from the Singakademie in Vienna to join them as their permanent director. This position was of short duration, but he was to remain in Vienna. By this time he had become a celebrated pianist in his own right and a

Facing page, above: The beautiful monastery of St Florian, on the Danube, where Bruckner was first a student, and later organist and choirmaster.

Facing page, below: Liszt with his daughter Cosima, who was later to marry the gentleman on her left, Richard Wagner. At the right of the picture (painted by Cosima's mother, the Countess Marie d'Agoult) is the German writer on music, Hans von Wolzogen.

Above: Bergen, Norway, the birthplace of Grieg in 1843.

respected composer, both of which activities allowed him to lead a life of relative ease.

As a pianist he made tours of Germany, Austria, Switzerland, Denmark and Holland. He refused an invitation to pay a visit to Cambridge University in England in order to receive an honorary doctorate, not daring to cross the sea. In 1896, at the age of 63, he was sent to Karlsbad for a health-cure during which it was discovered he was suffering from cancer of the liver. He returned to Vienna, where he died on 3 April 1897.

His output includes many works for solo piano, including a large number of arrangements, compositions for piano duet and two works for two pianos. A small number of organ works, many songs (including folk-song arrangements) and marvellous chamber music also came from his pen. In addition to the four symphonies, his orchestral works include the Tragic Overture, the Academic Festival Overture, the two piano concertos, the Concerto for Violin and Orchestra, the Concerto for violin, cello and orchestra, and Serenades and the Variations on a theme of Haydn. Brahms also composed large-scale works for chorus and orchestra, with or without soloists, of which the German Requiem is the best-known.

Wagner's birthplace in Leipzig.

Johannes Brahms

Throughout his entire life Brahms clung doggedly to traditional compositional forms and maintained for himself, personally and as a composer, an exacting sense of discipline. The musicologist Alfred Einstein described him as a 'musical thoroughbred' who never met with disappointments such as those experienced by the idealistic, innovative, decadent Richard Wagner. His disillusionments were of a different nature, namely those of a classical composer born too late. Brahms was extremely unsympathetic towards the new pathways taken by Liszt in his symphonic poems. Liszt's creations were one-movement orchestral pieces in which themes borrowed from literature were varied in a great number of ways. The renunciation of strict tonality, of which both Liszt and Wagner became passionate champions, was, to Brahms's way of thinking, outlandish. He had been thoroughly trained by his teacher Eduard Marxsen in the old-fashioned ways, deeply rooted in musical history from Palestrina to Beethoven. He had learned to use conventional sonata form and fugue, and studied Bach and Handel as did no other composer of his time.

Brahms was forty-three years old when he unveiled his first symphony before the public. For fourteen years he had carried it around in his head, though some of it had been written down. Brahms was careful, refusing to begin something whose consequences he could not foresee. And he realized that by publishing a symphony he might well 'burn his fingers'. In the first place, he sought to develop a personal orchestral sound in the instrumentation. His orchestration tends towards dark colourings. In the second place, Beethoven bothered him, in a positive sense. In the eyes of his contemporaries, Beethoven, with his ninth symphony, had achieved the acme of symphonic form; and Brahms, with his traditional orientation, was hesitant to stand in the former's shadow. He did compose for chorus and orchestra, notably in the *German Requiem*, but not for orchestra alone. Before publishing his first symphony, he tried out his purely orchestral skills by composing the *Variations on a theme of Haydn*.

Brahms made use of the usual complement of the symphony orchestra of his time: double woodwinds, an occasional third flute, four horns, two trumpets, three trombones, timpani and strings. His preference was always for the middle and lower registers of the instruments, particularly the resonant bass instruments. He used trombones not only for dynamic amplification, but also for soft chorale-like themes. Occasionally he made use of the tuba and double-bassoon to reinforce the bass line. The harp was absent from his scores, and string parts were often divided. Although at present modern instruments are naturally used to perform Brahms's symphonies, he himself wanted nothing to do with modern instruments. He held fast to the old natural horn and trumpet. His themes are always lyrical, sometimes reminiscent of folk music, sometimes motivic. The slow movements often have long-spanned themes. Brahms's style is distinguished by a frequent use of parallel thirds and sixths, and skilful use of counterpoint. Some maintain that in his contrapuntal working-out of themes he surpassed even Beethoven. Rhythmically, simultaneous use is frequently made of uneven rhythms such as two against three.

The success of the *Variations on a theme of Haydn* probably gave Brahms the courage to bring out his first symphony, to which he put the finishing touches in 1876.

Symphony no. 1 in C minor, opus 68

Brahms struggled with his first symphony for a long time. From a letter dated July, 1862, we know that he was then working on the first movement. In this letter, Clara Schumann quotes the first measures of the allegro. Six years later Brahms sent the theme of the last movement to his friend Clara Schumann with the greeting *Hoch auf'm Berg, tief im tal, grüss ich dich, viel Tausendmal*, a text which fits the theme. Fourteen years separate the beginning of the symphony and its first rehearsal, which took place in Karlsruhe on 4 November 1876. Even during this rehearsal he was hesitant about the work, making cuts on the spot and contemplating changes in the finale. The symphony was well-received by the public, and Brahms himself conducted performances in Mannheim, Munich and Vienna.

What Brahms had often feared came true: his approach *à la* Beethoven in the first and last movements caused him to be elected to the position of the 'third great B', the last in the well-known line of Bach, Beethoven and Brahms. Debates about the symphony flared up. He was accused of having 'lifted' the theme in C of the last movement from the finale of Beethoven's ninth symphony, the *Ode to Joy*. The conductor Hans von

Brahms at home.

Bülow defended Brahms, asserting that he had carried on the great tradition of Beethoven and proclaiming the symphony 'Beethoven's Tenth'.

Yet it is not amiss to speak of the work as a typical Brahmsian symphony. The first and last movements begin with a slow introduction which contains the thematic material. The rhetorical power of these introductions does in fact recall Beethoven. But the middle movements have nothing to do with the earlier master. In the place of a slow movement and scherzo, Brahms composed two movements with an intermezzo character. Notable is the violin solo in the second movement, a reminder of Schumann's fourth symphony with its violin solo in the romanze. The orchestration of the symphony is sometimes rather thick, less well-balanced than in the later symphonies.

Symphony no. 2 in D major, opus 73

The second symphony was given the nickname of *Pastorale*, though this is now rarely used. Many authors point to the 'country' quality of the work. The author Edwin Evans, who, for the benefit of musicians, provided a measure-by-measure rhythmic table for all of Brahms's orchestral *œuvres*, could not escape this same characterization, speaking of the second symphony as reflecting a mood which 'like it or not, carries us away to green meadows'. Another current of opinion considered the name *Viennese* to be more appropriate. Viennese, because the public of this musical city valued the symphony highly from the outset and because Brahms, in the first movement, seems to be giving an ironic wink to the Viennese waltz and Johann Strauss, whose music he held in high esteem.

No programmatic idea lies behind the symphony, in any event not one originating with Brahms himself. Brahms worked on the second symphony in the summer of 1877 in Pörtschach on the Wörthersee in Carinthia, and in the autumn of that same year in Lichtental near Baden-Baden. During his summer holidays in Pörtschach in the years 1877–79, Brahms clearly felt himself inspired. One work after another flowed from his pen. The Violin Concerto was composed in this period, as well as the Sonata for violin and piano, no. 1, opus 78. The period of creation necessary for his first symphony was as long as that required by his second symphony was short.

Initially Brahms caused some confusion regarding his second symphony. He proclaimed it to be a very sorrowful, melancholy work and advised his publisher Simrock to print a black mourning-band around the score. It proved however to be a buoyant and animated piece, full of melodic incursions, for which no mourning-band could be considered appropriate.

In the first movement, allegro non troppo, a lyrical theme unfolds containing all the elements on which the first movement is thematically based. The second theme is also lyrical, written in the characteristic parallel thirds, and supported by a pizzicato bass. The flowing horn solo in a bedding of strings just before the end, followed by the wink given to the Viennese waltz (played by woodwinds and strings), are also characteristic. In this symphony, Brahms added a tuba to the trombones. The second movement, adagio, was written in sonata form and immediately introduces two themes. One is played by the bassoons, and the other by the cellos. Both themes remain in contact, but are developed and varied in different ways, ending in an unexpected fugato.

The third movement, allegretto grazioso, was also a reason for the nickname of *Viennese* symphony. The ländler theme, introduced by the oboe, recalls Schubert, as do the alternations between major and minor. The movement unrolls in the manner of a serenade with two fast intermezzi, characterized by a shifting rhythm.

The finale, marked allegro con spirito, begins with a theme in which motifs from the first movement theme recur; these motifs disappear into the background as the second theme is introduced. In the coda Brahms

Beethoven's symphonies exerted an enormous influence on all later symphonists of the nineteenth century. Brahms's first symphony was nicknamed 'Beethoven's Tenth'.

made generous use of the brass. The three trombones bring the work to its conclusion with a sustained enunciation of the keynote. It is a robust movement whose rhythm and tempo scarcely flag as it rushes to its dramatic close.

Symphony no. 3 in F major, opus 90

Brahms completed the third symphony in Wiesbaden in the summer of 1883. The work presents certain enigmas. One of the theories of the poet Max Kalback, author of a substantial biography of Brahms, was that the two middle movements were originally intended as incidental music to Goethe's *Faust.* It is true that the composer was occupied with Goethe while working on his third symphony. His friend, the violinist Joachim, felt the finale to have a mythological origin. In a letter to Brahms, dated 27 January 1884, he wrote: 'I do not like to look for poetic backgrounds in music, but with this piece I cannot get the image of Hero and Leander out my mind. The image of the gallant swimmer passes again and again unbidden before my eyes.' Here Joachim was referring to the story from Greek mythology about Hero, priestess of Aphrodite, in Sestos on the Hellespont. Her lover, Leander, who lived on the other side of the Hellespont, swam across nightly to reach her. During a storm Leander was drowned and at the sight of his body cast ashore, Hero threw herself into the sea and was also drowned. Brahms did not react to Joachim's remarks, but clearly there was something in them. The deep friendship between Joachim and Brahms was troubled at this time, but in the third symphony Brahms's musical motto keeps returning. This is the notes F-A-F, the first letters of the phrase *Frei aber Froh.* And this phrase was a variant of Joachim's motto, F-A-E, meaning *Freu aber Einsam..*

The first movement, allegro con brio, opens with the F-A-F motto in a dissident way, for the A is lowered to A flat, an immediate conflict between major and minor which continues throughout the movement. The second movement is an andante and begins with a simple melody played by the clarinets and bassoons. The trombones have their say, but trumpets and timpani are absent.

In the third movement, poco allegro, the cellos play a prominent role in the introduction of the theme, which is later repeated in various ways by horn, oboe and violins. In the finale, allegro, Brahms uses short motifs instead of melodic themes; these are developed rhythmically in various ways. The symphony comes full circle at the end as the F-A-F motif returns in the original key.

The world première was given by the Vienna Philharmonic Orchestra under the direction of Hans Richter, who with the same orchestra had also given the first performance of the second symphony.

Symphony no. 4 in E minor, opus 98

Brahms had begun his purely orchestral work with a set of variations, the *Variations on a theme of Haydn* (1873) and he concluded it with another brilliant variation-piece, the fourth symphony. For with the exception of the Double Concerto for violin, cello and orchestra, Brahms was to write no great orchestral work after his fourth symphony.

The fourth symphony, which came into being in Murzuschlag in Stiermarken in the summers of 1884 and 1885, was first performed in Hamburg by the symphony orchestra of Meiningen under the direction of Brahms himself. The work still requires attentive listening. Prominent contemporaries of Brahms had trouble with it and during a performance in Leipzig, the audience left the hall before the finale. Brahms cast the finale in one of the most complex forms of composition, one which since Bach and Handel had scarcely been used: the passacaglia. The passacaglia was originally an old Spanish or Italian dance. Opinions vary as to the origin of the word. Some see in it the Spanish words *pasar* (walk) and *calle* (street). Others point to a similarity with the Italian *gallo* (rooster). The latter might refer to the three-part rhythm of the dance, the rhythm of 'the rooster's halting gait'. In any

Facing page : An anonymous drawing of Brahms, now in the municipal museum in The Hague.

Bizet

Georges Bizet (1838–75) was born in Paris and died just outside the city three weeks after the première of his magnum opus, the opera Carmen. He grew up in a middle-class and musical environment, and entered the Conservatoire before the age of ten, where Gounod was one of his teachers. While there he wrote his only symphony, in C major, at the age of seventeen, though it was not performed until sixty years after his death.

As well as Carmen, whose failure was the most bitter blow of its composer's life, Bizet's orchestral music has kept his name prominent in the repertory: L'Arlésienne Suite (from incidental music he wrote for Daudet's play), and Jeux d'enfants (originally a piano duet) are favourites everywhere. Most of the rest of his two dozen operas however, apart from The Pearl Fishers and a once-popular Serenade from The Fair Maid of Perth, have so far been condemned to oblivion by posterity.

Bruckner

Anton Bruckner (1824–96) was born in the Austrian town of Ansfelden. His grandfather and father were both schoolmasters and Bruckner was destined to follow in their footsteps. A pupil in his own father's class, Bruckner showed himself to be an extremely gifted student and as he also proved to be musical, he was committed to the care of the music teacher Johann Weiss. An attempt was made to educate him in the most all-round way possible, so as to allow him to teach virtually any subject, including music. Under Weiss he learned the art of organ improvisation and studied the compositions of Mozart, Haydn, Bach and Handel. When his father fell seriously ill, Bruckner was called upon to return to his family in order to replace him as schoolmaster and music teacher, no mean task for a youngster of twelve. Upon his father's death, Bruckner left for the Volksschule in St Florian, where he followed a regular course of instruction supplemented by lessons in piano, organ, violin and music theory. In 1840 he moved to Linz in order to receive teacher training and worked as a student-teacher in various places. Meanwhile, time permitting, he devoted himself to music-making and composition. In 1848 he became organist at the Stiftkirche in St Florian. Following a successful performance of his Mass in B flat, Bruckner decided to leave teaching and dedicate himself full-time to composition and performance. In 1856 he became organist at the cathedral in Linz, a distinguished position which carried a stipend commensurate with the dignity of the post. But as a composer he remained very unsure of himself and so decided to study 'modern' compositional techniques and counterpoint. For the latter, Bruckner went to Otto Kitzler, conductor of the theatre orchestra in

event it is a slow dance with a continuous bass-line, over which various instruments improvise. The form was adopted and assigned strict rules by seventeenth- and eighteenth-century composers. One of the most famous is by J.S. Bach (for organ in C minor, BWV 582). Unlike a typical theme with following variations, in a passacaglia the theme is heard uninterruptedly, with variation supplied by secondary figures worked in above, below or within it. Symphonically it was a very unusual form and it almost seems as if in this movement Brahms wished one more time to display his classical training. The idea runs throughout the entire symphony, although it is only in the finale that this uncommon form is actually employed.

Brahms borrowed the theme from his great predecessor Bach, from the latter's cantata BWV 150 *Nach dir, Herr, verlanget mich,* from the section *Meine Tage in den Leiden, endet Gott dennoch zu Freude.* In the very first measures of Brahms's symphony elements of it are recognizable in the melody and the bass. Another recognizable figure is the descending succession of thirds. In the first three movements this manner of treating the melody returns repeatedly. In the first movement, allegro non troppo, all these elements are exposed and give to the entire symphony an elaborately cohesive character. The second movement, andante moderato, with a horn theme, is highly concentrated and economically written. Using various procedures, Brahms makes the most of every small melodic, harmonic and rhythmic figure. The third movement, allegro giocoso, is a sturdy rhythmic scherzo, neither charming nor light-weight, but storming onward to the big finale, in which the theme is introduced by the brass at full strength.

As the first performance showed, the fourth symphony was not an immediate popular success. The conductor Hans von Bülow championed the work, and took it on tour. When the Vienna Philharmonic played the symphony on 7 March 1897, Brahms, extremely ill, was in attendance. At the close of the first movement an ovation went up from the audience, and this was repeated after each of the successive movements. So four weeks before his death, Brahms received enthusiastic acclaim for this work.

Anton Bruckner

The nine – or rather, eleven – symphonies by Bruckner had little popular appeal in the composer's time, and caused a certain amount of misunderstanding. On the one hand Bruckner was an advocate of the innovators Wagner and Liszt. On the other, he reached backward to baroque methods of composition, particularly in his use of sequences, repetitions, to move from one theme or key to another. Bruckner paid little heed to the length of a symphony as established by Beethoven. He was a proponent of the large form, thus continuing the line of Schubert and following in the footsteps of Wagner. But his 'baroque' methods and refined contrapuntal treatment of themes stood in direct opposition to these expansive formal tendencies. Among Bruckner's teachers was Otto Kitzler, conductor of the theatre orchestra in Linz, whose performances of Wagner's *Flying Dutchman* and *Tannhäuser* made a deep impression on Bruckner and transformed him into a confirmed Wagnerian. He drew the antagonism of the Viennese critic Eduard Hanslick, who was devoted to Brahms and wanted nothing to do with Wagner. And Hanslick, a leading critic who set the tone, tore Bruckner's work to pieces, abetted, though somewhat in the background, by Brahms. Neither composer cared for the other's work. Bruckner did find an admirer and follower in Gustav Mahler, who made a piano arrangement of the third symphony and conducted the première of the sixth in 1899.

In addition to their exceptional length, Bruckner's symphonies are remarkable for the use of the long organ-like 'pedal-points' and long silences between various sections within movements. Bruckner himself jokingly called his second symphony the 'Symphony of Silences'. On a number of occasions he used three themes in the outer movements and sometimes in the slow movements as well. Such a third theme usually makes its appearance in unison passages, which has led some authors to see a connection with Gregorian chant, not so much in the melody as in its essential atmosphere. Another of Bruckner's frequently encountered hallmarks is the so-called *Gesangsperiode*: two melodies appearing simultaneously, the lower one treated contrapuntally in relation to the upper. This is especially true for the second themes of sonata-type movements. Bruckner was originally an organist, familiar with the works of Bach and, as a result, with counterpoint.

A typical Bruckner symphony begins with a quiet tremolo in the strings. From this a theme blossoms forth while the accompanying tremolo rises

Facing page: Brahms in his study, at the end of his life.

Above: The Belvedere, where in 1891 Bruckner was invited to live by the Emperor Franz Josef.

Linz, whose performances of Wagner's Flying Dutchman and Tannhäuser **had made a confirmed Wagnerian of the aspiring composer. He remained in Linz until 1868, the year in which his first symphony was given its première. He then moved to Vienna where he taught music theory and organ at the conservatory and paid regular visits to the Wagner-paradise of Bayreuth. As a composer he was frequently exposed to heavy criticism, but as an organist his career** was extremely successful. He was a much praised organ improviser and made a number of tours, including visits to France and Germany. Criticism of, and even outright hostility towards, his compositions owed much to his great admiration for Wagner and his borrowing of Wagner's ideas, while failing to develop his own individual style. Wagner's death in 1883 inspired Bruckner to compose the adagio of his seventh symphony. In 1891 Bruckner accepted a pension from the conservatory. Able to walk only with difficulty and subject to respiratory problems, he received an offer from the Emperor Franz Josef to come and live in the Belvedere Palace. He gave up all regular work and devoted himself entirely to the completion of the ninth symphony, a goal he did not achieve, despite the efforts he made up to and including the very day of his death, in Vienna on 11 October 1896. During the memorial service held in the Karlskirche, the adagio from his seventh symphony was played under the baton of Hans Richter in an arrangement for brass made by Bruckner's pupil Ferndinand Löwe. Johannes Brahms observed the coffin being carried into the church and left, muttering: 'Soon it will be my turn.' Scarcely half a year later he too was dead. Bruckner's body was interred in the Stiftskirche in St Florian. In addition to his nine symphonies, Bruckner composed a number of motets, organ works, a Te Deum, several Masses, a Requiem and several chamber works.

Saint-Saëns

Camille Saint-Saëns (1835-1921) was writing music by the time he was six years old. Born in Paris, he was an exceptionally gifted pianist, and was admitted to the Conservatoire for study in piano and organ when he was thirteen. His piano and organ career – he was organist at the church of the Madeleine in Paris – progressed splendidly, but as a composer he was not immediately appreciated. He was reproached for being too 'heavy', and was so easily and uncritically influenced as to be unable to develop any individual voice until later in his life. Of his three symphonies, the third, known as the Organ Symphony, has become far and away the most popular. He also wrote concertos for violin (3), cello (2), and piano (5), symphonic poems, including Danse macabre, and a great deal of chamber music. Of his thirteen operas, Samson et Dalila is the only one still to enjoy a measure of popularity. But most famous of all is Le Carnaval des animaux, a work which its composer was terrified would earn him a reputation for frivolity.

to a crescendo. In his finales Bruckner tends to follow the same procedure. Other characteristics are: an increasingly shorter and more highly-accented rhythm, a rhythmic use of the triplet, the frequent repetition of main themes for full orchestra with long rests between phrases, chorale melodies as third themes and the conclusion of a symphony with a long coda restating all the themes expansively.

Bruckner seems to have derived his orchestral colours from the organ. Sound-groups are blended to function almost like organ registers. In principle he thought in terms of a typical nineteenth-century orchestra. For the last two symphonies he used a double complement of wood-winds, four horns, two trumpets, three trombones, timpani and strings. And the larger forms he indulged in added forces, including piccolo, triple woodwinds, triple brass, bass tuba, timpani, harp and strings. (The eighth symphony includes a part for three harps.)

Although one generally speaks of Bruckner's nine symphonies, he in fact composed eleven. The Exercise symphony in F minor and the 'Symphony No. 0' in D minor were not considered seriously enough by him to be included in the numbering. Bruckner was working on the last movement of his ninth symphony on the day he died. He was unable to complete it.

Bruckner was a sensitive person and touchy in matters of criticism. The barrage of criticism he received drove him to rework his symphonies. Sometimes he did this himself, sometimes he delegated the work to his students. Revisions had mainly to do with the instrumentation and abridgement of, in particular, the sequential passages. Confusion about the various versions, or Fassungen, of Bruckner's symphonies is still great. His revisions may be summarized as follows:

The first symphony was written between 1865 and 1866 and received the nickname Linzer. The work was revised in 1868, 1877 and 1884. In 1890 Bruckner reworked the symphony for the fourth time, creating the so-called Viennese version. The first performance took place in 1868 in Linz under the direction of the composer.

The second symphony was written between 1871 and 1872. He reworked it in 1873 and conducted the first performance in that same year. Further revisions took place in 1875–76, 1877, 1878 and 1891.

The third symphony has three important versions. The first version was made between 1872 and 1873, and reworked in 1874. The second version was written between 1876 and 1877 and Bruckner conducted its first performance in the latter year. The third version was written in the years 1888–89.

The fourth symphony has two versions, the first dating from 1874, the second from 1878 and completed in 1880, the composer adding a new scherzo. The first performance took place under the direction of Hans Richter in 1881. Bruckner reworked the finale five times.

The fifth symphony was begun in 1875 and completed in 1876. The first two movements were revised by the composer in 1877–78. The first performance took place in Graz in 1894 under the direction of Franz Schalk, but the composer was too ill to attend the première.

The sixth symphony was written between 1879 and 1881. Several movements were played in Vienna in 1883 under the direction of Wilhelm Jahn.

The seventh symphony which Bruckner began in 1881, underwent several modifications after its completion in 1883. The first performance took place in Leipzig in 1884 under the direction of Arthur Nikisch. This is the only symphony which has remained virtually unchanged.

The eighth symphony exists in two versions. The first was written between 1884 and 1887, the second, between 1889 and 1890. In the same period Bruckner also returned to the first symphony, creating the so-called Viennese version.

The ninth symphony remained incomplete and unmodified. Bruckner began work on it in 1887. The last movement, adagio, dates from 1894.

The versions listed above are those made by the composer. Confusion is increased by revisions made by his students Franz Schalk and Ferdinand Löwe. They prepared the symphonies for publication and shortened them substantially. Halfway through the 1930s a heated discussion arose when, on the initiative of Max Auer, Robert Haas and Alfred Orel, among others, the original versions of the fifth and ninth symphonies were performed. Schalk and Löwe had little defence against the charge that they had mutilated Bruckner's symphonies. The original manuscripts of the fifth and ninth symphonies were lost at the publisher's. Knowing that his works had not achieved publication undamaged, Bruckner had fortunately bequeathed authentic manuscripts to the library in Vienna. On the basis of these, more or less original versions of his symphonies could be published and played. It would be too complex to treat all Bruckner's versions and the editorial modifications in this chapter; those interested are referred to the *Essence of Bruckner* by Robert Simpson.

In 1980, in Bruckner's home town of Linz, a symposium was held concerning these matters and published in 1981 under the title *Die Fassungen*. Here, insofar as possible, the original versions are taken as the most authentic.

In addition to the problem of the *Fassungen*, Bruckner's music gives rise to another difference of opinion. Some see in him a worthy musician who, in his symphonies, did not express himself to the best of his ability. True enough, they do not differ widely from one another.

Others see a religious character in Bruckner's orchestral work. The author Frank Wohlfart divided them into three categories. Symphonies nos. 3, 5 and 9 are the most sacramental. The relation to God and worship speaks most strongly from them because of their chorale-like themes. Symphonies nos. 4, 6 and 7 have a less exalted atmosphere and awaken an idea of sensitivity to nature. The first, second and eighth symphonies all share the same key of C minor, the 'fate key' of Beethoven's fifth symphony.

Symphony no. 1 in C minor – Linzer

Like Brahms, Bruckner was no longer young when he wrote his first symphony. He was forty-one when he completed it, and revised the work in 1890. The allegro begins in march time, leading to the introduction by the violins of a gentler melody. A quick, very loud climax follows. The woodwinds put forward a lyrical second theme, one of the so-called

Liszt

Franz Liszt (1811–86) was born in Hungary. He was a prominent and revolutionary figure in many areas of life: as a pianist he introduced innovative virtuoso piano techniques, as a composer he created the 'symphonic poem', as a writer he left to posterity an intelligent analysis of the music of his time. His pianistic gifts were unequalled, and he first made his reputation travelling Europe as the greatest virtuoso in the world. After many travels and wanderings as a concert musician, he retired from the concert platform and took up residence in Weimar, where he became director of the Musikhochschule. This was in 1848 and the previously tranquil town of Weimar was transformed into a centre of great prestige within the musical world. His unparalleled success earned him a great deal of money, allowing him to lead an untroubled and aristocratic existence. With his fortune he made generous contributions to various musical institutions and gave aid and support to a number of less fortunate fellow-musicians.

Between 1835 and 1839 he carried on a notorious relationship with the Countess Marie d'Agoult. The liaison produced three children, one of them being Cosima, who was later to marry Richard Wagner after a failed marriage Liszt's pupil, the conductor Hans von Bülow. In addition to an enormous output of piano music, Liszt wrote the Faust and Dante Symphonies, symphonic poems such as Les Préludes, and Mazeppa, church music, songs and two piano concertos. He also made a large number of piano arrangements of such works as Beethoven's symphonies, Schubert's songs and selections from Wagner's operas.

Liszt playing the piano for some friends, including (standing behind the piano) Berlioz and Carl Czerny.

Wagner in Bayreuth, accepting the congratulations of his admirer, Anton Bruckner.

Franck

César Franck (1822–90) was taken to Paris from his native Liège by his father, when the boy's gifts as a pianist had made themselves apparent at a very early age. At the Conservatoire, he astonished his teachers with his virtuosity, which was only hampered by a shy and retiring temperament. Perhaps for this reason Franck became progressively more involved with

the organ, where the performer is safely shielded from the public gaze. After graduation, he earned his living as an organist in Paris, though his majestic compositions for the instrument failed to achieve much popularity. Later he became professor of organ at his old alma mater, the Paris Conservatoire, and aroused the hostility of his colleagues Saint-Saëns and Gounod, for devoting much of his lesson time to the teaching of composition. (His pupils included d'Indy, Duparc and Chausson.) As a composer himself, Franck matured late, and his greatest music – including his D minor symphony – was written after the age of sixty. He died as the result of an accident with an omnibus, just as his compositions were beginning to win him the fame he so richly deserved.

Gesangsperioden. After a long sequential passage, a third theme is proposed by the trombones. The movement concludes with the same accentuated rhythm that began the work in the violins.

The second movement, adagio, begins with a low horn introduction over a dark rhythm played by the strings. After a theme from the cellos, the dynamics are quickly raised in a crescendo. The flutes, followed by the clarinets, introduce the next melody. At this point the violas repeat the accompaniment to the first theme, played earlier by the violins. The woodwinds remain important throughout the entire adagio.

The following scherzo, the third movement, makes a fresh, dance-like impression. A certain influence of the Austrian peasant dance can be felt. The simple theme is repeated many times and by means of ample repetitions leads to a contrasting trio with a lovely horn motif.

The finale is built around two energetic themes. The first has a 'Wagnerian' brass colour; the second is given to the more peaceful violins. The sound-level of this movement causes one to suspect the use of an extremely large orchestra, though this is not the case. The work ends in a happy, assertive C major.

Symphony no. 2 in C minor

Bruckner began this work in London in 1871. In this composition he makes an impression of someone with too many symphonic ideas at once, unable to develop all of them. The symphony was at first poorly received by both the public and the critics, and Bruckner struggled for a long time to adapt himself to the standards of others.

The Vienna Philharmonic Orchestra played the symphony twice, and then consigned the score and orchestral parts to the archives, judging it to be a work of little interest.

The moderato first movement opens with a characteristic *tremolo* from the violins, after which the cellos introduce a theme. The second theme is again a *Gesangsperiode*. The third theme is played by the woodwinds over a relentlessly rhythmic bass. In the development the three themes are handled contrapuntally.

The andante is written in a simple form, with two themes alternating. The first theme is initially played by the violins, and the second by the horn. At the end of this second movement there is a quotation from Bruckner's own Mass in F minor, taken from the *Benedictus*.

The scherzo is monothematic. The single theme is developed harmonically in a variety of ways.

The first theme of the following finale recalls the opening theme of the first movement. The two themes of this finale are handled by Bruckner in a broad and expansive manner. Again there is a quotation from the Mass in F minor, this time from the Kyrie.

Symphony no. 3 in D minor

The third symphony is one of the most Wagnerian, and was in fact dedicated to that composer. The first version of the work contains quotations from Wagner's operas, namely, *Die Walküre, Tristan und Isolde* and *Die Meistersinger*. Later Bruckner removed these quotations, but dedicated the work to Wagner and in doing so, pronounced the death sentence for the symphony, which was thoroughly damned by the fashion-setting, anti-Wagnerian critic Eduard Hanslick. Although not a direct quotation, the opening theme of the symphony strongly recalls the beginning of *Der fliegende Holländer*.

The first movement is not one of Bruckner's strongest compositions. He seems unable to develop the lovely opening theme. The second theme is a *Gesangsperiode*. Triplets predominate rhythmically in this movement, but the impression given remains static.

The succeeding adagio makes a classical-Romantic impression, with lovely string melodies. The tension built up from juxtaposition of musical ideas in this movement is finally resolved in a rapturous and tender conclusion.

The third movement is a boisterous dance, such as can also be heard in the first symphony, although this movement leaves behind a less passionate impression.

The first theme of the finale has its origin in the first theme of the opening movement. The second theme is played by the violins, supported by a chorale-like accompaniment in the brass. A third theme, played by the wind instruments, bears out the work's liturgical character with a deceptively innocent chorale melody.

Symphony no. 4 in E flat major – Romantic

The fourth symphony has become the most popular of Bruckner's symphonies. The work underwent its last revision in 1874. In 1954 Hans Redlich made a new reworking of it, prompted by the belief that so many years after the composer's death, it would be good to assemble all the successful parts in a new version.

The first movement, *Ruhig bewegt*, begins with the customary string tremolo, above which is sounded a motif played by the horn. Bruckner continues with this idea until the introduction of the second theme, consisting of an up-and-down melody of two 'long' notes, followed by a triplet, a rhythmic figure so typical of the composer, and pastoral in character. In the development Bruckner exploits these elements, in contrary motion, repetitions and miraculous harmonic transformations. The movement concludes with an extensive repetition of the first horn theme.

The andante which now follows is written in sonata form. After a short introduction the cellos begin the mournful first theme. The second theme is also unfolded by the cellos, and a chorale melody can be heard at the end of the exposition. Following the development and repetition of all the themes, the movement ends with a coda in which only the first theme is used, with solemn, quiet sounds upon the kettledrums.

The third movement, bewegt, scherzo , leaves behind the impression of a typical Austrian hunting party. The contribution of the horn recalls this strongly and the entire movement is dominated by the brass. The melody of the trio has its origins in the folk tradition and is reminiscent of the ländler.

The fourth movement, bewegt, doch nicht zu schnell, opens like the first movement, softly with dissonant harmonies. The introduction grows in tension and culminates in a dynamic forte with the customary triplets and emphatic use of the brass. The horn theme from the first movement

Wagner

Even today Richard Wagner (1813–83) remains probably the most controversial of all composers. Points of dissent are his so-called revolutionary spirit, his individual vision of Christianity and his anti-Semitism. His anti-Semitic writings have frequently, though somewhat exaggeratedly, been taken as the basis of Hitler's ideas on such matters. His life-style has also drawn criticism: he led a life of great luxury, a speculating 'swindler' who spent money like water, constantly borrowing and seldom repaying his debts. Wagner is of no significance whatsoever as a purely orchestral composer. His great strength lay in his operas, from such early attempts as Die Feën and Das Liebesverbot to his sublime masterpiece Der Ring des Nibelungen, and his creation Gesamtkunstwerk, a synthesis of music, literature, painting and theatre, all of it conceived, written and directed by one man: Richard Wagner. Wagner's influence on musical life was enormous, and he took no account of established values in regard to music. He put down on paper what he heard in his thoughts; nothing like this had ever happened before. The compulsive power of his approach found many followers – as well as opponents – among composers in Western Europe.

Berlioz

Hector Berlioz (1803–69) was the son of a doctor, and born near Grenoble in the French Alps. As a child he showed no special musical ability, and never achieved mastery of any instrument. It was not until he went to Paris to study medicine that be became infatuated with music and attended the Conservatoire. Unfortunately he also became infatuated with a neurotic English actress, Harriet Smithson, who was playing a season of Shakespeare in the city. The relationship gave him a love of Shakespeare's plays, which stayed with him for the rest of his life. (They married, and were divorced in 1840; Harriet was by then a truculent alcoholic.) But their stormy courtship also inspired his magnificent Symphonie fantastique, which he sub-titled 'Episodes in the life of an artist'.

But it is not for any great symphonic output that Berlioz is remembered. He was concerned with many forms of music, and possessed a unique talent for imaginative orchestration. Works such as his great Requiem, the operas Benvenuto Cellini and The Trojans, and the extraordinary concerto/symphony for viola and orchestra Harold in Italy (which he wrote for Paganini) are some of the inspired products of his marvellous imagination.

But as well as listening to his music, another delight for music-lovers is a shrewd and witty volume of memoirs he wrote, documenting his extraordinary life.

is heard again. After a pause, the strings introduce the second theme. In this movement Bruckner again struggles with the development of a surplus of thematic material. He creates themes open to too many possibilities and seems unable to make decisions. He obliges himself to keep to the classic sonata form, but it is clear that his ideas lie outside the boundaries of this form. Harmonically, marvellous things happen in this movement, recalling Wagner; and Bruckner concludes the symphony with the horn-call from the first movement.

Symphony no. 5 in B flat major

In the first movement Bruckner gradually builds up tension in the home key of B flat. The piece begins adagio with pizzicato cellos and double-basses and a melody in the bassoon and violas. The composer then drifts off into more remote keys. Not until the allegro does the main key sound in the minor mode. It is a dynamic movement, in which strings are often doubled in octaves, and have some enchanting melodies to play.

The adagio is more quietly balanced harmonically. The first theme begins in the minor, played by the oboe. The second theme consists of intervals of a seventh. Again there are wonderful melodic passages for the strings.

After a typical and frisky scherzo, there follows a finale with an unusual form. Like the first movement, the finale begins adagio. The allegro is a fugue. After the complete fugue, the brass bursts forth in a festive and thrilling chorale.

Facing page: Richard Strauss (seated), with his friend, the conductor Mengelberg. *Right:* A letter from Bruckner to his friend Rudolf Weinwurm.

Symphony no. 6 in A major
This symphony has frequently been judged a masterpiece, though it is perhaps less often performed than it deserves. The first movement, maestoso, opens very rhythmically, and the main theme dominates the entire movement. The adagio is made up of three contrasting elements: a wistful oboe melody, restrained but rhapsodic string passages, and a grim, purposeful march. The scherzo makes a poetic impression, but does have a ländler trio. The finale contrasts a busy march rhythm with less energetic tunes that Bruckner seems to have drawn from the countryside he loved so much.

Symphony no. 7 in E major
In the first movement the cellos, together with horn, violas and clarinet, play an exceptionally long and rapturous theme over an underlying tremolo. This dominates the entire movement: what follow are motifs rather than themes in the ordinary sense. The long, lyrical theme undergoes a number of harmonic transformations in this glorious hymn to nature.
The adagio contains many themes. While Bruckner was at work on his seventh symphony he was also occupied with the masses in F and D minor. Its tragic flavour was imparted by the news he received, while at work on this movement, of the death of his idol, Richard Wagner. For the first time he uses Wagnerian tubas, which play the movement's main theme as a quartet.
The scherzo is traditional, with a rhythmic but poetic trio for strings alone. The finale is characterized by a chorale melody as second theme, while the first theme bears a relation to the long melody from the first movement.

Symphony no. 8 in C minor
The eighth symphony is the last Bruckner completed. It was first performed in 1887, but again was not well-received. It is known that in this period Bruckner was no longer capable of coping with the rejections of conductors and critics, in addition to those of his own students. In the beginning of 1890 he revised the symphony and completed the revision on 10 March of that year. The winds play a very important role in the work, which is dominated by an inexorable 'fate' motif. A lyrical second theme tries to induce a gentler mood, but the remorseless rhythm of destiny returns to remove all optimism from this music.
The second movement is an invigorating scherzo, thus deviating from the expected succession of movements. The movement has an energetic theme, with a quiet trio. For the first time Bruckner uses a battery of harps.
The succeeding adagio is one of Bruckner's most interesting scores in terms of orchestration. The six-part division of the strings is particularly uncharacteristic of him. A dark main theme is alleviated by a chorale melody which constitutes the second theme, played by five tubas, and together these elements build the movement to a shattering climax. The finale is likewise on an enormous scale, and contrasts a number of different themes which are brought together in the movement's glorious coda as if to show that man, ultimately, is the master of his own destiny.

Symphony no. 9 in D minor
The last movement of this symphony is missing, and so the symphony ends with an adagio. It is on a large scale, nevertheless. Bruckner marked the first movement misterioso. The themes are all developed at mighty length, with a grave and powerful coda. The scherzo, in which the timpani play a prominent part, offers a series of variants and repetitions of a grim-sounding theme. The final adagio opens with chromatic harmonies. Wagner again springs to mind because of the abandonment of strict tonality, but there is no weakness in this heavenly music, that was to be the last Bruckner ever wrote. He did not live to see the symphony performed.

R. Strauss

Richard Strauss (1864–1949) has no connection with the waltz king of Vienna. He was born in Munich, where his father was a horn player in the opera orchestra. During his student years, he received much help and encouragement from Hans von Bülow, who in 1885 procured for him the prestigious job of assistant director of the celebrated Meiningen orchestra. The next year he became third conductor at the Munich Opera and worked hard to perfect his conducting skills, while at the same time writing some attractive, if not outstandingly original, music. It was not until 1889 that he produced

example, Strauss used orchestras of enormous size, and had detailed 'programmes' in mind for each of them. His fame grew all the time: in 1898 he became conductor of the Royal Opera in Berlin, and co-director of the Vienna Opera at the end of the First World War.
After his orchestral successes (and failures), Strauss turned to the composition of operas; between 1900 and 1940 he produced more than a dozen masterpieces for the stage, such as Der Rosenkavalier, Elektra, Salome (to a translation of Oscar Wilde's play) and Arabella. Many of these were written in inspired collaboration with the poet, Hugo von Hofmannsthal. Salome, incidentally, shocked audiences

his first major work, the 'tone poem' Don Juan.
In this and other orchestral works, Till Eugenspiel, Also sprach Zarathustra, Don Quixote and Ein Heldenleben for

with its frank portrayal of the heroine's lasciviousness, and Kaiser Wilhelm II declared that it would do the composer much damage – damage which, Strauss remarked, paid for his villa at Garmisch.

Part of the manuscript of
Tchaikovsky's last
symphony, the
Pathétique.

Tchaikovsky at about the
time of his disastrous
marriage.

6
Tchaikovsky, Dvořák and Sibelius

The nationalists

1848, a year of rebellion, with the February uprising in Paris and the subsequent revolts in Germany and Austria, was not without repercussions in the world of music. Nationalistic sentiments, unleashed by the struggles for liberty, readily lent themselves to expression in musical terms. Chopin, in the first half of the century, was one of the earliest to give utterance to such feelings, followed, in some cases considerably later, by Smetana and Dvořák in Czechoslovakia, Bernard Zweers in Holland, Jean Sibelius in Finland and Mikhail Glinka in Russia.

Nationalism developed variously with each composer, never manifesting itself twice in exactly the same way. In Tsarist Russia, a group of five composers, comprising Alexander Borodin, Mily Balakirev, César Cui, Modest Mussorgsky and Nicolai Rimsky-Korsakov (in addition to their hero Glinka), laid great emphasis on the national character in their music, finding their inspiration in the national folk idiom, in Russian history or in the beauties of the Russian countryside.

Tchaikovsky's was a case of another sort. Like his teacher Anton Rubinstein, composer of six no longer performed symphonies, he opposed the blatant expression of nationalistic feeling, considering this to be superficial and searching for a more direct connection with the Western musical tradition. His symphonies excel, not in matters of form, but in their strikingly melodic nature. That these melodies often derived from folk music Tchaikovsky freely admitted, arguing for their appropriateness not as evocations of nationalistic sentiment but as simple mementos of his early youth in the country. Tchaikovsky thus takes his place in history as a 'Western' Russian nationalist, exhibiting a Western European approach to composition, yet nationalistic in spite of himself, due to this persistent use of Russian musical elements.

Anton Dvořák's development took place along different lines. At that time Czechoslovakia was part of Austria, but the year 1848 saw the emergence of strong patriotic feelings in Bohemia and Slovakia, sentiments which received great encouragement from Northern Italy's successful secession from the mighty Austrian empire in 1859.

The cry was increasingly heard for a national theatre in which dramatic and operatic productions would be performed in the Czech language. In November 1862 this dream became a reality. Bedřich Smetana, at the forefront of Czech composers, energetically devoted himself to the organization of a national musical life and the composition of typically Czechoslovakian works, operas in the native language and symphonic poems with nationalistic ties, of which *The Moldau* from his *My Fatherland* is the most celebrated example. Within the national patriotic struggle an internal feud was also smouldering between Slovakia and Bohemia. Although Dvořák in his first three symphonies did not concern himself overtly with nationalism, once he had come under Smetana's influence by studying the older composer's works in detail, the expression of Bohemian ideals and atmosphere began to be heard in his compositions. In his fifth symphony of 1875, despite its conspicuous debt to Beethoven, this tendency is unmistakable. Dvořák's so-called 'Slavic period' is generally conceived of as ending with the sixth symphony of 1880, but the Bohemian element is by no means absent from the subsequent symphonies. Even the ninth, the famous *From the New World*, written in 1893 shortly after the composer's arrival in the United States, represents a mixture of the new American and the old Bohemian worlds.

Of the three composers under discussion, Jean Sibelius is probably the only one who, for a considerable period at least, can be regarded as a conscious exponent of nationalism. Freedom to make use of the national language was a continual point of contention in the wars of independence waged in the second half of the nineteenth century. Already as a schoolboy Sibelius became fascinated with the great Finnish national epic, the *Kalevala*. This, together with Nordic mythology and nature poetry, in which he professed an extreme interest, formed an inexhaustible source of musical inspiration. In 1892 Sibelius married Aino Jarnefelt, daughter of an influential military officer and leading advocate of the use of the Finnish tongue. This milieu and the struggle for independence from Russia served to intensify Sibelius's national consciousness. Only in 1904 did he distance himself from expressly nationalistic Romanticism. The label of 'nationalist' is due not only to Sibelius's use of folk material, but more importantly, to the atmosphere, so difficult of description, which his music distils.

The symphonies of Tchaikovsky and Sibelius may be seen as high points in their respective national symphonic traditions, those of Dvořák, as the basis for a new national symphonic order. Tchaikovsky and Dvořák are alike in their utilization of conventional forms, in contrast to Sibelius who pursues an entirely individual course in each of his symphonies. Of the three, Tchaikovsky is prominent as an orchestrator, Sibelius as an innovator and Dvořák for his eclecticism.

Tchaikovsky

Tchaikovsky himself was well aware that whatever distinction his symphonies possessed, they were not shining examples as regards form. His strength lay, not in the development of long movements with well-knit structures, but in the realization of shorter, simpler forms, the scherzo, the waltz or the march. This 'deficiency', as he called it, undoubtedly arose from his strong affinity for melodic invention. Not only his symphonies *per se*, but all his large-scale instrumental compositions are based chiefly upon lyricism and melody, enriched by appropriate harmonies and orchestral colouring. To his patroness Nadezhda von Meck he expressed regret that so much of the melodic material he devised had to be discarded or completely reworked in obedience to the practical dictates of form. Hardly surprising then, as he continued throughout his lifetime to struggle with the classical ideals of orderliness and structural organization, that his admiration for Mozart knew no bounds.

Always averse to the mere stringing-together of 'empty' phrases and harmonies, he developed an antipathy towards programme music, music based upon an underlying story. Music, for Tchaikovsky, must itself have something to say, without external allusions.

Tchaikovsky did not take an active part in the contest then current in Western Europe between the adherents of Brahms, with his respect for classical design, and those of Wagner, with his rejection of this tradition in favour of freer, more organic structures. But he did nonetheless take sides by choosing the conventional symphonic form as the vehicle most suitable for the expression of his Romantic musical ideas.

Mozart remained for Tchaikovsky a kind of master teacher on paper, but his true source of inspiration was the lyric stream of Russian folk music and Italian opera. He professed a great liking for the operas of Verdi and

Tchaikovsky

Piotr Ilyich Tchaikovsky was born in 1840 in Wotkinsk, a remote area of Russia, and died in St Petersburg in 1893. His father was director of the state mines in Wotkinsk. The Tchaikovsky family showed little interest in culture and was not musically inclined. In the charge of his governess the ten-year-old future composer left for St Petersburg where he began studies in law. Interested in music as he was, he took piano, voice and music theory lessons. At nineteen he left law school and took a job as a functionary in the Ministry of Justice. Three years later he resigned and registered as a student at the newly-founded conservatory in St Petersburg, whose director was Anton Rubinstein. A few years later he left St Petersburg to accept a position as teacher of music theory at the equally new conservatory in Moscow. This appointment was due to the intervention of Anton Rubinstein who recommended to his brother Nicolas, the conservatory's new director, that he engage Tchaikovsky's services, taking him into the family. This occurred literally, as Tchaikovsky lived for a considerable time in Nicolas's home. In 1877 Tchaikovsky was given the opportunity to stop teaching in order to concentrate entirely on composition. This he could permit himself because his new rich admirer-friend, the widow Nadezhda von Meck, supplied him with a yearly income. In addition to composing, he worked as a music journalist for a Russian paper. Shortly before he met Nadezhda von Meck (in writing alone, they never met in person), he was married for a very short while to Antonina Milyukova. The alliance lasted ten weeks. The relationship with von Meck lasted until 1890. She broke off all

ties with him on the pretext of no longer having sufficient financial means. Tchaikovsky travelled frequently and far. He visited Italy, England, France, Switzerland, the United States, and heard Wagner in Bayreuth.
Much speculation surrounds his death. The official version is that he died from cholera after drinking a glass of contaminated water. Unofficial sources speak of suicide, and the most recent information points to his being sentenced to take poison by a secret tribunal as a result of a homosexual

relationship with a nephew of the Tsar. One piece of evidence against the cholera theory is the fact that Tchaikovsky's body lay in state, whereas this was strictly forbidden for those dead of cholera, due to the danger of contagion. He was buried in the artists' cemetery on the Alexander Nevsky Prospect in St Petersburg.
In addition to symphonies he wrote a large number of chamber works, ballets, concertos and operas, the latter including Eugen Onegin, Mazeppa and The Queen of Spades.

Rossini, frequently performed in St Petersburg at that time; and with Bizet's *Carmen*, which he came to know during a short stay in Paris, he maintained an almost love-sick infatuation throughout his life. This opera's permeating atmosphere of inevitable fate transmuted into musical terms of frequently sparkling tunefulness, vitality and even gaiety, a contradictory atmosphere so similar to the character of Tchaikovsky's own music, could hardly fail to captivate him.

Tchaikovsky's masterly technique as an orchestrator is of the first importance. The author Preston Stedman gives seven typical characteristics which combine to produce Tchaikovsky's highly individual and expert orchestral sound-colouring:

1. Rhythmic motifs are generally given to the brass and woodwinds.
2. Expressive melodies are played in octaves, usually by strings or woodwinds.
3. Orchestral families are kept strictly apart and only instrumental groups which accord well are used simultaneously.
4. Scale passages frequently serve to decorate important melodies or harmonic figures, most notably when leading to a climax.
5. Strings are often required to play pizzicato.
6. Melodies for woodwinds are preferably given to the instruments' lower register.
7. All instruments are assigned equal importance.

Tchaikovsky wrote all his symphonies for the typical symphony orchestra of his time, without recourse to the larger forces called for by such composers as Wagner or Mahler.

Anton Rubinstein, hailed in his lifetime as a great symphonist, is remembered today as the teacher of Tchaikovsky, a much greater one.

Acrobats in Admiralty Square, St Petersburg.

Riots in Prague in 1848. That fateful year saw revolutions all over Europe, often culminating in fierce fighting against the powers of the great Empires. Prague was no exception, and was the scene of a famous bombardment before being brought back to order.

The Winter Palace at St
Petersburg in about
1836, the year that
Glinka's opera *A life for
the Tsar* – a milestone
in Russian music – had
its first performance.

Right: Rimsky-
Korsakov, and the
sumptuous cover of his
Sadko, opus 5.

A religious procession in Kursk, by Ilya Repin. The rich Russian folklore and the intense Orthodox religion were important sources of inspiration to the Russian nationalist composers.

Bedřich Smetana (1824-84) as a young man. His opera *The Bartered Bride* (1863) is the comic masterpiece of Czech music.

Slavonic dancing in Moravia. Dvořák was very sensible to Slav aspirations, and much of his music, such as the Moravian Duets, celebrated his native folklore.

Symphony no. 1 in G minor, opus 13 – Winter Dreams

Tchaikovsky's work on his first symphony resulted in a case of almost total nervous exhaustion as he laboured ceaselessly far into the night in order to produce his first symphonic creation. Despite his dislike of programme music, he did give a loose programme to the work by himself calling it *Winter Dreams* and assigning a title to each of the first two movements, 'Winter Daydreams' and 'Forlorn country, misty country'. The country was most certainly Russia, the use of a country or place as a musical 'hero' having been foreshadowed by Mendelssohn with his *Scottish* and *Italian* symphonies and his *Hebrides* overture.

In February 1866 Tchaikovsky began work on the symphony, which was always to retain a special place in his heart. Having orchestrated the entire work between June and November of that year, he showed it to his teacher Anton Rubinstein, with whom he entertained extremely cordial relations and who had recently procured for him a teaching position at the Moscow Conservatory. Rubinstein condemned the work out of hand. Tchaikovsky approached the director of the Conservatory, Nicolas, Anton's brother, requesting a public performance of one movement of the symphony, the scherzo. The request was granted, but the performance was not a success. Tchaikovsky took the advice of Anton Rubinstein to heart and rewrote the symphony in accordance with his recommendations. The final version was completed in 1883 and first performed in Moscow on 1 December of that year, under the direction of Nicolas Rubinstein. Neither in the West nor in Russia has the first symphony achieved firm status in the repertory, although, despite its many formal imperfections, it remains a fresh and charming work. The third movement, scherzo, marks the beginning of a new tradition in symphonic history, a true dance movement, its trio Tchaikovsky's first symphonic waltz. The last movement, which makes use of the folk song *The garden is in bloom*, can be considered one of the first examples of the so-called 'festive Russian finale'. In his subsequent symphonies, the sixth excepted, Tchaikovsky also favoured such exuberant finales. Tchaikovsky himself regarded *Winter Dreams* as a valuable souvenir of his cherished youth.

Symphony no. 2 in C minor, opus 17 – Little Russian

Tchaikovsky began work on his second symphony in 1872 while staying with his sister Alexandra and brother-in-law Lev Davidov on their estate in Kamenka in the Ukraine. Not surprisingly, a few Ukranian folk tunes are present in the work, accounting for its nickname of *Little Russian*, i.e. Ukranian, given to the symphony by the critic Nicolai Kashkin. The score was met with great enthusiasm by fellow composers who were adherents of nationalistic expression in music. Yet it had not been Tchaikovsky's intention to express himself in a nationalistic manner. He regarded the folk-songs only as promising melodic material for symphonic treatment and in the entire work only three actual folk tunes can be isolated.

The first movement begins with a lengthy introduction, andante sostenuto. A solo trumpet, followed by a bassoon, against pizzicato accompaniment form cellos and basses, play a Ukranian variant of the folk melody *On the banks of Mother Volga*. At the conclusion of the movement, this melody is again quoted in its entirety. The rest of the melodic material is original. Two of the most striking original themes make their appearance in the brilliant allegro vivo and are developed along traditional lines.

Prompted by the success of his first opera, Tchaikovsky began a second in 1869. But this second attempt, *Undine*, was a failure and retaining only a few successful sections, he destroyed the score. One of these commendable fragments was the wedding march intended for the opera's third act. Tchaikovsky used this march as the second movement of his symphony. In place of the expected slow movement we encounter an andantino marziale. The first theme, introduced by the clarinets and

Rubinstein

Anton Rubinstein (1829–94) was a pianist and composer who had received his training in Berlin. As a pianist he was a strong competitor of Franz Liszt, and was instrumental in setting up the conservatories in St Petersburg and Moscow. His brother Nicolas was a first-rate pianist and conductor.
Anton Rubinstein is of minor importance as a composer. His Melody in F **is practically his only composition which is still known, although he did write six symphonies and some symphonic poems, including one entitled** Russia.

Cui

César Cui lived from 1835 to 1918. He was the son of a French army officer who had remained in Russia and a Lithuanian mother. He received his musical education from Moniuszko. Cui was a qualified engineer and worked in this capacity. In addition he was not only a composer but also a music journalist for Russian, French and Belgian publications.

An early ninetheenth-century view of St Petersburg, then one of the most beautiful cities in the world.

Balakirev

Mily Balakirev, born in 1837, began his studies as a mathematician and applied himself to musical studies and composition on the side. He worked as a pianist and music teacher in St Petersburg. In 1857 Mussorgsky and César Cui became his students. Four years later Rimsky-Korsakov joined the group and again a year later,

Alexander Borodin. In 1868 he became director of the music academy in Leningrad and conductor of the city's orchestra. For several years he withdrew completely from musical life and took a job with the railway. In his last years of composing he wrote a great deal of piano music. His most important works include the oriental fantasy Islamey for piano, various overtures on Russian national themes and several symphonies which are no longer performed.

bassoons, is a dark–hued military melody. The second theme provides a rhythmic response to the first, and the third theme is again a folk song, *Spin, fair spinner*, a melody Tchaikovsky had treated in his earlier collection for piano duet, *Fifty Russian Folk Melodies*, published in 1868–69.

The third movement of the second symphony is a spirited scherzo whose fluctuating rhythm (3/8, 2/8) recalls folk music, though the material is original. The main theme of the fourth movement is another Ukranian folk song, the then very popular *The Crane*, followed by a series of variations. A strongly rhythmic second subject forms an appropriate counterbalance to the popular melody.

The first performance of the second symphony took place on 7 February 1873 in Moscow. Tchaikovsky reworked the entire first movement in 1879. The final version, as we now know it, was first heard in St Petersburg on 12 February 1881.

Symphony no. 3 in D major, opus 29 – The Polish
The third symphony hardly represents a high point in Tchaikovsky's symphonic output. Rather than an example of deeply-felt creative genesis, the work was for the composer a form of creative therapy necessary after another of Anton Rubinstein's harsh judgments, stated in no uncertain terms, this time of the composer's first piano concerto. It is the only symphony in a major key and the only one having five movements. In this work, Tchaikovsky gave himself almost entirely over to strict formal considerations and was later to look back on it as a decisive step forward in his struggle with form. The fifth movement, in the style of a polonaise with the marking tempo alla polacca, gave the symphony its nickname, *The Polish*, despite the total absence of any other Polish elements, or even of Russian folk melodies.

The symphony begins with a funeral march leading into an allegro brillante. The second movement resembles an Austrian ländler and bears the marking alla Tedesca. Notable here is the generous use of pizzicato in the strings accompanying the melody. The following movement is an andante elegiaco, its themes typically Tchaikovskian in their melodiousness. The fourth movement is a short, brilliantly orchestrated scherzo which recalls Mendelssohn, and the fifth movement is the above-mentioned virtuoso polonaise. The first performance took place in Moscow on 19 November 1875, under the direction of Nicolas Rubinstein.

Symphony no. 4 in F minor, opus 36

The story of the birth of the fourth symphony marks in two respects a significant point in Tchaikovsky's life. It was at this time that he began his long correspondence with Nadezhda von Meck. In 1876 he received from her an insignificant musical commission, but the contact thus established was to grow into an extensive and intimate exchange of over a thousand letters. Under the one stipulation that they were never to meet, the extremely wealthy Madame von Meck undertook to furnish Tchaikovsky with an income sufficient to provide for his material needs, permitting him to set aside his teaching and to devote himself entirely to composition. As an expression of this strange intimacy, Tchaikovsky dedicated his fourth symphony to Nadezhda von Meck, inscribing 'Dedicated to my best friend' on the title page of the score, in accordance with her wishes to remain anonymous. In his letters the composer refers again and again to 'our symphony'.

It was also at this same time that Tchaikovsky, in order to put a stop to (partially imagined?) rumours regarding his homosexuality, took the decision to marry. Perhaps he even hoped, by means of this marriage, to find a solution to his struggle with homosexuality itself. In any event, on the spur of the moment he married a young student who adored him, Antonina Milyukova. Within a few weeks the marriage proved disastrous and Tchaikovsky was nearly driven to suicide, a prompt divorce his only salvation.

Again in spite of his rejection of programme music, Tchaikovsky provided this symphony with a programme, explaining the argument himself in letters to Nadezhda von Meck. The first movement, andante sostenuto; moderato con anima, begins with a sweeping fanfare indicative of irrevocable fate 'which hangs like a sword of Damocles above our heads'. This same fanfare brings the movement to its conclusion. The oboe, which plays the melancholy theme of the second movement, andantino in modo di canzona, represents the composer's own disposition, the sorrowfulness and pain of the past. The third movement, scherzo, pizzicato ostinato, portrays dreaming, fantasies providing an escape from reality. The pizzicato sections are inspired by the sound of the balalaika. This movement's trio, with its drunken oboe melody, is 'the memory of inebriated farmers', as Tchaikovsky wrote to Madame von Meck. The fourth movement, allegro con fuoco, is an uncommon explosion of passion and fire. Critics have frequently objected to this finale, reproaching Tchaikovsky for having created nothing more than a piece of noisy vulgarity, but if we are aware that the composer had in mind a faithful rendering of a typical Russian revel, we must admit that the musical portrayal conforms admirably to reality. The main theme of the finale is again a folk song, *A birch stood in the meadow*. The fate motif of the first movement suddenly re-emerges, but does not succeed in extinguishing the celebratory fervour.

The world première took place in Moscow on 22 February 1878 under the direction of Nicolas Rubinstein.

Symphony no. 5 in E minor, opus 64

For the first time, it was Tchaikovsky himself who, on 17 November 1888, conducted the first performance of one of his own compositions. Ten years elapsed between the premières of the fourth and the fifth

Tchaikovsky photographed with his bride in 1877.

The title-page of
Tchaikovsky's *Manfred*
Symphony, dedicated to
Balakirev.

Below: Tchaikovsky, by
this time the grand old
man of Russian music.

symphonies. In the intervening period Tchaikovsky had devoted
himself chiefly to opera, both as composer and conductor, acquiring a
certain international renown and making, as guest-conductor, a tour
throughout Europe. His diary speaks of meetings with Brahms, Dvořák,
Gounod, Grieg and Massenet. At the conclusion of this journey, he took
up residence in a house in the country near the village of Klin, a tranquil
setting which afforded him great pleasure and allowed him to find the
necessary discipline for intensive composition. In a few summer months
the fifth symphony had been written, and although Tchaikovsky did not
rate it as highly as the fourth, it has become one of his most popular
works. Again Tchaikovsky seems unable to completely avoid a
programmatic idea behind the music, several notations making the programme, at elast for the first movement; quite clear: 'Complete
abandonment to fate, or rather the inscrutable ways of Providence.
Allegro: murmurs, doubts, complaints, reproaches to XXX! Must I
throw myself into the arms of faith?'
Whether or not Tchaikovsky with XXX had in mind a specific person is
unclear. More unlikely he was referring to his greatest problem, his
homosexuality. If we consider the first movement in the light of the
aforementioned notations, the beginning of the movement, andante,

can be called the 'Destiny theme', introduced by the clarinets. The following allegro con anima, also put forward by the clarinets, expresses the 'murmurs and doubts'. For the rest Tchaikovsky leaves us in uncertainty, although the 'Destiny theme' repeatedly recurs throughout the work. It is said of the second movement, andante cantabile, con alcuna licenza, that it is expressive of love which cannot be attained. Tchaikovsky however gives no indication to this effect. The movement begins with an imperishable horn melody, followed by a counter-melody introduced by the oboes. It is a highly emotional section, full of drama and tenderness, dynamic outbursts and unremitting changes of tempo. Midway through, the 'Destiny theme' reappears. The theme of the third movement, valse, allegro moderato, derives from a song which the composer had heard in the streets of Florence. The waltz's trio begins with spiccato violins which later return to embellish the re-capitulation of the principal waltz theme. Here again we find, very near the end, a reminder of the 'Destiny theme', softly played on low clarinets. The finale begins with the 'Destiny theme' in E major rather than minor, the first step toward the victoriousness which characterizes the entire movement. After the introductory andante maestoso, a rhythmic allegro vivace flares into life, building to a bombastic but triumphant conclusion.

Nadezhda von Meck, Tchaikovsky's friend and patron, whom he never met.

Symphony no. 6 in B minor, opus 74 – Pathétique

Tchaikovsky's final and most important symphonic work is the sixth symphony. The name *Pathétique*, suggested by his brother Modest, came to replace the original name given to the work by the composer himself, that of *Programme symphony*. A symphony with a story, but not one to be told in words. Tchaikovsky confided to his cousin Vladimir Davidov that the programme arose from deep personal feelings and that during the symphony's composition he often found himself in tears. The day before the première Modest paid a visit to his brother at home and discovered him worrying anxiously about the problem of a suitable name, as the score was to be sent off that same day to the publisher. 'Tragic,' suggested Modest at first, then, 'Pathétique'.

The idea for the symphony was born during a concert tour. At the beginning of 1893 Tchaikovsky conducted in Brussels, then went on to Cambridge where he joined the illustrious company of Grieg, Bruch and Saint–Saëns as the recipient of an honorary doctorate. In Cambridge he conducted *Francesca da Rimini*; in London, his fourth symphony. Back in Russia, he directly set to work on the elaboration of his ideas and in a matter of weeks the symphonic score was ready for performance.

A group of Tchaikovsky's friends bidding farewell to the composer as he leaves Tiflis for a trip to France (1886).

Dvořák

Antonin Dvořák was born in 1841, the son of a café owner and village butcher. The only trace of musical schooling in his early life was his active participation in the village orchestra. Only when he was fourteen years old did he begin to receive regular musical instruction. Talented as he showed himself to be, he went on to a music academy in Prague, the Organ School. His studies were paid for by an uncle who was a man of means, after which he played the viola and worked for eleven years in the orchestra of the Czech opera. In 1873 he married Anna Čermákrová, a contralto in the opera's chorus. They had six children, several of them dying young. From the moment he left the Organ School he devoted himself to composing. A nationalistic work for chorus and orchestra, entitled The Lands of

Tchaikovsky conducted the première in St. Petersburg on 28 October 1893. The title page of the manuscript bears a dedication in Tchaikovsky's own handwriting to his beloved cousin Vladimir 'Bob' Davidov.

Although we officially know very little about the programme behind the sixth symphony other than that it moved the composer profoundly, it is allowable to speculate on the probabilities governing these emotions. Three years earlier Nadezhda von Meck had written to Tchaikovsky, breaking off their relations. A year later his sister died and at the same time he was confronted with the deaths of three good friends. It is perhaps likely, though we have no way of knowing for certain, that his own death greatly occupied his thoughts.

In any event the sixth symphony is a symphony in which death plays an undeniable rôle. Notes found among Tchaikovsky's papers after his death indicate that the symphony was an expression of 'life, love, disappointment and death'.

The first movement, allegro non troppo, begins with a low bassoon melody, supported by threatening harmonies from the strings and giving rise to the first theme. The well-known second theme, often referred to as the 'love theme', is introduced by the strings, undergoes a development involving many changes of tempo and subsides into a slow pianissimo played by a bass clarinet. A startling outcry from the full orchestra ushers in an allegro vivo which, after substantial development leading to a climax, is followed by the melody of a burial hymn deriving from the Russian Orthodox liturgy. The first movement is brought to a close by brass and woodwinds accompanied by pizzicato strings.

The second movement, allegro con grazia, is an orchestral waltz, distilling an airy charm, but at the same time by no means alien to Tchaikovsky's despondent temperament. The 5/4 time signature gives the waltz a halting character which continues throughout, even in the trio, as if the music were locked within an impenetrable and relentless circle.

The third movement, a march, allegro molto vivace, has been considered by some critics to be a funeral march and is certainly one of the most marvellous that Tchaikovsky conceived. The movement builds with intensely dramatic tension, variations on short motifs rising through descending scales for full orchestra to a tremendous climax.

The fourth movement, adagio lamentoso, is an unusually lengthy section for the conclusion of a symphony. The strings begin with a downward leaping theme and the entire movement is characterized by descending melodies and changes of tempo. The symphony ends with a hushed pianissimo bassoon melody over darkly coloured ostinato strings.

In addition to the six symphonies, Tchaikovsky composed a truly programmatic symphony, the *Manfred Symphony*, inspired by Balakirev, who himself devised the programme, based upon Lord Byron's dramatic poem. It is an elusive programme, full of earth, air and water, Alpine sprites and magical enchantments. The symphony is not a particularly inspired composition and Tchaikovsky himself remained ambivalent towards it. This elusive quality, together with the work's great length and difficulty, has caused *Manfred* to be seldom performed.

At the beginning of the 1960s sketches were found for an eighth symphony in E flat major, dating from 1892. The work was reconstructed by Bogatreiv and given in performance, but has not gained acceptance as a true symphonic creation of Tchaikovsky.

Antonin Dvořák

Dvořák's style is characterized by a continual alternation between the 'Germanic' style and nationalistic sentiments manifested in the use of folk material. Modality and rhythms rooted in the folk tradition are a constant feature of his nine symphonies.

Dvořák was influenced by many other composers, but chiefly by

Brahms, whom he much admired. Yet Beethoven's influence can also be clearly heard in short pithy motivic statements or the long-spanned themes of the slow movements. Schubert provided a rich lyrical stimulus and is recalled in certain modulations and the manner in which themes are repeated. Some harmonic progressions bring Wagner to mind.

Dvořák made no clear decision to compose in a nationalistic way. Nor did he choose sides in the then prevailing contest between followers of Brahms and followers of Wagner and Liszt. He constructed his symphonies along traditional lines, while indulging in freer compositional techniques by writing a fairly large number of symphonic poems. The influence of Smetana on Dvořák's nationalistic manner of composing has already been mentioned.

Orchestral composition absorbed Dvořák throughout his lifetime, the orchestra apparently being the best 'instrument' with which he could express his creativity. His chamber and vocal music was written either in periods of repose or concurrently with orchestral works and operas.

Dvořák is a less interesting orchestrator than Tchaikovsky, clear and transparent but more conventional. His fundamental guideline was that everything must sound natural. A theme written for a particular instrument must conform to the individuality of that instrument. A violist himself, Dvořák wrote beautifully for strings, and his experience as a member of the village orchestra in Zlonice gave him a great affinity for wind instruments. He showed a predilection for the infrequently heard alto oboe and bass clarinet, and used horns, trumpets and trombones not only to supply harmonic weight, but for the introduction of themes. Harmonically, Dvořák may be thought of as a traditionalist.

The ninth symphony, *From the New World*, has become the most popular of Dvořák's symphonies – to the detriment of the other eight. And unjustly so, for the eighth symphony especially is most certainly its equal, and in fact each of them has its individual charm.

Dvořák is the typical nineteenth-century symphonist, avidly taking in all outside influences, yet developing his own personal, spontaneous, even occasionally naive style. Confusion due to various instances of deferred publication still exists as to how the symphonies should be numbered, and the numbering given is that of their order of composition.

the White Mountain, was a success and procured him enough money to take the risk of leaving his job with the orchestra in order to apply himself chiefly to composition. His career progressed smoothly. In Vienna he made the acquaintance of Brahms and of Hans von Bülow, who was to champion his work. Dvořák travelled and was repeatedly acclaimed. In Cambridge he became an honorary doctor of the university and he was awarded this

same tribute by the university of Prague in 1890. From 1892 to 1895 he was director of the conservatory in New York and after he returned to Prague, he became artistic director of the conservatory there. Dvořák wrote symphonic poems, chamber music, concertos, works for chorus and orchestra, for a cappella choir, short works for orchestra (including the celebrated Slavonic Dances), operas such as Rusalka and Armida, many songs and works for piano solos.

Dvořák's autograph of the first page of his 6th symphony, in D major.

Borodin

Alexander Borodin was nine years old when he composed the piano polka Hélène. He was born in 1833, the son of a member of the nobility named Gedeanov. His exceedingly youthful interest in music was ignored and he was obliged to study medicine. He finished his studies in 1858 and became an army doctor. As a composer he was largely self-taught. In 1864 he became professor at the academy of medicine in Leningrad. His best-known composition is the opera Prince Igor, whose ballet music, the Polovtsian Dances, has become world-famous. In the Steppes of Central Asia is also regularly performed. He wrote two symphonies, and a third was completed by his fellow composer Glazunov. Borodin died in Leningrad in 1877.

Glazunov

Alexander Glazunov was a composer who became known as such at a very early age. In Weimar Franz Liszt performed one of his symphonies, which Glazunov had written at the age of sixteen. Glazunov left the Soviet Union in 1928 because of problems with the authorities, and established himself in Paris. He was born in 1865 and died in 1936. He was a composer of much chamber music, ballets, choral works and eight symphonies.

Symphony no. 1 in C minor, opus 3

The score of Dvořák's first symphony, written in Prague between 14 February and 24 March, 1865, was entered in a competition in Germany and mislaid. It was not until twenty years after the death of the composer that the work was rediscovered, and received its first performance in Brno on 4 October 1936. Dvořák remained unperturbed by the loss of the symphony, remarking, 'I'll simply write another one'. The symphony bears the name of *The Bells of Zlonice*, although there is no indication of this on the manuscript. The composer is reported to have mentioned this name to his students in Prague and it is by no means unthinkable that he may have associated the work with his youth in Zlonice. The symphony, with its extremely long finale, shows definite influences of Beethoven and Schubert.

Symphony no. 2 in B flat major, opus 4

The second symphony, inhabiting the world of Wagner and Liszt, is formally speaking Dvořák's weakest. The outer movements contain such a wealth of thematic material as to give an overall impression of excessive density and inadequate development. The score, completed on 9 October 1865, was fully rewritten in 1888 and received its first performance in Prague on 11 March of that year.

Symphony no. 3 in E flat major, opus 10

During the ten years which separate the second and third symphonies Dvořák concentrated on composition in other musical forms, writing much chamber music and two operas. The three-movement symphony was given its name of *Eroica* because of its ultra-Germanic character, and the shadows of Schubert, Beethoven and Wagner are indeed never far away. The symphony was completed on 4 July 1873 and received its first performance soon afterwards in Prague under the direction of Smetana.

Symphony no. 4 in D minor, opus 13

In this symphony, despite certain echoes of Wagner, Dvořák began to find his personal voice, with the emergence of nationalistic sentiments expressed in both melody and rhythm and orchestration of exemplary clarity and transparency. The slow second movement is significant in Dvořák's work as an example of the free-variation form. The third movement was played in public in 1864, and although the work was completed in its entirety in that same year, it did not receive its world première until 6 March 1892 under the direction of the composer.

Symphony no. 5 in F major, opus 76

This symphony was dedicated to the conductor Hans von Bülow, who described Dvořák as 'together with Brahms the most inspired composer of his time'. It is the most Czechoslovakian, or rather, the most Bohemian, of Dvořák's symphonies, unmistakably rooted in folk lore, the Furiant rhythm of the first movement's second theme being an obvious example. A work of youthful élan, it exhibits scarcely a trace of imitative neo-Romanticism. The orchestration was completed on 23 July 1875 in Prague, where the first performance was given on 25 March 1876.

Symphony no. 6 in D major, opus 60

A performance on 16 November 1879 of the *Slavonic Rhapsody No. 3*, given by the Vienna Philharmonic under the baton of Hans Richter, prompted the conductor to request that Dvořák write a new symphony for the orchestra. Thus the first signs of international recognition were on their way. The work has its origins in folk music. The traditional scherzo is replaced by a Furiant, a typical Czech dance, partially based on an actual folk melody. Despite echoes of Brahms – the same key signature as the latter's second symphony and a similar spirit in the final movement – the symphony fully inhabits Dvořák's own world.

Dedicated to Hans Richter, who considered this a great honour, the work was first performed in Prague on 25 March 1881.

Symphony no. 7 in D minor, opus 70

Dvořák's reputation continued to grow internationally and in 1884 he was given honorary membership of the London Philharmonic Society, which at the same time commissioned from him a new symphony. This was completed on 17 March 1885 and taken into the repertory of three conductors, Hans Richter, Hans von Bülow and Arthur Nikisch. Each of them gave successful performances, notably three in Boston under Nikisch, but it was Dvořák himself who first introduced the work to the public in London on 22 March 1885.

International recognition, the stimulus of the commission and the requirement Dvořák imposed upon himself to achieve a level of craftsmanship equal to that of Brahms in his third symphony combined to produce in the composer exceptional enthusiasm and single-mindedness as he completed work on the symphony. Moreover, he had set himself the challenge of adding a great work to Czech musical culture, and the entire composition radiates the exhilarating freshness of the Bohemian countryside.

Symphony no. 8 in G major, opus 88

Two features of the eighth symphony are immediately prominent, the variety of sentiments expressed, the wholesome, robust virility of the outer movements contrasting with the poetic, meditative mood of the middle two, and the conspicuous Slavic character, stronger than ever before, which infuses not only the melodies, but rhythms and harmonies as well. Dvořák wrote the symphony following a period of intensely emotional exertion while seeking rest and a renewal of energies in his house in Vyoská in Bohemia with its much-loved garden and surrounding woodlands and meadows. His intention was to produce a symphony unlike any that had gone before, to prove himself capable of developing thematic material in a totally original way. In this he

Rachmaninov

Sergei Rachmaninov (1873–1943) is extremely well-known as the composer of solo piano works and piano concertos. But his compositional activities went further than piano playing and composing for that instrument. He wrote chamber music, choral works, a symphonic poem, songs and three symphonies.

Above: The composer and pianist Rachmaninov (right) with Eugene Ormandy, conductor of the Philadelphia Orchestra 1938-80. *Left:* A letter to Dvořák from Hans von Bülow. 'Next to Brahms you are the most excellent of composers', he affirms.

Zweers

Bernard Zweers (1854–1924) is referred to as the father of Dutch composition. He was an avowed nationalist. His vocal works have only Dutch texts. His third symphony, To My Fatherland, **is still known. One of his choral works is still a favourite of male choirs,** The Big Dog and the Little Cat.

PHILHARMONIC SOCIETY OF NEW YORK

FIFTY-SECOND SEASON, 1893-1894.

Synopsis of Compositions

TO BE PERFORMED AT THE

Second Public Rehearsal and Concert

ON DECEMBER 15th and 16th, 1893, AT

✳MUSIC HALL✳

ANTONIN DVORAK:
Symphony No. 5, E minor, op. 95 (Manuscript.)
"FROM THE NEW WORLD."

Above: An advertisement announcing the première of Dvořák's Symphony 'From the New World'.
Right: Folk dances were the inspiration of many Slav composers in the nineteenth century.

succeeded admirably, for although he retained the traditional symphonic form, he contrived to charge the customary structures with enormous ripeness, naturalness and novelty of expression.

The first movement, allegro con brio, opens with a stately and ceremonious chorale, giving way to a second theme for cellos and winds, which returns as a motto figure throughout the movement, although never serving as developed thematic material. Marked use is made of the Mixolydian mode, suggestive of neither major nor minor, endowing the work with an unmistakable folk character.

In the second movement, an adagio in C minor, a dark mood predominates. Several critics have pointed to the similarity between this atmosphere and that of another of Dvořák's compositions, *In the Old Castle*. The stormy, agitated middle section of the adagio is followed by the return of the poetic theme in the violins.

The allegretto grazioso third movement is much lighter in character, free of emotional outbursts. An elegant and charming theme is introduced by the violins and undergoes a number of chromatic transformations. The finale, allegro ma non troppo, is eminently robust and again strongly recalls the folk tradition. After a cheerful opening fanfare by the trumpets, the rigourously rhythmic main theme is announced by the cellos, followed by a series of masterly variations. A fast coda brings the work to a spontaneous close.

The symphony was written between 6 and 23 September 1884 in Vyoská, the orchestration completed on 8 November in Prague. The première was given in that city of 2 February 1890, followed by performances in London and Frankfurt, all under the direction of the composer.

Symphony no. 9 in E minor, opus 95 – From the New World
This, the most popular of all his symphonies, was completed on 24 May 1893, shortly after Dvořák's arrival as director of the conservatory in New York, a position he held from the latter part of 1892 until the spring of 1895. In the *New York Herald* of 12 December 1893 Dvořák refutes the opinion, then generally current, that he had made widespread use of negro themes. 'I borrowed not a single one of these melodies. I wrote my own themes, applying characteristics of Indian music and developing them by the use of modern rhythms, harmonies, counterpoint and orchestral colour.'

The 'American' element is most noticeable in the overall atmosphere: the Bohemian in busy Manhattan; an avidity for all things new.

The first performance took place in Carnegie Hall on 16 December 1893 and was immediately an overwhelming success.

Jean Sibelius

As stated earlier, of the three composers treated Sibelius was the one most conscious of his national background, evidenced by his symphonic poems *Finlandia, En Saga* and *Four Legends from the Kalevala*. In his symphonies, however, he turned away from nationalistic programme music to follow a highly individual path. His orchestral *œuvre* shows Sibelius to be a master of the orchestra with a deep instinctive understanding of form and a highly original approach to it.

None of Sibelius's symphonies serves as a prototype from which a general principle can be taken which would characterize them all. He never addressed himself twice in the same way to the problem of symphonic composition, arriving at a unique, though not always equally approachable style. Certain distinguishing features of his manner of composition can however be noted: a definite preference for minor key signatures, short motivic themes, frequent use of a descending fifth in the melodic line, usually falling on an unaccented beat, and the continual recurrence of darkly hued, sustained, static chords in the brass. As to the magnitude of the orchestra, Sibelius's music calls for little out of the ordinary. Woodwinds are doubled with added bass clarinet in the sixth symphony, together with four horns, three trumpets, three

Sibelius

Johan Julius Christian Sibelius, better known as Jean Sibelius, was born in Tavastehus, Finland in 1865 and died in the same country in Järvenpää in 1957. He came from an academic milieu, his father was a doctor, and during his school years he developed a great interest in the Kalevala, the Finnish national epic. Another great source of inspiration for him was nature, and he loved the nature poetry of the Swedish poet Runeberg. Later he studied composition with Martin Wegelius, a confirmed adherent of Wagner with little respect for Tchaikovsky, who had strongly impressed Sibelius in his younger years. In 1889 he went to Berlin for further study. Armed with a letter of introduction from the composer and pianist Busoni, he then went to Vienna in order to meet Brahms, but Brahms refused, and Sibelius returned to Finland less than two years later. In 1892 he married Arno Järnefelt, daughter of a leading propagandist for the Finnish language. His first sizeable work, the choral symphony Kullervo, was a great success. International recognition followed at the turn of the century. His work was played at the World's Fair in Paris and at the Proms under Sir Henry Wood. After 1925 he wrote no more works of significance. Only several light works came from his pen, written for money in order to pay for the large debts which resulted from his luxurious and self-indulgent life style. In addition to Kullervo and the seven symphonies, Sibelius wrote symphonic poems, including Finlandia, overtures, suites, chamber music, and a few works for other combinations of voices and instruments.

Smetana

Bedřich Smetana (1824–84) was a composer, pianist and founder of the music school in Prague, a school which flourished thanks to financial assistance from Franz Liszt.
He spent a number of seasons in Gothenburg in Sweden, conducting the orchestra there, but he always remained a steadfastly nationalistic Czech. His best-known works are his string quartet From My Life, **the** opera The Bartered Bride **and his cycle of symphonic poems** My Fatherland **which includes the world-renowned** Moldau.

Rimsky-Korsakov

Nicolai Rimsky-Korsakov, born in 1844, was a naval officer as well as a brilliant composer.

During a sea voyage he wrote a symphony which proved to be a great success when performed. He became a pupil of Balakirev and threw himself wholeheartedly into composing. He was a very important teacher and conductor, whose most famous pupil was Igor Stravinsky. He was also the author of a book on the art of instrumentation which is still highly regarded. He wrote three symphonies, chamber music, choral works, operas, concertos and symphonic poems, including Scherezade. He died in 1908.

trombones, timpani and strings. The first symphony calls for slightly larger forces, adding tuba, triangle, bass drum, cymbals and extra timpani.

The first two symphonies were written in what is referred to as Sibelius's Finnish period, the first, performed in Helsinki in 1894 and 1897, composed in the shadow of Tchaikovsky's *Pathétique*. The third is a product of composer's classical period. The fourth, dating from 1911, took shape at a time of unrest, and of personal malaise due to illness and the threat of the First World War. The fifth symphony, completed 8 December 1915 on the occasion of the celebration of the composer's fiftieth birthday, has been seen as an even more telling example of ominousness expressed in musical terms. The sixth and seventh symphonies date from the years after the war, years of full maturity.

After 1925 Sibelius composed no works of significance. In the early 1920s he may have began work on an eighth symphony, but even if it were completed, no trace of it has ever been found. His first large-scale piece for orchestra, the symphonic poem *Kullervo*, was suppressed by Sibelius during his lifetime and only rediscovered in the 1960s.

The first, second and fifth symphonies, as well as the one-movement seventh, are regularly performed. Less well-known is the fourth, a starkly powerful work, nonetheless, filled with intensely personal ideas and an unmitigated sense of brooding.

Symphony no. 4 in A minor
Reaction to the fourth symphony, first performed early in 1911, was more one of bewilderment than of approval. This was the first large-scale work Sibelius wrote following his serious illness. Suffering from cancer of the throat, he underwent an operation in 1908 which could scarcely fail to confront him, a dedicated *bon vivant*, with the sober questions of life and death.

The symphony's four movements are held together by a dominating motif which returns in each, the triplet. Sibelius seems to be foreshadowing his seventh symphony, which consists of a single continuous movement. Various symphonic elements recur in the fourth symphony, recalling the Wagnerian use of leitmotif.

In the first movement, tempo molto moderato, quasi adagio, seven basic motifs can be isolated, two of them being especially significant. The first is the triplet, used melodically as well as harmonically, the second is a

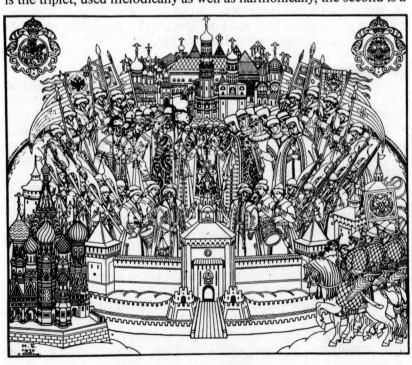

A caricature of the Czech composer Martinů by Ondrej Sekora.

Mussorgsky

Modest Mussorgsky, world-famous for his Pictures at an Exhibition, **was born in 1839 and was an officer of the regimental guard in St Petersburg. He appears to have been an excellent pianist, and listening to the original piano version of** Pictures at an

Exhibition, **this is easy to believe. As a composer he was almost entirely self-taught. In 1859 he left the army to establish himself as an independent composer, but failed. His lack of compositional facility made the progress of his work too slow and too uncertain for building a career. He accepted a government job to earn a living, but took to heavy drinking and died from alcohol abuse in 1881. As a composer he is important for his operas, of which** Boris Godunov **is the best-known.**

short rising melody in major and minor thirds. After a brief development of these two ideas, the remaining figures are introduced. The almost primitive orchestration gives no evidence of a search for colouristic effects, the various motifs and fragments following one another without benefit of colourful linking material.

The second movement, allegro molto vivace, has the character of a scherzo, though Sibelius himself did not qualify it as such. The movement contains a large number of short themes, succeeding one another in various dance rhythms and in the majority of which the triplet again plays an important rôle. Despite the cadences of the dance, the movement displays no buoyancy or light-heartedness.

The third movement, il tempo largo, is one of the loveliest, as well as one of the most complex slow movements in all of Sibelius's symphonies. After some preliminary material based on short motifs, in which the triplet is again prominent, the main theme is stated by unison strings, an expansive melody constructed of smaller fragments.

The fourth movement, allegro, is also complex in structure. The main motif can be traced to the beginning of the symphony, with short melodies and triplets constructed largely of major and minor thirds. After an intricate development, the work dies away with soft indeterminate chords in the strings.

In Finland there was no great symphonic tradition before Sibelius. Neither have any significant works been written since his death. Sibelius seems to have been a unique high point.

In Russia however the symphonic tradition continued. Tchaikovsky's younger contemporary Glazunov composed eight highly Romantic, fairly unoriginal symphonies. Rachmaninov wrote three symphonies which are weaker than his piano concertos and Scriabin wrote his in a mystical-impressionistic style. In the Soviet Union Tchaikovsky is still regarded as a shining example for many composers, although no one has attained his greatness, unless an exception is made for Shostakovich, who, with difficulty and under political pressure, succeeded in developing a personal symphonic style.

In Czechoslovakia, Bohuslav Martinu was at first strongly under the influence of Smetana and Dvořák. He wrote his symphonies in America, but they are clearly Czech in character. In the compositional world of Czechoslovakia in the 1980s nationalism, often fostered by political circumstances, quietly persists. Martinu's six symphonies have a deeply-thought and intense musical feeling, and are loved by all who know them. Of no. 1, the American critic Virgil Thomson wrote: 'The shining sounds of it sing as well as shine . . . personal indeed is the delicate but vigorous rhythmic animation . . . the singing syncopation that permeates the whole work.'

Facing page (centre): A set design for a 1930 Paris production of *Boris Godunov*. Thanks largely to Diaghilev and the Ballets Russes, Russian music of all kinds was especially popular in France.

Mahler

Although the life of Mahler (1860–1911) has been the vehicle for a somewhat subjective film, it is not the stuff of which romances are usually made. Rather it is the story of a brilliant executive, an administrator who by the age of 37 had been appointed to one of the most prestigious posts in the musical world. Much of his music was composed between appointments at various opera houses throughout German-speaking Europe, or else, during his incumbency at the Vienna Opera House, at his lakeside holiday home at Maiernigg, near Klagenfurt.

He was born in Kalište, then part of the Austro-Hungarian Empire, and went to school in Iglau, now Jihlava in Czechoslovakia. He was the second child of twelve children, of Jewish parents. Five of his siblings died in infancy, a sixth child died at thirteen, a seventh of a brain tumour, an eighth committed suicide, and the surviving brother emigrated to America to escape importunate creditors. That left Gustav Mahler himself, and two sisters, who were his family security after his parents died. This depressing necrologue, though unremarkable a century ago, may have contributed significantly to the dark side of Mahler's creative development, or neurosis, as the practitioners of the new science of psychiatry were to term it.

As a child, Mahler showed promise as a pianist of talent, and his father supported his entry into the Vienna Conservatory, where he displayed a marked gift for composition. He left the Conservatory in 1878 to pursue a University course in musical philosophy, but this was discontinued. In 1880 he took up his first musical post as Musical Director for a summer season appointment in Hall, near Innsbruck. From that small-time job (during which, incidentally, he completed his first major work, Das klagende Lied, a cantata for voices and orchestra, originally intended as an opera) Mahler climbed steadily up the ladder of success. Those who engaged him were impressed by his drive and confidence; those subordinate to him were to find him intolerant and ambitious.

The following year he was at Laibach (Ljubljana, now in Yugoslavia) followed by an appointment at Olomutz, after which he returned temporarily, in 1883, to Vienna.

This was a significant time for Mahler; he visited Bayreuth and was profoundly affected by Wagner's Parsifal, and it was also the year when he finished the song-cycle Lieder eines fahrenden Gesellen (Songs of a travelling Journeyman), the result of a blighted love affair. An appointment at Kassel in Germany, which gave him the opportunity to conduct opera of a wide variety of styles, revealed his dissatisfaction with the inadequate, and two years later he took an appointment in Prague with a more competent company. But shortly afterwards the director went on tour leaving Mahler in charge, and Mahler began to shape the resources at his command. Although

7

Mahler

The music

Most listeners have been beckoned to Mahler's music through one of two doors: the shadowy adagietto of the fifth symphony (the *Death in Venice* music) or the giant architecture of the eighth – the *Symphony of a Thousand*. The universal acclaim now quite properly accorded to Mahler is actually a very recent phenomenon, due in no small measure to the success of that haunting film, the beauty of Venice being sensitively matched with music which was, at that time, relatively little known. A generation or two ago, Mahler's lack of popularity was due, on the one hand, to the conservatively-minded distrusting anything modern, while the modernists disparaged anything that savoured of a bygone era. Now, having stood the test of time, Mahler's music receives the veneration paid to old and respected masterpieces.

With the music of the masters such as Bach, Mozart, or even Beethoven, the craftsmanship, construction, and cleanliness of melodic line can be seen on mere perusal of the written music; but with Mahler, the heart-beats and the agony are not to be found on the page, but only by listening to, and experiencing, the sound of the music. One obstacle to the enjoyment of Mahler is the sheer length of the works; they are mountainous, to be sure, but the best view from a mountain is from the summit, not the foot.

At first, Mahler wrote lengthy descriptive explanations embodying non-musical imagery as programme notes for his symphonies – but these effusive 'programmes' were later discarded, even scoffed at, by the composer, who said that the music should be able to stand up without the crutch of a narrative. Even regarding the one movement of all his symphonies which was actually written to a programme – the 'Huntsman's Funeral' in the first symphony – Mahler declared 'it is quite irrelevant to know what is being portrayed; it is only important to grasp the mood of what is being expressed.'

And yet . . . Mahler was to find that music was not enough to express his moods. In the second, third, and fourth symphonies, and later in the trilogy which included the eighth, ninth, and *Das Lied von der Erde* (Song of the Earth) he calls upon voices to express the emotions he portrayed in words. And when he could not find, in existing literature, the texts to express his thoughts, he wrote the words himself.

In 1897 he wrote: 'Whenever a plan for a great musical structure occurs to me, I always arrive at a point where I have to call in words to convey my musical ideas. It must have been the same with Beethoven in his ninth' (wherein Beethoven adds his own words as an introduction to Schiller's poem). He may at the time have been planning his fourth symphony. But then, following the fourth, he embarked on the purely instrumental group of symphonies – the fifth to seventh – perhaps as if to prove to himself that he could write without the necessity for verbal expression. More remarkable is the fact that a composer who spent his life working with opera should never, despite several false starts, have written one himself.

The symphonies

One of the ways in which Mahler expresses the agonies of his mind is through the appoggiatura – a clear fingerprint of the composer. This musical device is the placing of a note of melody slightly higher than the accompanying chord, with which it clashes harmonically, before the melody settles on to its rightful resolution. It is like a billiard ball tantalizingly perched on the edge of a pocket before at last sinking into place – or else, as might happen in the music of later Mahler – rolling away instead, thus creating new possibilities of musical tension.

Mahler is justly renowned for his use of the orchestral palette; the huge orchestra he uses is not novel – Richard Strauss had employed similar forces before him – nor are the forces used merely for the effect of their sheer volume. Rather, it was to provide a greater degree of shading in the tone-colours. Flutes are used for their ethereal, rather than pastoral quality; over a choir of trombones in sombre harmony a single trombone utters a plaintive cry; bassoons, in their higher registers become plangent rather than comic. In forte passages, clarity of line is preserved by handing the melody to a single, strident, trumpet. He often intentionally used the banal to effect musical irony. Again, the obvious example is the third movement of the first symphony, but the numerous trumpet calls that resound through his music are echoes, perhaps, of the bugles at the Iglau barracks. Mahler revealed that a formulative incident in his creative development occurred when he was a child; his parents caught in a violent quarrel, the distressed young Mahler fled from the house into the strains of an organ grinder's *O du lieber Augustin*. That is why, on

lack of time prevented his composing, the germs of the first two of his symphonies were being nurtured. Ideas for his Resurrection symphony (no. 2, not completed until 1894) were being incubated as early as 1883. From Prague he moved to Leipzig, as assistant to Artur Nikisch, eventually leaving this post to work on his symphony no. 1. His first real directorship came in 1888, when he took over the Opera House at Budapest, whose music at that time was in a somewhat parlous state. He agreed to stay for ten years, and although his productions there increased his reputation, winning the admiration of no less a personage than Brahms, he stayed only two years. For the next six years, in the closing decade of the nineteenth century, he spent a happy time at Hamburg in a less demanding job which gave him the opportunity to produce the long-gestating Resurrection symphony, and the third symphony in D minor. A visit to London with a troupe from Hamburg to play selections from German operas at Drury Lane and a guest appearance at Covent Garden took place in 1892, but much more significant a happening during that period was his conversion to Catholicism, which played such an eventful part in his development as a creative artist. Then in 1897 Mahler went to Vienna. The appointment, opened to him on his formal conversion to the Catholic faith, was to have a tremendous impact on both Mahler and his public. His ten years there, firstly as Kapellmeister at the Court Opera, and then as its Artistic Director, were to be be known as the opera house's 'golden age' while to the world at large he became regarded as a Viennese composer. Burning with tremendous zeal, living only for music, he hired and fired as the necessity took him, oblivious to the personal feelings of those who were there to make the notes sound. It was a time of his greatest creative output, the masterful canvases produced including the fourth to the eighth symphonies. Another significant personal event was his marriage to Alma Maria Schindler, who gave him the support he needed during this period of intense – perhaps too intense – activity. Never having been really comfortably off, his eventual decision to leave Vienna was tied up with the need to make provision for his retirement, and he thought that he could do this by going to America. He made several visits to the USA between 1907 and 1910, taking up the post of the conductorship of the New York Philharmonic Society in 1908. He introduced Smetana's Bartered Bride, and Tchaikovsky's Queen of Spades, but by 1910 the position was deteriorating. Unfortunately, his natural acerbity did not endear him to society, and perhaps the vital flame was guttering. Offhanded with people first, and next with the music under his direction, he became too ready with tactless excuses. Madame Mahler complained to the press that in Vienna not even the Emperor dared dictate to him, but in New York he was at the beck and call of ten ladies (the Board of the Philharmonic Society) who ordered him round like a puppet. Then Mahler's health declined rapidly, and after a collapse, he returned to Vienna with only a few months to live. Although his symphonies are built round transcendental questions, the queries, it has been said, savour more of the neurotic than the deeply philosophical. 'Will the meaning of Life be revealed by Death?' he asked his friend, Bruno Walter.

He had a superstitious dread of finishing a ninth symphony, for neither Beethoven, Schubert nor Bruckner completed a tenth. For this reason alone, he entitled his ninth Das Lied von der Erde no doubt thinking by such means to avoid the taboo. That done, he went on to write his ninth-numbered symphony, which was to be his last, the so-called tenth remaining incomplete at his death, at the age of 50, in May 1911.

hearing those trumpet calls, one must be prepared to ponder, are these the trumpet calls of fate, or ironic echoes of the banal trivia of everyday life? At least, that is what Mahler asks us to do. While the giant tapestries of his symphonies were being woven in his brain, the composer, as administrator of an opera house, would be constantly caught up in the humdrum world of bills and box-office, and the endless disputes between artist and artisan.

The symphonies fall neatly into three periods – the classification is Mahler's own, but apparent enough on the most cursory inspection. The three groups are symphonies 1 to 4, 5 to 7, and the final group, including *Das Lied von der Erde*. In fact, a neater classification is made by putting the first symphony in a category of its own – a kind of introduction to the others which then fall into three trilogies, the central one being the purely instrumental symphonies.

The first symphony, the *Titan*, in D major, is closely linked with the song-cycle *Lied eines fahrenden Gesellen* for which Mahler wrote not only the music, but the words as well (he had not yet encountered the collection known as *Des Knaben Wunderhorn*.) The conformist nature of this first work can be seen in the conventional four movement construction, and the fact that the first three movements never stray far from the tonic or related keys. Even the last movement, with its incursion into the remote key of D flat pays lip-service to Beethoven's ninth by the reiteration of themes from other movements.

Apart from linking themes, there is a predominant motif, a falling fourth, which runs throughout the work. In the first movement, played by the woodwind against held strings, it suggests the 'Titanic' Austrian scenery; played rapidly it becomes a cuckoo call; played boldly by the brass, a military theme. In the popular third movement based on *Frère Jacques* in a minor key, the fourth is a persistent bass.

The first trilogy, symphonies 2 to 4, not only have a common emotional link – the search for spiritual assurance – they are unusual in that they each have movements including voices, using texts drawn from *Des Knaben Wunderhorn* (an anthology set by many other composers, including Brahms). According to Mahler's friend and biographer Bruno Walter, in the second symphony he asks the reason for the tragedy of human existence, in the third, he is assured of the almighty love that forms all things, while the fourth is a declaration of the certainty of the heavenly life. The strivings for spiritual recognition found their resolution when Mahler became a Catholic; after his conversion, he wrote the fourth symphony which reveals the Paradise offered to the soul after death.

The second symphony, *The Resurrection* calls upon gigantic forces: an enormous string section, with several harps, is needed to support quadruple woodwind, a vast brass section (with an additional brass band) an array of percussion, organ, female soloists and full chorus. He was not to employ such vast resources again until his eighth symphony. The full contingent is however reserved for the climactic fifth and last movement – *a dies irae* and jubilant hymn in juxtaposition. Neville Cardus regarded the third symphony as a true test of the Mahler enthusiast. There are six movements, and the first lasts for nearly three-quarters of an hour. Such a complex structure defies conventional analysis, but the multitude of short themes has been likened to the structure of early Mozart movements where contrasted groups of motif-like phrases take the place of well-contrasted themes. This expansive first movement (called in the original programme note 'Summer Marches In') is followed by a contrasting pastoral minuet, a bucolic scherzo, and a sombre aria. The fifth movement begins with an unusual choral effect, a women's chorus singing against boys' voices imitating the tolling of bells. This tolling persists for most of the movement, in which the violins are silent throughout. As the bells fade away, the well-

Roussel

Born in Tourcoing, Northern France, Albert Roussel (1869–1937) was orphaned at seven, and brought up by his uncle and grandfather. He entered the Navy where in his spare time he made his first attempts at composition. A musical fellow officer suggested that he ought to pursue his studies more seriously, whereupon Roussel resigned his commission and entered the Schola Cantorum under the composer d'Indy. His time in the Navy had given him the opportunity to visit Indo-China, which made a deep impact on his musical development. Following a further private visit to Cochin, China and India in 1909 he embarked on his opera-ballet Padmavati. During the First World War he enlisted, serving with the Red Cross and Motor Transport, then after the conclusion of the war, once again began to compose. His idiom is marked by the interweaving of melodic lines, rather than an overall harmonic structure. His greatest works date from his later life, from his fifties onwards, and include the second symphony in B flat, commenced after the end of the war, the virile third symphony in G minor, which appeared in 1922; and what is sometimes regarded as finest if not his most popular work, the fourth symphony in A major, commissioned by the Boston Symphony Orchestra.

The Vienna Opera House,
an engraving from 1838.

tailored finale begins with a soft string passage. Mahler planned a
seventh movement for the symphony, which would have been an anti-
climax to this great work, but rejected it, using the material instead for
the fourth, the final symphony in the trilogy, described in more detail
later.

The fifth symphony begins the purely orchestral second trilogy.
Although in five movements, it is divided into three 'parts', the third part
– the fourth and fifth movements – beginning with the popular adagietto
for harp and strings.

The sixth symphony uses an unusual device – a major chord followed by
a minor one, portraying the fall from optimism to despair, to make the
connecting link between the subject matter of the symphony. The finale
is another movement of extreme length, often a barrier to the understanding of this complex work whose thematic development captures
the growth of Mahler's own musical development.

The seventh symphony is again in five movements, and displays many
traits of Mahler's later style: shifts of tonality bringing the work to a close
in a key unrelated to the one in which it commenced, thus achieving a
directional impulse. Here too, are uncompromising contrapuntal lines
which led, not just to an awareness of the tonal possibilities, but in the
hands of Schoenberg, into a whole new school of musical construction.
Now, seemingly having proved that he could express his feelings in
music without the aid of words or voices, he embarked on his massive
eighth symphony, and although two more symphonies were to follow it,
by any standard it must be counted his greatest achievement. It consists
virtually of two huge choral cantatas, the first a setting of the hymn *Veni*

The artist Otto Böhler's impression of Gustav Mahler on the podium.

Schoenberg

Arnold Schoenberg (1874–1951), the founder of the Second Viennese School and inventor of the 'twelve-note' method of composition was vitually self-taught. As a child he had violin lessons, and when a young man, lessons in counterpoint from a friend. His earliest attempts at composition were, he admitted later, pastiches – mere copies of pieces he admired. But after the death of his father he was very much influenced by the opinions of friends in his circle, and gained the conviction to resist convention in his music. A performance of a string quartet gave him the confidence to proceed with the early masterpiece, the sextet Verklärte Nacht written in the amazingly short time of six weeks. When it was first performed it was regarded as controversial and uncompromising, though today its highly chromatic, even luscious, writing is unexceptional. But this was an early work, and there was a long way to go. It was the period of Mahler's later symphonies, which pointed away from tonality, and this was the direction which Schoenberg took.
Early pieces were beginning to arouse hostility, yet it was not until 1908 that the first works which totally broke with tonality, Six little Piano Pieces, appeared. In 1913 he conducted a concert which included his own early Chamber Symphony and works by two of his pupils – Anton Webern and Alban Berg. The riot which ensued broke up the concert, before the final item, Mahler's Kindertotenlieder could be performed.
Since the classical structure of a symphony was based on sonata form, and this, virtually by definition, relies on well-defined tonal centres, it follows that in the 'new music' the concept of a symphony was going to need redefinition. Thus Schoenberg's Chamber Symphonies are quite different from those of the classical and Romantic schools. The same quandaries faced his pupils; Berg wrote nothing with the title 'symphony' and Webern only one, minimal, piece.
In addition to his treatises on twelve-note music, Schoenberg also wrote several text-books on conventional harmony. A curious anecdote concerns Schoenberg's superstitious fear of the number 13. During his last illness, he believed that if he could survive July 13th, he would recover. He died 13 minutes before the day expired.

Nielsen

Carl Nielsen's (1865–1931) compositions were in great vogue during the middle of this century, but knowledge of his music outside his native Denmark was virtually restricted to his symphonic music. In fact this represents just a fraction of his output, which includes chamber music, choral works, solo instrumental music (including a symphonic suite for piano) and two full-scale operas.

Nielsen came from a large, and consequently poor, family, and in his early working life he was a shepherd boy. But his musical talents showed in his playing the violin for street dancing, and his joining the town band in nearby Odense when he was fourteen. His popularity prompted friends to help him take up full-time musical studies, and he entered the Royal Conservatory, Copenhagen, under Nils Gade in 1884. After two years he left to join a theatre orchestra, but was later awarded a travelling scholarship to visit Germany, Italy and France. It was in Paris that he met his future wife, the Danish sculptress Anne Marie Brodersen.

He had by now sketched the first movement of an unfinished symphony which was to become his Symphonic Rhapsody. Much of his completed music of this time was instrumental or chamber music, but he embarked on his first symphony proper (in G minor) in 1892, completing it in 1894. The second symphony, the Four Temperaments in which each of the movements is allied to one of the four 'humours' – the slow movement Melancholy for example – dates from the next decade, and already shows one of the hallmarks of his style – the simultaneous playing of passages in different keys. In 1908 he became conductor of the Royal Opera, which no doubt influenced his decision to use wordless voices in his third symphony. He left the Royal Opera in 1914 to concentrate on conducting and composition. His Fourth Symphony, The Inextinguishable, written between 1914 and 1916, during the First World War, is probably his best known. It is worth noting that the 'nicknames' of his compositions, such as Sinfonia espansiva for the third, were apparently coined by Nielsen after writing the works in order to make them more widely understood; the parallel is Mahler's writing 'programmes' for his symphonies. Symphony no. 5, which has a cadenza for the side-drum, is only in two movements, but generally regarded as his finest work. The title Simple Symphony for his sixth, and last, is regarded as a somewhat ironic title. Though his music shows polytonality, it never strays far from a defined key scheme.

Creator Spiritus, and the second the closing scene of Part II of Goethe's *Faust*. Eight solo voices, double chorus and organ, with appropriately enormous orchestral forces have earned this symphony the nickname *Symphony of a Thousand*. It was the first of Mahler's works to achieve unanimous acclaim.

Eight months after its first performance, Mahler was dead. He never heard his next works. The first of these, *Das Lied von der Erde,* to translations of Li Po and other Chinese poets, is altogether different in both structure and concept from anything he had previously written. Dark and delicately orchestrated, the use of the pentatonic scale gives a faint suggestion of the exotic. Here too, is the extension of tonality which was to be its dissolution.

His last complete symphony, the ninth, is again in the conventional four movements, but the whole structure is innovative. It begins, not brashly, but with a lyrical easy-moving andante comodo, and ends, not with a grand finale, but with a sustained adagio movement finishing on hushed strings.

There were sketches of a tenth symphony which Mahler's wife Alma could not bear to destroy (as Mahler willed). Instead, sufficient material

remained to enable movements from the work to be performed. It is intensely personal, and the manuscript ends with anguished words of farewell from the composer to his wife.

The fourth symphony

Although Mahler is usually associated with massive works, the smaller scale of the fourth symphony enables us to look at this work in some detail. It is Mahler's happiest symphony, and after the enormous resources of the second, and the intellectual demands of the third, the fourth symphony comes almost as a respite. It is not only that the orchestra is reduced in numbers, but its forces are used sparsely and delicately, the overall texture founded, as in the classical symphony, on the strings instead of the wind. Furthermore, the naive lines and the skilful counterpoint show the symphony to be an extension of Haydn, rather than Beethoven. Two melodies are quoted, *Es sangen Drei Engel* associated also with the third symphony, and one from the *Wunderhorn*, on which the quiet last movement is built, *Wir geniessen die himmlichen Freuden*. The first movement is constructed from a number of folk-like themes, unequivocally major, uncluttered by chromatic notes or accidentals, which never stray far from the tonic or related keys. The effect is of childlike simplicity. Sometimes themes run together hand-in-hand so that it is difficult to say what the predominant theme is at certain points; rather, it is the pairs of themes which are the signposts, their inextricable links being part of the thematic texture. Three themes, however, act as a guide through the movement, although there are in fact at least five forming the opening section. The opening clucking melody soon turns into a rapid musical figure which is a thread through most of the movement. Another important distinctive theme (marked *Ton!*) for the cellos tells us that we are nearing the end of the exposition. The development section introduces a happy flute theme – the symbol of childhood. The second movement is a light ländler-type movement, in which Mahler compensates for the reduced size of the orchestra by using several curious devices and effects, including a solo violin tuned a tone higher to give an antique 'fiedel' sound. There is a suggestion that this movement owes something to Saint-Saëns's *Danse Macabre*, but the 'Freund Hein' who leads the children through Limbo into the world beyond is not the Devil, but a kind of spiritual Pied Piper.

The symphony's slow movement is its third; but it is marked only poco adagio, for a movement too grave would be out of place for a child's entry into Paradise. It is one of the loveliest movements in all Mahler's music. It begins with the lower strings alone; the violins enter, their melody being taken up by the oboe as a counterpoint to the opening theme. From then on the texture thickens and the movement takes the form of variations of increasing complexity which reveals the adult Mahler, yearning perhaps for his lost childhood. The movement leads triumphantly to the gates of Paradise, marked by sustained brass chords against which the horns call, with the timpani beating confidently. The strings descend, harp arpeggios leading to an unusual cadence (the chords of E, C, and D) leaving only the faintest whisper of woodwind and strings to close the movement. The final movement begins with a clarinet introduction, after which the soprano soloist sings of the heavenly paradise. The clucking figure of the first movement returns; the end is a quiet lullaby. It marks not just the close of the movement, and the symphony itself, but the end of the trilogy – even the passing of childhood. The work is now even more impressive, for we, with hindsight, know what music still lay ahead. Not even Mahler knew that.

Elgar

Though Elgar (1857–1934) is Britain's only symphonist of the classical and Romantic periods, and a late starter at that, the two symphonies are not the best known of his works. The huge popularity of the Pomp and Circumstance marches at one extreme, the almost reverential awe accorded to The Dream of Gerontius at the other, with such masterpieces as the Enigma Variations and the Cello Concerto in between, have elbowed the academically respectable symphonies to one side. Too derivative, the modernists declared. Only three years, but a noticeable growth in creative development, separates the two symphonies. The first, in A flat, was given its first performance in 1908 at the Free Trade Hall in Manchester under Hans Richter, to whom the work is dedicated. It was written while Elgar was fulfilling the only academic post in his life, the Chair of Music at Birmingham University. Its interest lies in the thematic material for the whole symphony being built from the simple melody which opens the first movement. The second symphony is regarded as a much maturer work, though it was received less enthusiastically, perhaps because the emotional content, whilst suited to the symphony's stated purpose (a memorial to King Edward VII) was, in a way, anti-climatic: it begins gloriously, and ends with quiet restraint. Elgar was virtually self-taught as a composer. His early skills he had from his father, a musical general factotum. After a short spell in a legal office, Elgar concentrated on making music his career, performing in a provincial orchestra, teaching the violin, and doing musical hackwork. Serious acclaim did not reach Elgar until he was forty; much of the main driving force in bringing Elgar's music to public notice was due to his wife, eight years his senior. When she died, Elgar seemed to lose his creative spirit and he began to lead the life of a country gentleman. When, however, he mentioned off-the-cuff that he had written a third symphony but that nobody wanted it, there was a public outcry. Money was advanced for its performance, and Elgar found himself having to write the symphony which he had only sketched out. At his death two years later, only fragments of each movement had actually been written.

8

The twentieth century

'It is not music's job to
express anything', said
Igor Stravinsky;
'Composers combine
notes. That is all.'

'It seems to me that since Beethoven ample proof has been given of the
uselessness of the symphony.' These words are those of none other than
the French composer Debussy, who continues: 'Even with Schumann
and Mendelssohn it is merely a respectful repetition of the same forms
but lacking the same power. Yet the ninth was a brilliant guidepost, a
magnificent attempt to expand and liberate habitual forms by giving

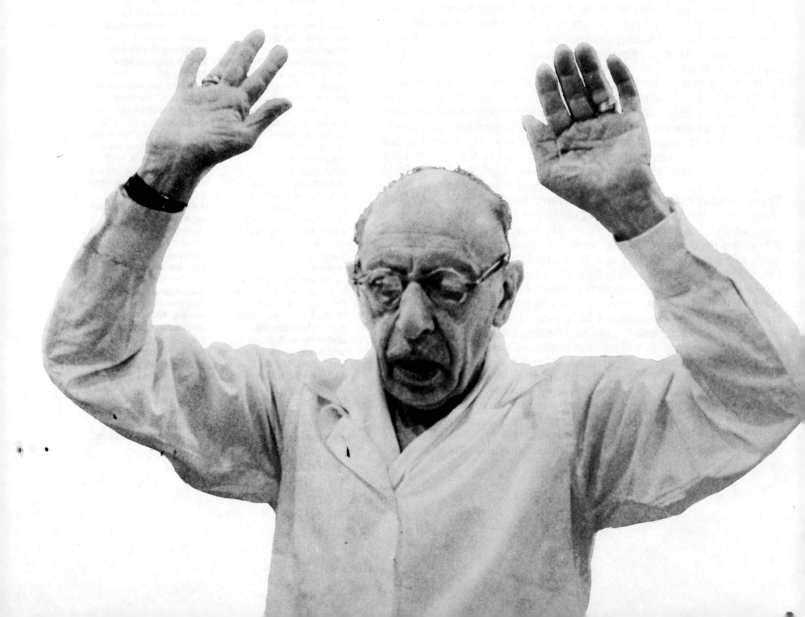

them the harmonious dimensions of a fresco … Beethoven's true lesson was not to conserve old forms, nor to follow slavishly in his footsteps. But to look through open windows towards the freedom of the sky …'

These observations, the remark regarding Mendelssohn's and Schumann's symphonic art aside, are not only typical of Debussy; they suggest the place of the symphony itself in music in the twentieth century, particularly in Western Europe. The most important principles of symphonic form and structure have always had their basis in the reliable mainstay of tonality. The tones making up a symphonic composition are distributed according to a set system around a ground-tonality or tonal centre, and are of varying degrees of importance. The entire compositional coherence of a symphony rests upon there being in each movement a continuous ebb and flow around this tonal centre, as the music moves either to escape it temporarily or to be drawn back. Traditionally, a set relationship also exists between each of the various movements.

From the beginning of the twentieth century, however, the sovereignty of tonality has been on the decline. Composers have been searching for other methods of achieving cohesiveness in their compositions. Some have gone very far indeed and abandoned all the traditionally observed relationships among the notes, with atonality as a result. The most important representatives of this trend are the composers of the second Viennese School, Schoenberg, Berg and Webern. Others, less radical, have made use of freer forms of tonality, or sought ways to employ two or more tonal centres simultaneously in the same composition (Darius Milhaud). The consequences are these: where tonality has suffered its greatest crisis, the symphony has suffered its greatest crisis as well; where tonality has remained unchallenged (largely Eastern Europe), the symphonic form is still an important means of musical expression.

To return to Claude Debussy – he wrote no symphonies. Yet he gave admirable support to the opinions quoted above by creating *La Mer*, which he sub-titled 'Symphonic Sketches', pointing on the one hand to the painterly effect (wind, sea, light, colour, atmosphere), and on the other to the symphonic latitude and liberation he so fervently advocated. Although he stayed well away from the academic rules of symphonic composition, his development of the musical material can be called symphonic in that there is a clearly contrasted thematic structure, a recognizable symphonic design with an introduction, scherzo and rondo-finale. *La Mer* has no traditional tonal centre, but seems to be seeking one throughout.

Arnold Schoenberg, in his chamber symphony no. 1 opus 9 (1906), found a highly personal solution to the problem of form. To begin with, this work brings into question the suitability of a large orchestra as the primary medium for the presentation of symphonic form. Written for fifteen solo instruments (ten winds and five strings), it represents a reaction against the supremacy assigned to the strings by the nineteenth century. Schoenberg does not only strike at the 'big sound', but also at full-scale structural expansiveness. He compresses the structure of this five-movement work into what may be loosely considered an example of the classical sonata form. The first of the five continuous movements is an allegro exposing the main themes, the following scherzo introduces new themes, the third movement can be seen as a development of the material from both these sections, and it is in turn followed by an adagio which presents further new figures. The fifth movement acts as a reprise of the themes from the first and fourth movements. Although Schoenberg does challenge nineteenth-century practices, he nevertheless concurs with the need for thematic coherence among the various movements. In this respect he belongs to the Romantic school. The symphony as a formal problem was only of moderate interest to Schoenberg. In addition to this opus 9, he completed in 1939 a second chamber symphony, opus 38, on which he had worked extensively while

Prokofiev

Serge Prokofiev (1879–1953) was born in the Ukraine. He began composing at the age of seven and studied privately with Reinhold Glière before, at the age of thirteen, he was admitted to the conservatory in St Petersburg. There he studied with Liadov, Rimsky-Korsakov and Tcherepnin. At this time he created a sensation as a pianist. His performance of his Piano Concerto no. 1 won him the Anton Rubinstein prize. In 1918 Prokofiev left his own country. He remained in the West until 1927, travelling through Germany, Italy, Spain, Belgium and America, performing chiefly his own compositions arranged for piano. Important compositions from this period are The Love of Three Oranges, **the Symphony no. 2, the Quintet in G minor and the Overture in B flat.** Between 1927 and 1936 he spent periods of varying length in Russia and the West. Only in 1936 did he decide to again definitely take up residence in the land of his birth. This marked a period of great creativity: Romeo and Juliet, Peter and the Wolf, **the second violin concerto, and piano sonatas nos. 6, 7 and 8.** Prokofiev died on 5 March 1953, the same day as Stalin. His music was banned by musical officialdom in his own country and not reinstated until 1959.

Britten

Benjamin Britten (1913–76) was born in Lowestoft (Suffolk) on 22 November, and at the age of twelve became a pupil of Frank Bridge. Later he studied composition with John Ireland and Arthur Benjamin. Early in the 1930s his works were already being performed. From 1935 to 1939 he worked in close cooperation with W. H. Auden, who supplied him with librettos for films, theatre and radio. Britten was a pacifist, and during the war he lived and worked in the United States. He was one of the co- founders in 1947 of the English Opera Company, and in 1948 the Aldeburgh Festival was inaugurated at his instigation. Britten was an excellent conductor and pianist. He conducted many of his own works and was the regular accompanist for the tenor Peter Pears, with whom he began an especially fruitful collaboration upon his return from America. Britten died in 1976. In addition to chamber music, songs, choral works and orchestral pieces, Britten left behind a large number of important operas, of which Peter Grimes, set on his beloved Suffolk coast, is probably the best- known.

Benjamin Britten accompanying the tenor Peter Pears.

composing the first. The other two important representatives of the second Viennese School also devoted little attention to the symphony *per se*. According to the musicologist Hans Redlich, Alban Berg's Three Pieces for Orchestra, opus 63 should be considered as 'Berg's active discussion of Gustav Mahler's conception of the symphony'. Anton Webern, in his symphony, opus 21, has only two movements. The first is a combination of sonata form and double canon, so subtly put together as to be scarcely discernible to the ear.

Apart from his symphony no. 1, opus 1, a youthful work written between 1905 and 1907 and thoroughly bound by academic restrictions, Igor Stravinsky made four essays into symphonic form; this statement, however, needs qualification. The symphonies for wind instruments (1920) do not constitute a symphony in the classical-Romantic sense. Stravinsky harks back to an earlier meaning given to the word, signifying 'to sound or play at the same time'. The work, dedicated to the memory of Debussy, exhibits no conformity with any of the symphonic conventions. Its single movement is constructed from six elements made to cohere by motivic inter-relationships.

Neither is the *Symphony of Psalms* (1930) to be considered as a true symphony. Rather it should be regarded as a musical document portraying the drawing-together of the symphony and the oratorio in the twentieth century. Together with the two orchestral symphonies, the symphony in C and symphony in three movements, it marks Stravinsky's neo-classical period. The term 'neo-classical', must here be taken to refer to an orientation towards models considered 'classical', without in any strict manner conforming to the style of that period. The *Symphony of Psalms*, for example, might more accurately be labelled 'neo-baroque'. Of the three movements, prelude, double fugue and sinfonia-allegro, the first two may be seen as a reflection of the baroque principle of form: an introduction wedded to the subsequent primary section. This main section looks back to Bach in its large-scale vocal and instrumental design. Symphonic cohesion is achieved in two ways, firstly by the appearance in all three movements of a particular motif, an intervallic figure of two interlocking minor thirds, and secondly by reminiscences of the introduction in the finale.

Stravinsky composed the symphony in C in the years 1938–40 while delivering a series of lectures at Harvard University on, among other things, form and structural principles. It was his intention to demonstrate in the work his belief that certain principles of form remain valid regardless of composition. He took as his point of departure the smaller orchestra of the Viennese classicists, finding his chief model in Haydn, though certain features of the first movement (in sonata form) point to Beethoven. The symphony in C has four movements: the outer movements are interrelated, the second movement, larghetto concertante, is an arioso for solo woodwinds, and the third, allegretto, is a dance movement, with the succession minuet-passepied-minuet, exhibiting a definite scherzo character. As in the *Symphony of Psalms*, the cohesive element for the entire work is an intervallic figure, this time consisting of a rising second and a descending fourth. The first movement's main theme arises from this motif and returns in the coda as a chorale-like conclusion. A significant characteristic of the symphony in C is its concertante quality, exemplifying the way in which twentieth- century composers detached themselves from the pathos of the nineteenth.

The Symphony in three movements, from the years 1942–45, is also a concertante work. As in the *Symphony of Psalms* and the symphony in C, Stravinsky here again attempts to explore the formal principles of classical scores without adopting the musical vocabulary of their time. Structurally, old models are brought together to form a novel unity. In the first movement it is chiefly sonata form which is used to distinguish the symphonic and concertante elements in two separate expositions. Both elements are jointly recapitulated. The middle movement, a homage to Rossini, forms the core of the composition. It was originally written to accompany film footage taken of occupied China during the Second World War. It is a sensitive andante in three-part form (ABA), in which the melodic part for harp and the equally solo-like flute part are given free room for expansion. Noteworthy in the instrumentation is also the repeated use of timpani and piano, which lends particular strength to the keen syncopated rhythms of the outer movements. These rhythms inevitably recall *Le Sacre du Printemps*, written thirty years earlier. But the finale also foreshadows to a certain extent the strict serial style which Stravinsky would later adopt.

In contrast to Stravinsky, who occupied himself with the phenomenon of the symphony only during his neo-classical period, his countrymen Prokofiev and Shostakovich espoused the form throughout their compositional careers. This surely has something to do with the fact that Stravinsky settled outside Russia after the revolution, whereas Prokofiev, after a fourteen-year stay in the West, returned; and Shostakovich spent his entire life in the country of his birth. In eastern Europe, particularly in Russia, tonality has remained the basis of all music-making, and this holds true today. Therefore the symphony has continued to occupy a position of importance in Russian musical life. Of Prokofiev's seven symphonies, only the first, the so-called *Classical*, has proved to be an unqualified success. Written in the troubled period before the outbreak of the Russian Revolution of 1917, it offers, in its purity and simplicity, a reaction against the excesses of late Romanticism. As Stravinsky was later to do in composing his symphony in C, Prokofiev took a Haydn symphony as his point of departure. Prokofiev however went much further, composing his symphony as if it were in fact by Haydn, without actually plagiarizing him. The outer movements are constructed according to the classical sonata form and provide a frame for a larghetto in three-part song-form and a gavotte, which replaces the classical minuet, giving an overall form perfectly within the classical tradition. Prokofiev's desire in composing his second symphony (opus 40, 1924) was to write a work of 'iron and steel' and no greater contrast to the first symphony is imaginable. The composition is modelled on Beethoven's last piano sonata, opus 111. The tormented mechanical restlessness of the work makes it almost inaccessible. With the third and fourth symphonies, Prokofiev attempted to transfer music previously written for his opera *The Flaming Angel* and for several ballets, to the symphonic form. The third symphony is predominantly sombre in colour, but of exceptional formal clarity. The fourth, on the other hand, is the most cheerful of them all. For the first time, in this symphony's finale Prokofiev offers a response to the positivism required by the Soviet authorities. Music must not exist for its own ends, but must function as an audible stimulus for the people. The finale is understated, but at the same time concludes ostentatiously: a cynical response.

The positivistic concept also colours the last movements of Prokofiev's fourth, sixth and seventh symphonies. In the seventh and last, dedicated to the youth of the Soviet Union, this ultimately leads to a level approaching that of mediocre light music. But it is Prokofiev's fifth symphony which is indisputably his masterpiece. A classical equilibrium reigns throughout. It is a score patterned on the classical-Romantic model and exhibiting great expressive power and melodic richness. The stately sobriety of the first movement is followed by a nervously fluttering scherzo. The third movement, adagio, begins gravely, but an abrupt shift into the major mode gives it a more benevolent character. Thematic elements from the first section of the adagio are reproduced in the finale.

The fifteen symphonies of Dmitri Shostakovich give every indication of being direct descendants of the nineteenth century. His first symphony can only be described as the ingenious undertaking of a nineteen-year-old. Here Shostakovich seems clearly to have had his origins in the world of Tchaikovsky and Bruckner, although Prokofiev's symphonic ideas

Ives

Charles Ives (1874–1954) was born in Danbury, Connecticut. His early musical education was from his father, an amateur musician who had been a military bandleader during the Civil War. Musically Ives's father was something of an eccentric, making his son sing 'Swanee River' in E flat while accompanying him in C – 'to stretch his ears'. Young Charles took to his father's love of dissonance and polytonality like a duck to water. At Yale, his music teacher (the composer Horatio Parker) was shocked and nonplussed at the musical ideas and irreverence of this brilliant young man who found Chopin 'soft' and Mozart 'effeminate'. Ives graduated from Yale in 1908, the same year that he married Harmony Twitchell, and embarked on a prosperous career in insurance that enabled him to retire at the age of fifty-five. As a musical initiator, he was generations ahead of his time, using tone-clusters, polyrhythms, microtones (intervals smaller than two adjacent notes on the piano), jazz and random elements in his music years before any of the 'serious' European masters. Socially he kept very quiet about his activities as a composer, and refused all royalties on his music – which he published at his own expense. In later years however, when fame (much to his displeasure) had reached him, Ives tried to explain his outrageous harmonies and anarchic approach: 'I found I could not go on using the familiar chords early. I heard something else', he commented.

have not left him untouched. (Shostakovich wrote his first symphony only six years after Prokofiev wrote his.) The work provides ample evidence of Shostakovich's early mastery of form and instrumentation. This is particularly true of the first three movements, in which there is not only a continual shifting of tempi but also an ever-increasing extravagance of musical thought. The finale, in which unremitting variety is raised to the level of a formal principle, does not wholly succeed in fulfilling the promise of the earlier movements. The second and third symphonies, entitled *To October* and *The First of May* respectively, are both in a single movement with a choral conclusion. Both are a result of questing and experimentation, neither particularly successful in matters of form. Yet the musical expression is spacious and daring. Passages such as those at the beginning and end of the second symphony, containing no trace of a tonal basis, remain unique in Shostakovich's output.

The fourth symphony, opus 43, was not heard until 1961, a quarter of a century after its composition, as Shostakovich withdrew it following the first orchestral rehearsals. Again the composer embraced the classical-Romantic principle of form, and the musical language of Tchaikovsky, Bruckner and Mahler. The first movement is written in true sonata form with an emormous development section, complete with the quasi-baroque concertante interpolations so widely favoured at the time. Characteristic of the symphony as a whole is the way in which Shostakovich spotlights individual instrumental groups, a procedure similar to that employed by Mahler and Ives. The conclusion of the second movement is a masterpiece of instrumentation, its graceful string figures artfully combined with explosive percussion. The finale shows the composer juxtaposing passages of extreme contrast in a short space. A vehement beginning is followed by a waltz and pastoral sections, in which the cuckoo's cry is to be heard, and the work ends with a long melancholy coda. The fifth symphony, bearing the programmatic title *The Stabilization of Personality*, is essentially a late-Romantic work incorporating Wagnerian harmony. As in the sixth symphony, the motto of optimism, *From darkness into light*, dictated by the Soviet authorities, tends towards triviality. The seventh and eighth symphonies reflect various war-time events in a patriotic way. Fascinating in the first movement of the seventh symphony is a protracted ostinato which takes

The conductor Eugene Ormandy (in a dark shirt) with, on his left, the cellist Mstislav Rostropovich and Dmitri Shostakovich.

the place of the development. As in Ravel's *Bolero*, this *ostinato* works toward an enormous climax, but the character is much more sinister. Symphonies eleven to fourteen, like much music written in the years between 1950 and 1970, were conceived as programme music. No. 11, opus 103 (1957) commemorates the year 1905, the year of revolution, in which Rimsky-Korsakov made his liberalism explicit. The twelfth symphony, *The Year 1917* (opus 112, 1961), was dedicated to Lenin. Symphony no. 13 (1962) is not only of a programmatic nature but vocal as well. A chorus declaims poems by Yevgeny Yevtushenko, including his famous *Babi Yar*, with its denunciation of anti-semitism. When Premier Krushchev withdrew his support of Yevtushenko, Shostakovich's thirteenth symphony also disappeared. The fourteenth symphony, for soprano, bass and chamber orchestra, is a song-cycle in which the increasing asperity of the musical idiom is closely bound up with the textual content. In the fifteenth symphony (1971), Shostakovich does not strive for profundity. A gentle sound predominates. This and the many instances of persiflage, such as the quotation of Rossini's William Tell theme, exclude the work from the influence of true symphonic art. The only symphony completely within this tradition is the ninth, which can be regarded as a pendant to Prokofiev's *Classical Symphony*.

Just as the symphony in Russia could flourish thanks to the dominance of tonality, so in the rest of Europe the symphony could only blossom where confinement to a tonal centre was still held in esteem. Such a group of composers centred itself around Paul Hindemith. Hindemith used the denomination 'symphony' for the first time in 1937, employing it more and more frequently as he became increasingly conscious of his place in musical history. In total he uses the classifications of 'symphony' or 'symphonic' eight times.

Best-known is the symphony *Mathis der Maler* (1934). From his opera of the same name about the sixteenth-century painter Mathis Grünewald, who was ever in conflict with the authorities, Hindemith extracted three symphonic episodes. These were inspired by pieces of Grünewald's Isenheimer altar in Colmar: Angelic Concert, Burial, and the Temptation of St Anthony. Hindemith tastefully works two chorale melodies into the symphony: in the first movement, *Es sangen drei Engel ein süssen Gesang* and in the third, *Lauda Sion Salvatorem*.

The process for *Die Harmonie der Welt* was the reverse: Hindemith later used this symphony, which treats the life and work of the scholar Johannes Kepler, as a basis for an opera. The symphony provides a clear link with the sound and expressive world of Bruckner. This is also true for the *Symphonische Tänze*, which may well have been intended as dances, but provide an example of a true symphony in their interrelation. The symphonic procedure is also visible in *Symphonische Metamorfosen Carl Maria von Weberscher Themen*, in which four pieces for piano duet are so reorganized, transformed and enriched in a variety of ways, as to allow one to speak of a proper symphony. Less successful is Hindemith's attempt to transfer his ideal of *Spielmusik* to the symphonic form, as in the symphony in B flat for concert band, the *Sinfonia Serena* and the symphony in E flat. These all have a concertante character coupled with the application of polyphony. Admittedly this combination leads to a number of surprising and original solutions to problems of form, such as the partial layering of originally separate structural elements and the use of fugal components.

In the footsteps of Hindemith and his concertante polyphony followed Karl Amadeus Hartmann, Johann Nepumuk David and, to a certain extent, the Swiss composer Arthur Honegger. Hartmann joins Hindemith's techniques of construction with the late-Romantic tradition of Bruckner and Mahler. His eight symphonies are without exception charged with tragic expression and extremely elaborate as regards constitution. Polyphonic structure for Hartmann is a very sophisticated affair, which derives from three basic rules. According to

When Ravel's *La Valse* was not performed by the Ballets Russes, after Diaghilev had commissioned the work, the composer was deeply hurt. He refused to shake hands with the impresario, who then challenged him to a duel. The matter was settled bloodlessly, however, if not amicably.

La Danse des Morts

Paul Claudel   Arthur Honegger

Editions Maurice Senart. Paris.

The cover of the score of Honeggers' *Dance of Death*.

Arthur Honegger, once a member of the group *Les Six* in Paris, outlived the public's taste for his closely-woven musical textures.

these, melodies lend themselves primarily to: 1. variation 2. fugue and 3. all possible forms of imitation (for instance, from back to front, or in contrary motion from high to low using the same pattern of intervals). By these and other means he often achieves shattering climaxes in an expanded tonal idiom with extremely well-thought-out constructions. For example, under the title of *Toccata variata*, in the second movement of his sixth symphony, Hartmann presents three fugues, bound together by means of variation-techniques, and by accelerating the metric impulse and thickening the polyphonic structure, he achieves enormous intensity using melodies which are in themselves quite simple.

The symphonies of the Austrian composer Johann Nepomuk David are all monothematic, built out of a single motif. In order to avoid the risk of monotony this might produce, David exploits constructional procedures similar to those used by Hartmann, and with a Bach-like polyphony.

The symphonic art of Arthur Honegger is on the one hand firmly rooted in the nineteenth century, yet his harmonic idiom, joining an expanded tonal sense to an archaic-sounding diatonic system, allows him to achieve an authentic style. His connections with the past emerge above all in the breadth of his melodic invention, his retention of the three-part symphonic form (with the exception of the *Monopartita* of 1951) and his inclination towards the programmatic. Not only did Honegger come to the symphony via the symphonic poem, the last three of his five symphonies were assigned programmes: *Symphonie Liturgique* (1946), *Deliciae basiliensis* (1946) and *Di Tre Re* (1947). The first movements of his symphonies always demonstrate a very personal approach to sonata form. In the first symphony, the three themes of the exposition are sounded simultaneously in the recapitulation. The first movement of the second symphony has two development sections. The first movement of the fifth symphony has no development, but two groups of themes and a recapitulation. The second symphony, which Honegger wrote while deeply concerned with the events of the Second World War, exhibits his strong urge towards 'autobiographical' music. It is written for string orchestra with a solo trumpet in the finale.

Like Honegger, Albert Roussel stands at the frontier between two epochs. In his four symphonies Roussel proceeds along the path from programme music to an absolute symphonic form. The first symphony, from 1908, bears the title *Poème de la forêt*. High points are the third symphony of 1930 and the fourth (in A major) of 1935, both of which have maintained a place in the repertory. Echoes of Mahler can be heard in the Romantic understructure of these symphonies, but the rugged motive power, the daring melodies and a preference for great masses of sound recall Prokofiev and Stravinsky.

The symphonic work of Honegger's contemporary Darius Milhaud falls into two distinct groups. Between 1917 and 1923 he wrote six symphonies for reduced forces (the sixth, for example, is for vocal quartet, oboe and cello). Each of them is a short ironic piece of raillery, poking fun at established symphonic forms and procedures. Only in 1939 did he address himself to large-scale symphonic form. He wrote thirteen symphonies, some calling for a chorus (no. 3, *Te Deum*, 1946; no. 13, *Pacem in Terris*, 1966, from the encyclical of Pope John XXIII) and some with titles (no. 8, *Rhôdanienne*, 1957; no. 12, *Rurale*, 1961). In these works Milhaud shows himself to be an impressive and imaginative orchestrator.

Among twentieth-century French symphonists, mention must also be made of Henri Dutilleux and Henri Barraud. In his first symphony (1951), second symphony *Le Double* (1959) and *Métaboles pour orchestre* (1964), by making use of expanded tonality Dutilleux achieves works which are virtuoso and strictly organized, as well as clear and transparent. The second symphony owes its name to the fact that the principle of concerto grosso is applied within the symphonic form: a

Darius Milhaud (1892-1974), whose witty essays in polytonality gave his music a considerable vogue.

small ensemble, a concertino of twelve instruments, confronts the full orchestra.

Dutilleux and Barraud have in common their attempt to bridge the gap between the various twentieth-century currents, from impressionism up to and including serialism, even endeavouring to bring these different worlds into contact with each other. Barraud however bases his style more explicitly on the strict contrapuntal methods of Hindemith, which gives his works a darker quality than those of his colleague.

An isolated case is the ten-part symphony *Turangalîla* by Olivier Messiaen. Although the work does not fit into any traditional symphonic conception, because of its thematic relationships, scope and power, it has its place in the world of the symphony.

The American composer Charles Ives wrote four symphonies, the first two in the period before 1900 and the last two well after the turn of the century. The fourth symphony, which Ives wrote in the years 1911–16, is indisputably the most important. It is a four-part composition for large orchestra with two pianos and a mixed chorus in the first and final movements. The work bears little relationship to traditional symphonic form. With the exception of the third movement, a conventional fugue, the symphony seems consciously to be pointing towards the future. After a majestic and monumental opening (based on the poem *Watchman, Tell us of the Night* by Lowell Mason), there follows a lengthy allegretto of an extremely sombre and oppressive nature. After the fugue, this atmosphere is again evoked in the fourth movement. Noteworthy in Ives's method of composition is the division of the orchestra into independent, sometimes even spatially separated, sound-groups. The consistent use of these independent groups leads to a frequent piling-up of various rhythms one above another simultaneously and the occurrence of elaborate polytonal and polyphonic situations. A great deal of the melodic material is borrowed from, or even quotes directly, American tunes, whether instrumental or vocal. These include, for example, *Yankee Doodle; Hail Columbia, the Gem of the Ocean; Joy to the World* and *In the Sweet By and By*. In addition Ives also re-uses material from his own earlier compositions.

The collage-technique which Ives employs is also used by the American Elliott Carter in his *Symphony of Three Orchestras*, written in 1976.

Samuel Barber composed his first single-movement symphony in 1935–36. The work breathes a Romantic atmosphere with certain influences

Copland

Aaron Copland (b.1900) is one of the foremost composers to come out of the United States. After receiving his earliest music lessons from his sister and studying piano with V. Wittgenstein and Clarence Adler, he received instruction in composition from Rubin Goldmark, a nephew of the well-known Karl Goldmark and, in Paris, from Nadia Boulanger. In 1924 he returned to America where he took an active role in contemporary musical life. Copland assimilated jazz elements into his music, and later added both North and South American folk elements. After 1950 his work also shows signs of twelve-tone techniques. In addition to his compositions, Copland wrote a great deal about music: What to Listen for in Music (1938), Our New Music (1941), Music and Imagination (1952) and Copland on Music (1960).

from the young Prokoviev. In this symphony Barber made a startling formal discovery. Although written in one continuous movement, the composition contains a scherzo and adagio which are worked into the development of the large sonata form of the whole, after which the exposition themes again make their appearance.

The second symphony (1944–47) also adheres to the Romantic tradition. The first movement (allegro ma non tanto) is in true sonata form with three clearly defined themes, a development and a recapitulation. This is followed by a pastoral andante un poco mosso and the work concludes with a passionate allegro risoluto, The symphony was, however, withdrawn by the composer.

Less important as a symphonist than either of these Americans is Aaron Copland. Yet his *Dance Symphony* of 1925 must be mentioned, a work in which, like Hindemith, he succeeded in adapting dances to the symphonic form while maintaining their dance-like character.

Leonard Bernstein, who has won greater fame as a conductor than as a composer, has three symphonies to his credit. The first and third are bound up with elements of the Jewish liturgy. The first *Jeremiah*, dates from 1942 and is based on Hebrew melodies. The first movement, which uses the Jewish vocal patterns of the *Amidah* and *K'rovoh*, symbolizes Jeremiah's prophecy of the destruction of Jerusalem. The second movement portrays the mocking reaction of the corrupt priests, symbolized by jazz rhythms, while the main theme of the first movement is proclaimed distortedly braying horns. The third movement harks back to the first, but what then was presented as prophecy now is sounded as a lamentation, with passages from Jeremiah's eponymous book sung by a mezzo-soprano.

The second symphony, *The Age of Anxiety*, is based on a poem by W. H. Auden. Bernstein divides the poem into two three-part sections: a prologue with two series of variations, followed by an elegy, 'The Dirge', a scherzo 'The Masque', and an epilogue. The work has a programme: four people philosophise about their own future and the future of the world. The third symphony, the *Kaddish* (1963), exhales an atmosphere similar to the first. Notable in the build-up of melodies and structures is a compositional technique, which approaches that of Johann Nepomuk David or Willem Pijper: small units are used as building-blocks to create larger lines which constantly renew themselves, piece by piece, without breaking the over-all musical coherence.

For a long time it seemed as if Dutch symphonic music, heavily influenced by late German Romanticism, might suffocate under the burden of its own rigidity. Fortunately a few composers, though still dependent upon the Romantic idiom, experienced an impulse towards innovation. Hendrik Andriessen wrote five symphonies and one symphonic étude, characterized by classical construction and a French sound-palette with room for Romanticism à la César Franck and impressionism in the manner of Debussy.

Also the composer of five symphonies, Jan van Gilse perpetuated the German Romantic idiom of Richard Strauss.

Henk Badings, who composed no less than fifteen symphonies between 1930 and 1970, also has based his work on the German tradition. In matters of form and instrumentation he demonstrates strong ties with the past as well as a certain individuality.

Whereas the sound-worlds of Andriessen and Badings appear uninfluenced by the developments advanced by the Viennese School, Stravinsky and Bartók, the innovations coming out of Vienna and Paris proved to be of great significance for Willem Pijper and Matthijs Vermeulen. Although both of them held the opinion that the direction taken by the Viennese School, with its emphasis on atonality and the twelve-tone system, would provide consequences ultimately unacceptable for such aspects of composition as form, rhythm and melody, leading finally to a disintegration of sound as we know it, they were sufficiently stimulated to develop their own structural principles. Pijper and Vermeulen also have in common a great admiration for Stravinsky, even though this finds expression in their symphonic work in widely divergent ways.

Vermeulen's seven symphonies, written between 1914 and 1965, are characterized by a continual use of 'polymelodies', various melodies appearing simultaneously in the different instrumental groups, each retaining its own independence. Vermeulen combines this with a forceful motoric drive, from which ear-catching rhythmic or metrical accentuation is absent, but thick orchestration obscures the compact structures and undifferentiated lines.

Willem Pijper's works demonstrate a greater refinement. His use of a great variety of unexpected rhythmic and metrical shifts results in a continual revivification of structure. While with Vermeulen harmony as an important musical ingredient is sacrificed to the 'polymelodic', Pijper achieves a true polytonal harmony in which different keys appear at the same time. A very personal aspect of Pijper's compositional methods is the 'germ-cell system', which he himself developed: a minute motif, itself extremely unobtrusive, permeates and influences large sections, or even the entire composition, as all musical components (melody, rhythm, harmony, etc.) are grafted onto it. Pijper's best-known symphony is his third and last. It bears the motto: 'if I can not reach heaven, then I will raise hell.' With satanic rage, hell is indeed raised by the full orchestra in the finale; from the outset a climax begins to build, becoming almost unbearable near the end, followed by no sense of resolution, and leaving behind a feeling of despair. In the 1950s Dutch composition was heavily influenced by Pijper's music.

During the same period, through the work of Kees van Baaren and his students, the twelve-tone system and serialism also became influential, with their emphasis on the confinement of all musical parameters into ordered series. Since the beginning of the 1970s, a reaction against this has produced a return to tonality, though it is a tonality charged with a different and more personal character.

Peter Schat, who in his earlier compositions turned his back purpose-

Vaughan Williams

Ralph Vaughan Williams (1872–1958) received his instruction in composition from Max Bruch and, much later, from Maurice Ravel. Originally an organist, he found himself increasingly attracted to composition. In 1918 he became a professor of composition at the Royal College of Music. Like Bartók, Vaughan Williams made an extensive study of folk music. He studied, collected and arranged a large number of English folk songs; they had a profound effect upon his own compositions too, particularly in the field of orchestral music.

In his own country, Vaughan Williams belongs to the most influential composers of his generation. His reputation became definitively established with the Sea Symphony (1910), and his great hymn, 'For All the Saints', remains one of the most popular in the English canon.

The lively rhythms and enchanting tunes in Aaron Copland's music have won him admirers all over the world.

fully on all traditional forms, composed a symphony in 1978 in which he attempted to reach a synthesis between classical form and non-traditional elements: twelve-tone techniques, uncommon instruments within the orchestra and unusual metres. Younger composers such as Tristan Keuris, whose *Sinfonia* (1972) was an overnight success, and Jan Wagemans (symphony, opus 3, 1972), have kept the symphonic form alive in Holland.

In Great Britain, after Edward Elgar, the most important exponent of English late Romanticism, Ralph Vaughan Williams, attracted attention as a symphonist. Nationalistic tendencies, deriving from an early interest in folk song, are present in most of his symphonies. Actual folk material is seldom quoted; rather the music breathes a melodic atmosphere

Hindemith's descriptive symphony *Mathis der Maler* is among the most enduringly popular of all his works.

evocative of the folk spirit. His links with the traditions of the sixteenth and seventeenth century polyphonists are apparent in his harmonies, often based upon the old modes, and in his clearly constructed counterpoint. His first three symphonies – *Sea Symphony* (1905–10), *London Symphony* (1914) and *Pastoral Symphony* (1922) – are written in an easily assimilable style. In the fourth symphony (1935), Vaughan Williams makes a sudden departure from this folk-influenced style. The work is violent and dramatic, full of dissonance and dark sounds. With his fifth symphony (1943) he returns to his familiar musical language with its folk character. The sixth, seventh and eighth symphonies share, in addition to unconventional formal structures, an increasing use of dissonance and harmonic tension. In his ninth symphony (1956–57) Vaughan Williams succeeds in exploring new sound possibilities: there are important passages for saxophone trio and for flugelhorn.

Eleven years his junior, Arnold Bax, with seven three-movement symphonies to his credit, characterized his music in the following words: 'My music is the expression of emotional states.' Bax is a perfect example

Right: Arnold Schoenberg, a self-portrait painted in 1910. As well as being one of the most revolutionary of composers, Schoenberg was a remarkable painter, a member of the 'Blaue Reiter' school. His music was championed in America by Leopold Stokowski (*left*), conductor of the Philadelphia Orchestra.

Stravinsky studied law in his birthplace, St Petersburg, and had lessons at the same period with Rimsky-Korsakov; the impresario Diaghilev heard some of his early works and comissioned a ballet. With *The Firebird* (1910), the 28-year-old composer leaped into world-wide prominence.

The avant-garde composer Karlheinz Stockhausen is mystified by the strong animosity his work arouses in many listeners. 'My music makes sense to me', he says.

Luciano Berio. In his *Sinfonia*, the experimental Italian composer combined elements of Bach, Wagner, Martin Luther King and the Swingle Singers.

Jean Sibelius. Like Rossini before him, Sibelius retired from composition in middle life and wrote little more.

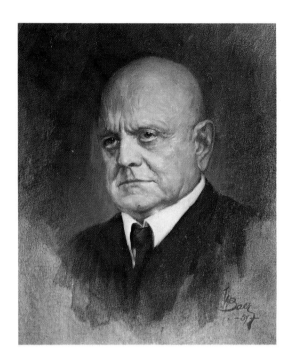

The Moldau, Prague, by Kokoschka.

Pijper

Willem Pijper (1894–1947) was not only a composer but also a teacher and music critic. As critic for the Utrechts Dagblad **(1918–23), he took as his quarry Jan van Gilse, conductor of the local orchestra, and pursued him mercilessly in his columns. After teaching theory and composition at the Amsterdam Conservatory from 1918 to 1930, he was appointed director of** **the Rotterdam Conservatory and remained in this position until his death.**

of a 'threshold composer', someone standing midway between the old and the new. He shares with Vaughan Williams his affection for old traditions, but impressionism by no means left him untouched. His work is therefore somewhat ambiguous, colour and form hover between the Romantic and the modern. A more interesting symphonist of the same generation is Havergal Brian, composer of thirty-two symphonies, twenty-one of which he completed after the age of 80 (he died at the age of 86). Brian's musical language is compact and functional. His early symphonies lack the compactness of his later work and are remarkably ambitious. His music is classically tonal, sober and meticulously crafted. Michael Tippett too, in his four symphonies, seems preoccupied with the possibilities of the classical form. The fourth symphony in particular is intense, melancholy, and deeply felt. It is a profoundly moving work, and most rewarding to come to know.

The most prominent British composer during the years after the Second World War is undoubtedly Benjamin Britten. His talent revealed itself very early: the delightful *Simple Symphony* for strings, published in 1934, is based upon material from compositions he wrote between the ages of nine and twelve. His two greatest contributions to the symphonic

Elgar never completed his third symphony. In this sketch for the Adagio, the opening bars are surmounted by the beginning of his Piano Quintet, opus 84.

repertory are the *Sinfonia da Requiem* (1940) and the *Cello Symphony* (1963).

William Walton wrote two magnificient symphonies, the first including a splendid scherzo marked con malizia. Among the younger generation of British composers, Malcolm Williamson, born in Australia, stands out in the symphonic field, with his remarkable second symphony (1969), in which he manages to unite traditional symphonic form with highly modern techniques, serialism among them.

In his six symphonies, which he himself calls 'orchestral pieces given the name of symphonies', the German Hans Werner Henze devotes himself to the same problem, that of resolving the conflict between sonata form and the twelve-tone system. He often finds his solutions in variation techniques. In his second and third symphonies he uses the form of the chaconne. His fourth symphony, originally created as the finale of the opera *König Hirsch* (King Stag), is a one-movement work with a cyclical form. The finale of the fifth symphony consists of a series of variations on music from the second part of the work. When Henze uses sonata form, as in the first, fourth and fifth symphonies, his approach is free in the extreme, allowing him to develop well-ordered, logical structures which escape the repressive bonds of traditional rules of structure and development. Henze's attitude towards the twelve-tone system is also characterized by a very free approach, enabling him to achieve a colourful palette of widely expressive means, musical transparency and flowing, almost lyrical lines, fused with dense, compact contrapuntal and motivic structures. His sixth symphony is constructed in a particularly interesting way. There are no actual themes as such, but rather a number of associated musical elements which emerge again and again in the various movements, rhythmic, intervallic and harmonic structures which, in their endless variation, acquire ever-new dimensions.

The Polish composer Witold Lutoslawski has found a highly individual

The extraordinary wailing of the Ondes Martenot was used to great effect in his *Turangalîla Symphony* by Messiaen. Most listeners will be familiar with the sound through early American Science Fiction movies, however.

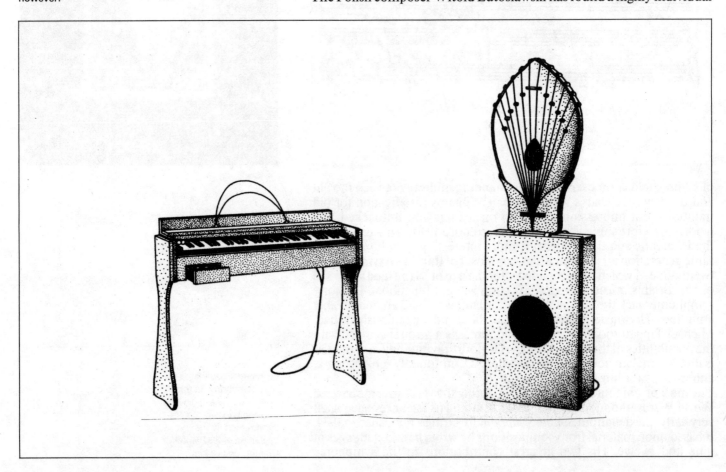

way of disengaging himself from the dictates of form. After his neo-classical first symphony, written in 1946, he turned to the twelve-tone system. His second symphony, dating from the years 1966–67, is based on this system, with the addition of 'aleatoric counterpoint' *i.e.* that the plurality of voices is only partially set down, with the result that a certain element of chance is built in to the music played by the ensemble, initiated either by the conductor or individual members of the orchestra. Naturally there can no longer by any talk of themes, exposition, development, etc. But coherence and compactness still give the work a symphonic allure, to which in any event the oldest definition of 'symphony' is applicable: 'sounding together'.

Stockhausen's *Refrain*, an elegant example of today's graphic notation.

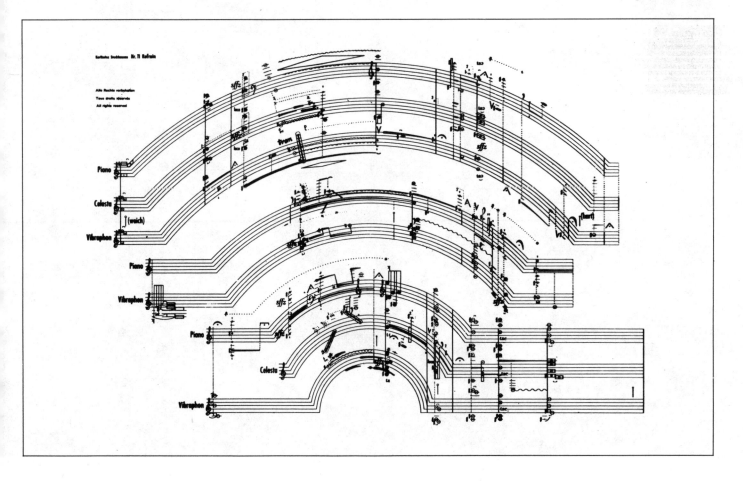

9

A guide to the great conductors

Abbado

Abbado knew already at the age of eight what he wanted to become. 'Someday I want to conduct Debussy,' he wrote in his diary. He completed his studies at the age of nineteen at the conservatory in Milan with a degree in piano, and, two years later, in conducting and composition. He continued his study of conducting with Hans Swarowsky: 'Vienna was extremely important to me,' recalls Abbado when discussing his student years. Along with his fellow-student Zubin Mehta, he sang in the chorus the St Matthew Passion, the Brahms Requiem, the Mozart Requiem – 'all of them experiences which later helped me as a conductor.' When he won the Mitropoulos competition for young conductors in 1963, he declared that Arturo

Toscanini and Victor de Sabata exemplified for him the ideal opera conductor and that Wilhelm Furtwängler, Bruno Walter and Dmitri Mitropoulos were guiding forces in the area of symphonic interpretation.
By now Abbado himself has become an example of the ideal modern conductor. His artistic credo is summed up in two statements: 'I do not feel like a magician wielding a conductor's baton, but like an intermediary who must express musical matters as clearly as possible.' And: 'I want to help the audience to understand music.' The latter has been put into practice at La Scala in Milan where, since Abbado's arrival as artistic director, most of the rehearsals have been open to the public.

Claudio Abbado, born 26 June 1933, the son of an Italian musician, studied piano, composition and orchestral conducting at the Conservatory of

Milan and the Musikakademie in Vienna. In 1958, along with his fellow-student Zubin Mehta, he won the Koussevitsky Prize in Tanglewood (USA). In

1963 he took first prize in the Dmitri Mitropoulos competition for young conductors in New York. Success was quick. He became a frequently requested

guest-conductor at the Vienna and Salzburg Festivals and was appointed to a number of honorary posts (principal conductor of the Vienna Philharmonic,

'Principal Guest Director' of the London Symphony Orchestra and artistic director of La Scala in Milan).

Ansermet

Swiss conductor. Late in life Ernest Ansermet claimed that he did not at first choose music as a profession because he was lazy about practising. He became instead a mathematician, tachning at Lausanne University from 1905-09. Throughout this period he studied harmony and counterpoint, learning symphonic scores and taking every opportunity to observe the great conductors of the day. 'Conducting is not a

profession', he once said, in justification of his self-acquired skills.
He began his career as a conductor in Montreux in 1911, moving to Geneva in 1915. That same year he became conductor of Diaghilev's Ballet Russe on the recommendation of Igor Stravinsky, a recent acquaintance. When the Swiss musical establishment collapsed after the First World War, Ansermet filled the vacuum with his own creation: L'Orchestre de la Suisse Romande. This orchestra was formed to serve French-speaking Switzerland, but from

the beginning it had a cosmopolitan nature. Few of its members were Swiss, and its repertoire was boldly avant-garde. From 1918-66 Ansermet conducted L'Orchestre de la Suisse Romande, becoming in later years synonymous with this one ensemble. He was eventually in a position to turn down lucrative and glamorous offers of work from America, a country that was scarcely aware of his existence before the Second World War. Such a reputation was hard won. In the years immediately following the First World War Ansermet tirelessly championed the works of his contemporaries. Today he is particularly associated with Stravinsky; for a time he premiered nearly all of Stravinsky's works, including *The Soldiers Tale, Pulcinella*, the *Symphony of Psalms*. Among his many other first performances were Falla's *Three-cornered Hat*, Satie's *Parade* and Honegger's *Pacific 231*. He was so devoted to the music of Debussy that he admitted he would pay for the privilege of conducting it. Ansermet was unaffected by fame and critical of conductors whose showmanship

was a performance in itself. 'I have never played to the public', he said. His own performance was nevertheless full of character. As befits a pioneer of modern music, he was a meticulous technician, developing a special conducting style for the rapidly-changing rhythms of Stravinsky. Bearded and severe, his appearance on the podium was described by the composer Virgil Thomson as 'a cross between Agamemnon and the King of Spades'.
In spite of all his efforts in popularizing contemporary music, Ansermet had no sympathy with Arnold Schoenberg's school of twelve-tone composition. He found it occasionally ingenious but musically heartless, the product of 'dead theory'. In *Les Fondements de la Musique* (1961), he wrote a massive refutation of serial music, drawing upon deep religious beliefs and all his musical, mathematical, and philosophical resources. 'In music the artisan comes after the artist, not before', he wrote, revealing that behind the analytical and modern mind lay a profoundly old-fashioned soul.

Born in Switzerland in 1883, he did not begin conducting until 1911. Working from 1915 with the *Ballet Russe,* he gave many important

first performances including Ravel's *La Valse,* Satie's *Parade,* Falla's *Three-cornered Hat,* and several works by Stravinsky including *L'Histoire du Soldat,*

Renard and *Les Noces*. Ansermet founded L'Orchestre de la Suisse Romande in 1918 and remained its conductor until 1967. As well as his interpretations of

Stravinsky, his performances on record of French music, particularly Debussy and Ravel, are outstanding. He also enjoyed a fine

reputation in the opera house, and was noted always for the meticulous clarity of his approach to complex contemporary scores.

Barenboim

Israeli pianist and conductor. At the age of seven Daniel Barenboim gave his first public recital in his native Buenos Aires. He concluded the program with seven encores, stopping only when he had exhausted his repertoire. The child is father of the man. Today, both as pianist and conductor, Barenboim is one of the most exuberant and tireless of modern musicians.
His parents, who were of Russian-Jewish origin, moved to Israel in 1952, but Barenboim's precocious talent was fostered in Europe. He studied conducting with Igor Markevitch and piano with Edwin Fischer in Salzburg, composition with Nadia Boulanger in Paris, while in Rome he graduated from the Accademia di Santa Cecilia. The great Wilhelm Furtwängler called him a phenomenon. And all before his fifteenth birthday.
In 1955 Barenboim played a Mozart

concerto in the Royal Festival Hall, and two years later he made his American debut with the Symphony of the Air under Leopold Stokowski. His career as a concert pianist was well under way, but as a conductor he had to wait until 1964, when he began a long and fruitful relationship with the English Chamber Orchestra. Conducting from the piano, Barenboim performed and recorded the twenty-seven Mozart concertos with the ECO. 1967 was an astonishing year. He played all thirty-two of the Beethoven sonatas at the Queen Elizabeth Hall in London, celebrated a popular (and highly publicized) marriage with the English cellist Jacqueline du Pré, toured the United States with the Israel Philharmonic and, with the New Philharmonia, appeared for the first time in Europe as conductor of a symphony orchestra. The following year, when Istvan Kertesz fell ill, he made his New York conducting debut with the London Symphony Orchestra. 'Mr Barenboim is a born conductor', wrote Harold C. Schonberg in the New York Times. Since then his right to a musical existence apart from the piano has remained unquestioned.

As any lingering resentment of the teenage wunderkind subsides, his musical opinions are treated with increasing respect. In 1975, after years of guest appearances, Barenboim became permanent conductor of

L'Orchestre de Paris, expanding his largely Germanic repertoire to include the works of Berlioz, Saint-Saëns and Debussy. His many recordings with this orchestra, added to an already vast discography, have made him the most inescapable of modern musicians and, in early middle age, one of the 'grand old men' of music.

Born in 1942, the Israeli Barenboim was a child prodigy as a pianist. He began conducting in 1964, and has pursued this career side by side with that of a pianist ever since. Performances of Mozart operas have won him great acclaim; and as a symphonic conductor, since becoming Artistic Director of L'Orchestre de Paris (1975) he has explored and made recordings of the nineteenth-century French repertoire, nobably Berlioz and Saint-Saëns. Barenboim has a great ability to control and bring out the form in such large-scale orchestral works, which he performs with a rare and passionate sensibility.

Beecham

Beecham had little formal training and was at times a laughably poor technician. He was immensely rich and felt no shame in hiring his own orchestras when no one else would employ him. He was often careless and inconsistent during performance. He treated many great masterpieces with contempt and appeared to revere what was second rate. He was vain, insufferably rude and unbelievably extravagant. Yet, unlike most 'amateur' conductors, he could make even a poor orchestra play, for one evening at least, like the best in the world; with the best orchestras he created some of the century's most memorable performances.

He was born in Lancashire, heir to the fortune amassed by his father in the manufacture of 'Beecham's Pills'. His musical training was private, but at the age of twenty he felt confident enough to stand in as conductor at a local concert in place of the venerable Hans Richter. Confidence was a quality Beecham never lacked. While still in his twenties he went to London, where his father sponsored his expensive education in conducting.

In 1910 opera became his passion and Covent Garden his plaything. He was eventually responsible for over 120 productions, including works by Strauss, Delius, Debussy and Ethel Smyth. Financial problems forced him to retire

completely for three years in 1920, but by then his apprenticeship was over, and on his return he was recognized as England's foremost conductor. He formed the London Philharmonic Orchestra in 1932 and with this group established his reputation on the Continent.

During the war he travelled throughout Australia and the United States, often urging mediocre orchestras into performances well above their normal capacities. In England again in 1946 he established the Royal Philharmonic Orchestra. By now his musical Midas-touch was infallible, and the new orchestra quickly matured to become one of the best in Europe.

Beecham the savage wit has been a subject of legends since long before his death. (In a relatively genial moment he could accuse his Tristan of making love to Isolde like "that estimable quadruped, the hedgehog".) Beecham the musician is more of a mystery. His memory was extraordinary and his repertoire vast. In Haydn and Mozart he inevitably discovered a freshness and grace that came as a revelation to audiences. Bach he disregarded entirely; Beethoven he found awkward; Mahler he treated like an unpleasant odour. Of all modern composers, he reserved his greatest affection for Frederick Delius. Claiming that his "barbarous age" could never properly appreciate music with such "a sense of regret and craving for beauty", Beecham betrayed a tenderness that his acerbic intellect too often concealed.

One of the most important British conductors, Beecham was born in Lancashire in 1879. Though much of his best-remembered work was done in the opera house, his symphonic career was also distinguished. He founded the London Philharmonic Orchestra (1932) and the Royal Philharmonic Orchestra (1946).

Van Beinum

'Just wait! Someday I will be standing on the conductor's podium in front of that orchestra,' the fourteen-year-old van Beinum is reputed to have said while attending a concert by the Concertgebouw Orchestra. These words, uttered in youthful enthusiasm, were to prove true. In 1929 he was invited to conduct one of the summer concerts and made such a favourable impression that, after a few more guest appearances, he was offered a permanent contract. The concert in 1931 which marked his assumption of his new position as alternate conductor amounted to an immediate musical declaration of faith: on the programme was Bruckner's eighth symphony, at that time infrequently performed. Van Beinum's manner of conducting was expressed by a member of

the orchestra in these words: 'He turned our orchestra into one enormous chamber music ensemble. Everything was mild, rounded and refined.' Eduard van Beinum himself referred to this approach as 'freedom in bondage'.

He considered himself to be an integral part of his orchestra: 'A conductor does not stand above the orchestra but is in essence simply one of its members.' His ambition was to make music along with the other members of the orchestra, rather than with the orchestra as a whole, at the same time preserving each person's individual freedom within the limits of the total body.

When dealing with soloists or individual members of the orchestra, van Beinum never forced his own vision of a work upon them, but tried continually to reach a balanced compromise and be a simple intermediary between listener and composer.

The Dutch conductor Eduard van Beinum (1901–59) began his musical career as a violist, going on to study orchestral conducting at the Amsterdam Conservatory. From 1926–31 he was conductor of the symphony orchestra in Haarlem. In 1931 he was appointed assistant conductor of the Concertgebouw Orchestra in Amsterdam, and in 1938 took his place beside Bruno Walter and Willem Mengelberg as alternate conductor. From 1945 until his death in 1959 he was principal conductor of the Concertgebouw Orchestra. He made a great many concert tours and was appointed conductor of the Los Angeles Philharmonic Orchestra in 1956. Van Beinum was widely known as a Bruckner interpreter and conductor of music by such French masters as Roussel, Debussy and Ravel. In addition he paid particular regard to composers of his own time and a large number of works by Dutch composers received world premières under his direction.

Bernstein

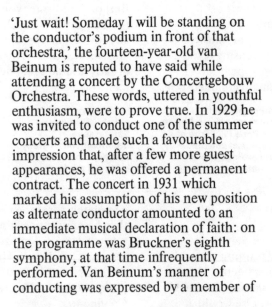

The concert in which Leonard Bernstein replaced Bruno Walter was broadcast by radio throughout the United States. After the initial disappointment of having an almost completely unknown young man substitute for the famous Bruno Walter, the audience grew extremely enthusiastic, overwhelmed by the mastery with which Bernstein controlled the orchestra. This won him instant fame. From 1945–48 he was musical director of the New York City Symphony; from 1951–55 he conducted classes in composition at the Berkshire Music Centre; in this same period he taught at Brandeis University. After becoming chief conductor of the New York Philharmonic in 1958, he was, in 1969, given the title of honorary conductor for life, in appreciation of his many merits. The boldness with which Bernstein began his career has characterized his entire

professional life. In Hungary he interpreted Bartók, in Vienna, Mahler and Beethoven. Bernstein's approach to music-making before an audience has often been criticized for its showmanship; he conducts not only with his hands but with his entire body. But for anyone having an ear for the musical flow of his interpretations as well as an eye for his athletic movements, there can be no doubt as to the seriousness of his approach and the depth of his dedication. For Bernstein music is an art which cannot be exercised in isolation, in a studio for example. He makes music for listeners whose presence he must sense. He is convinced that only then can great interpretations be achieved, that musicians must be able to see those for whom they are performing. This explains why he currently makes his recordings before a live audience. No careful fabrication aimed at perfection, but honest and forthright music-making, with all the necessary risks this entails.

Leonard Bernstein was born on 25 August 1918 at Lawrence, Massachusetts, the eldest of three children. Neither of his parents, Russian emigrants who had taken refuge in Boston, was particularly musical. In 1943 he became assistant conductor of the New York Philharmonic and that same year made a spectacular début, replacing the ailing Bruno Walter and taking over his entire programme unchanged. In 1958 Bernstein was appointed musical director of the same orchestra, making him the first American, exclusively trained in his own country, to be offered such an important position.

Böhm

Böhm was descended from a family of physicians and lawyers. While still engaged in legal studies, he began his musical career in 1917 as a coach at the opera in his birthplace of Graz, Austria. In 1921 he was appointed principal conductor of the State Opera in Munich, and in 1927 he became *Generalmusikdirektor* in Darmstadt. Next he went to the Hamburg opera, after which he succeeded Fritz Busch at Dresden in 1943. Through the intervention of Richard Strauss, Böhm was engaged by the Vienna Opera that same year. After the war, like his colleagues Furtwängler and von Karajan, he was forbidden to conduct. In 1947 he was given the direction of the *Konzerthausgesellschaft* and the *Gesellschaft der Musikfreunde* in Vienna. From 1950 to 1953 Böhm was active in the German opera season in Buenos Aires. In 1954 he returned to the Vienna State Opera and in 1962 he made his first appearance in Bayreuth with a performance of *Tristan und Isolde*. In 1968 Böhm published an autobiography entitled *Ich erinnere mich genau.*

Böhm's manner of conducting can best be described in the celebrated words of Richard Strauss: 'A conductor actually need do nothing at all with his left hand. Best would be if he simply left it in his coat pocket! At most this hand should be used to give a small sign when playing is too loud, but this can also be accomplished with an almost imperceptible glance.'

The conductor Karl Böhm died on 14 August 1981, just before his eighty-seventh birthday. Born at the end of the nineteenth century (18 August 1894), Böhm worked personally with such composers as Richard Strauss and Alban Berg. Strauss entrusted to Böhm the first performances of his operas Die Schweigsame Frau (1935) and Daphne (1938). But primarily Böhm was a great Mozart interpreter. It was he who brought Così fan tutte back into the standard repertory after almost a century of neglect.

Boulez

As a musician, Pierre Boulez for a long time considered himself to be first and foremost a composer rather than a conductor. In fact he was more or less obliged to become a conductor in order to perform his own compositions. His approach to music and instrumental techniques differed so greatly from customary practices that it was difficult for him to find conductors capable of rehearsing and performing his works. Since the mid-1960s, however, Boulez's career as a composer has shown a rapid decline. At the same time, music-lovers came to value the impressive interpretations for which, thanks to his well-developed musical intellect, he was responsible. Boulez's conducting continually reveals the instinctive feeling for form of a strongly analytical musician. Especially in recent years, he has combined this talent with a warm, Romantic musician's heart and as a result his interpretations have increased in power.

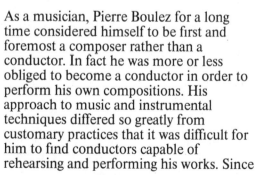

The French conductor and composer Pierre Boulez was born in Montbrison (Loire) in 1925. Initially he took up the study of mathematics and the technical sciences, but abandoned these subjects in favour of music. He studied composition with Olivier Messiaen and René Leibowitz. The latter put him in touch with the ideology of the Viennese School. In 1946 he became musical director of the experimental theatre company headed by Jean-Louis Barrault, who actively supported him in the organization of a concert series of avant-garde music: Domaine Musical. In 1963 he took up a position as conductor-in-residence and visiting professor at Harvard University in America. In 1971 he was under contract to both the BBC Symphony Orchestra in London and the New York Philharmonic.

Davis

In 1964 Davis left Sadler's Wells and addressed himself increasingly to the symphonic repertory. After a period of guest conducting he was appointed principal conductor of the BBC Symphony Orchestra (1967–71). During this time Davis became immensely popular with young audiences thanks to his appearances at the 'Last Night of the Proms'. Since 1971 he has been a much sought-after guest conductor the world over. In that year he made a successful appearance with the Berlin Philharmonic; in 1972 he became permanent guest conductor of the Boston Symphony Orchestra, occupying for several years a similar position with the Concertgebouw Orchestra in Amsterdam. Davis is a conductor of forceful enthusiasm, rather than of balanced versatility, which gives an indication of his weaknesses as well as his strengths. Mozart, Berlioz, Stravinsky and Tippett find in him an excellent advocate, due to a combination of inspired vitality and technical accomplishment. Davis's interpretations are lively, passionate, fresh and imaginative. In 1980 he was knighted for his services to music.

Because his piano-playing abilities were judged insufficient, Colin Davis, born 25 September 1927, was refused entrance to the conducting class of the Royal College of Music. When, however, a group of fellow-students founded the Kalmar Orchestra, Davis was regularly invited to direct. His appearances in this capacity led to an invitation to conduct for the Chelsea Opera Group, where from the early 1950s his Mozart interpretations won him considerable praise. In 1957 Davis was appointed assistant conductor of the BBC Scottish Symphony. In the following years he drew attention through a number of spectacular substitutions for leading conductors, such as Klemperer in 1959 for Don Giovanni **and Beecham in 1960 for** Die Zauberflöte. **In 1961 he was appointed music director of the Sadler's Wells Opera, where he not only gained admiration for his interpretations of accepted works but also for his championing of less accessible repertoire.**

Dorati

Antal Dorati was assistant conductor of the Budapest Opera from 1924 to 1928, and in this last year also assistant to Fritz Busch at the Dresden State Opera. The next year he was appointed principal conductor of the opera in Munster, where he remained until 1932. From 1933 to 1939 he was conductor of the Ballets Russes in Monte Carlo, from 1939 to 1943 he worked in New York, first as music director of the Ballet Theatre, then as director of the New Opera Company. Until 1949 he was conductor of the Dallas Symphony Orchestra, after which he was appointed music director of the Minneapolis Symphony Orchestra (1949–60), succeeding Dmitri Mitropoulos. Many conducting posts followed: the BBC Symphony Orchestra from 1962 to 1966, the Stockholm Philharmonic Orchestra from 1966 to 1975, as well as the National Symphony Orchestra of Washington D.C. from 1970 onwards, and in 1974 the Royal Philharmonic Orchestra in London. In 1977 Dorati was named music director of the Detroit Symphony Orchestra.

With the Philharmonia Hungarica, founded in Vienna in 1957, he recorded for Decca, beginning in 1969, all the symphonies of Joseph Haydn. He has also made recordings of Haydn's operas. In addition to his great interest in the music of Haydn, he is sympathetic to much modern music and, particularly in America, has given the premières of many contemporary compositions.

The Hungarian-American conductor Antal Dorati was born in Budapest on 9 April 1906. From his fourteenth until his eighteenth year he studied at the Franz Liszt Academy in his birthplace with Béla Bartók, Zoltán Kodály and Leo Weiner. At the close of this period, having received honours in composition, piano and conducting, he began his career as a conductor.

Furtwängler

Furtwängler first drew particular notice as a conductor when he was given the opportunity to conduct one of his own works. Having to present a full evening's programme, he selected Bruckner's ninth symphony to supplement the performance of his own composition. Later he declared that only during the extensive preparations for this concert culminating in his appearance on the podium did he himself become aware of his talent for conducting. From that moment he gave up his aspirations as a composer and set to work developing his conducting techniques. His path was a long and difficult one. Assistant conductorships in Breslau, Zürich and Munich led to an appointment as Kapellmeister in Strasbourg and, in 1911, in Lübeck. In 1915 he became director of the opera in Mannheim, in 1921, concert director of the Tonkünstlerorchester in Vienna, and a year later, director of the 'Musikfreunde'. There then followed his important appointments in Vienna, Leipzig and Berlin. Upon the death of Nikisch in 1922, a successor was sought both in Leipzig and Berlin. The young Furtwängler's capacities were so valued he was given both positions, quickly rising to the top of German musical life. Furtwängler developed a personal conducting technique based on observation of the styles of Nikisch and Weingartner, whose movements were rounded and supple rather than angular. Furtwängler did not so much mark time, but seemed, as it were, to sketch the music in the air.

From 1922 until his death in Baden-Baden on 30 November 1954, Wilhelm Furtwängler, born in Berlin on 25 January 1886, was inseparably bound up with German and Austrian musical life. After study in composition and orchestral conducting with Josef Rheinberger and Max von Schillings, he began his career as director of the theatre in Strasbourg. Later he was conductor for the Berlin State Opera, then succeeded Artur Nikisch as conductor of the Gewandhaus Orchestra in Leipzig. After a time with the Vienna Philharmonic Orchestra he was given, in 1952, lifetime conductorship of the Berlin Philharmonic Orchestra, with which he had been regularly associated since 1922.

Giulini

In 1944 Giulini was assistant conductor to Fernando Previtali of the orchestra of the Italian Radio in Rome. From 1950 to 1953 he conducted the symphony orchestra of Radio Milan. During this time he made friends with Arturo Toscanini, with whom he studied from 1951 to 1957. From 1952 to 1956 Giulini was associated as conductor with La Scala in Milan, at first as assistant to Victor de Sabata, later as artistic director. In the period between 1956 and 1973 Giulini did not have his own orchestra, but appeared regularly as guest conductor with the London Philharmonic Orchestra, the Chicago Symphony Orchestra and at the festivals of Edinburgh, Glyndebourne, Lucerne, Vienna and Aix. In 1973 he was appointed principal conductor of the Vienna Philharmonic, a post in which he remained three years. In 1978 he succeeded Zubin Mehta as conductor of the Los Angeles Philharmonic Orchestra. Although he won international recognition through his interpretations of Italian works, in particular of Verdi's operas, he owes his present-day celebrity to his renderings of the great masters of the Romantic period, especially Mahler. Giulini prefers to conduct from memory, considering this a necessary condition for greater freedom during a performance, since there is no danger of distraction from looking at the score. His gestures, consonant with his early training as a string-player, are extremely ardent. He is an autocrat, allowing no misunderstanding of his intentions and rejecting discussion of his insights by members of the orchestra.

After studies at the Accademia di Santa Cecilia, where he took first prizes in viola (1936), composition (1939) and conducting (1941), Carlo Maria Giulini (b. 9 May 1914) made his conducting debut in 1944.

Haitink

Each of Haitink's predecessors as principal conductor of the Concertgebouw Orchestra contributed in their individual ways to the growth of this world-famous orchestra. Haitink seems to combine their most important characteristics. He possesses the pedagogical gifts of Willem Kes, first principal conductor of the Concertgebouw Orchestra, the interpretational art of Mengelberg and the attentiveness of Eduard van Beinum to perfection of ensemble and beauty of orchestral sound. Jo Hekster, a musician in the Concertgebouw Orchestra under

Mengelberg, van Beinum and Haitink, says: 'In comparing the three, I would always choose Haitink as the greatest. Expansive, with a dose of energy which is simply fantastic. The modern conductor, a man of our times . . . Haitink is in full control of his material. You can feel it from the very opening bars of a Mahler symphony. He has an overview of the totality of even the longest work. He doesn't slacken for one second. And when it's all over and he seems completely "emptied", you haven't got over your surprise at how well he managed his reserves. Orchestral musicians like a conductor who fascinates. Somebody who "gets to you". A real personality. Haitink is that kind of man.'

Bernard Haitink, born in 1929, finished his studies in Amsterdam in 1957 and was appointed conductor of the Radio Filharmonisch Orkest. Two years later he became conductor of the Concertgebouw Orchestra alongside Eduard van Beinum. Upon the latter's

sudden death, Haitink was his logical successor. Initially he shared this function with his colleague Eugen Jochum, but since 1964 he has been the sole principal conductor of the famous Concertgebouw Orchestra. He maintains many

contacts in England with the London Philharmonic Orchestra and with the Glyndebourne Festival Opera, of which he has been music director since 1978. Haitink's specialities lie in the Romantic repertoire (Beethoven, Brahms, Bruckner and Mahler), the orchestral works of

Debussy and Ravel and, more recently, the symphonies of Shostakovich.

Harnoncourt

Harnoncourt opts for the performance of Renaissance and Baroque music according to old principles on period instruments or copies 'not for historical reasons, but artistic ones. For music of any period can be presented in the liveliest and most convincing way only in the sound-terms of its own time'. Yet this artistic credo is not a hard and fast rule, and Harnoncourt readily makes concessions. He has for example given performances of J.S. Bach's Passions with the Concertgebouw Orchestra, which does not possess the required specialized technique for 'authentic' interpretations of Baroque music. An important project, with the Concertgebouw Orchestra, is a series of

recordings for Telefunken of the Mozart symphonies, in which he attempts to come as close as possible to the eighteenth century sound-world.

Anyone watching Harnoncourt, winner of the Ernst von Siemens music prize in 1974 and of the Dutch Erasmus Prize in 1980, will know immediately that he is completely untrained in matters of conducting technique. As one colleague rather baldly put it: 'It looks as though he is constantly hanging out the wash.' But with his unsophisticated gestures he succeeds in drawing from his players persuasive interpretations. His rhythmic and dynamic delivery have combined to form an interpretative style which has had a definite influence on traditional performance practices.

The Austrian Nicolaus Harnoncourt, born in Berlin on 6 December 1929, began his musical career as a cellist. After studies with Paul Grümmer in Graz and from 1948 onwards with Emanuel Brabec in Vienna, he joined the cello section of the Vienna Philharmonic (1952–69).

During this period he made an intensive study of early music and old instruments. In 1953 he founded the Vienna Concentus Musicus, an ensemble dedicated to authentic performance practices and playing techniques on original instruments. It gave its first public per-

formance in 1957. Since this time the Concentus Musicus has become famous throughout the world for recordings of works by Johann Sebastian Bach and Claudio Monteverdi.

Jochum

Jochum approaches each performance with extreme seriousness and dedication, and no sort of spectacular showmanship may be expected from him. He is an advocate of simple honest music-making, utterly faithful to the score. Working from these basic principles, he attempts to penetrate to the profoundest depths of a composition. This has won him a reputation as a leading Bruckner interpreter, and he has also been classed among the most important conductors of the Classic/Romantic repertoire, thanks in particular to his recordings of the complete symphonies of Beethoven, the symphonies of Brahms – for which he received the Brahms Gold Medal – and the twelve London symphonies of Haydn.

Eugen Jochum, born 1 November 1902, comes from a musical German family. His brothers, Otto and Georg Ludwig, were also conductors. By the age of four Eugen was playing the piano, and two years later the organ as well. He studied at the Music Academy in Munich (1922–25). He began his conducting career in this city in 1926, working successively in Lübeck, Mannheim, Duisburg, Kiel and Leipzig (with the Gewandhaus Orchestra). In 1932 he was appointed conductor of the Radio Symphony Orchestra of Berlin and likewise of the Berlin Philharmonic. Two years later he succeeded Karl Böhm as director of the Hamburg Opera and Karl Muck as General Music Director of the Philharmonic concerts, also in Hamburg. From 1949 to 1959 he conducted the Symphony Orchestra of the Bavarian Radio, which he had founded. Together with Bernard Haitink he was in 1961 appointed chief conductor of the Concertgebouw Orchestra in Amsterdam. In 1969 he was given the direction of the Bamberg Symphony Orchestra, and in 1975 he was named Conductor Laureate of the London Symphony Orchestra.

Von Karajan

Von Karajan became known as a strong-willed, highly individual personality. In 1941 he became conductor of the Berliner Staatskapelle, but true success came only at the close of the Second World War when he received appointments for life from various orchestras and musical institutions: in 1946, from the Gesellschaft der Musikfreunde in Vienna, four years later, from the London Philharmonic Orchestra, and in 1955 from the Berlin Philharmonic Orchestra. In 1948 he became artistic director of the Salzburg Festival, participating in the redevelopment of the Bayreuth Festival; in 1967 he first organized the Osterfestspiele and in 1973 he began the Whitsuntide concerts, both in his birthplace. No other conductor has had such an enormous impact on European musical life. No doubt exists as to the effectiveness of his gestures, which are extremely controlled, but differences of opinion exist as to the poetry and evocative power of his music-making. In the last few years certain mannerisms have crept into Karajan's conducting: artificially switched-on tempos, unusual accents and dynamic extremes.

Herbert von Karajan was born in Salzburg on 5 April 1908, son of a surgeon who was also a gifted amateur musician. From 1916 to 1926 he studied the piano and followed a general music course at the Mozarteum in the city of his birth, already making regular appearances as a pianist. He wanted to be a musician, but his parents obliged him to engage in technical studies at the University of Vienna, where within a few years he earned a degree in engineering. Music kept calling, however, and von Karajan entered the Musikhochschule, studying conducting until 1929 with Franz Schalk. He was appointed student conductor of the Ulm opera, where he was eventually made permanent conductor following a successful stand-in performance of Mozart's Figaro. He worked industriously in this position for seven years. Soon his star began to rise. From 1934 to 1941, he was employed in Aachen, first as conductor of the Staatsoper, later as Generalmusikdirektor, and during this period he was frequently invited for guest appearances in Salzburg, Vienna, Amsterdam, Berlin, Italy and Scandinavia.

Kleiber

Erich Kleiber was a versatile and highly developed artist. In addition to the violin, he also studied philosophy and art history before assuming the position of opera conductor at the German Theatre in Prague. Thereafter he filled similar positions in Darmstadt, Barmen-Elberfeld, Düsseldorf and Mannheim. His first big opportunity as a conductor came in 1923 when he was appointed to lead the Berlin State Opera and given unlimited powers. These he put to advantage, holding for example 150 rehearsals for the première of Alban Berg's *Wozzeck*, a sign of his seriousness and dedication as well as of his affection for contemporary music. In 1935 Kleiber emigrated to South America, first founding an orchestra in Cuba, then assuming the direction of the Teatro Colon in Buenos Aires from 1937 to 1949. From 1950 onwards Kleiber travelled the world giving guest appearances. In addition to the interest he showed in contemporary music, Erich Kleiber was known for his interpretations of the great classics, Haydn, Mozart and Beethoven.

Characteristics which earned admiration for Austrian conductor Erich Kleiber (1890–1956) were his decisiveness and feeling for proper proportions and justice. These characteristics induced Kleiber to take up residence in South America in 1935. He had always been opposed to the meddling of the Nazi regime in artistic affairs and could not accept being forbidden to perform new 'difficult' music (Stravinsky, Hindemith, Mahler and many others).

Kondrashin

Although Kondrashin began his conducting career in the world of opera, symphonic music attracted him still more, and from the 1960s onwards he devoted himself increasingly to the symphonic repertory. This quickly resulted in a gold medal from the Internationale Mahler Gesellschaft and an appointment as artistic director of the State Philharmonic in Moscow. From that time he was also often engaged as guest conductor by numerous leading orchestras in Western Europe and the United States. Kondrashin was an artist of great humility, who effaced himself in favour of the music he performed. This did not, however, mean that he was not at the same time a demanding perfectionist, desirous of performing every score with the utmost faithfulness. The demands he made resulted in an enormous intensity of approach. Most of Kondrashin's recordings are of Russian music, but in his years in Western Europe he recorded a number of other works, including radio recordings, and these are being made available as a proof of his artistry.

On 7 March 1981, having that same day given a performance in the Amsterdam Concertgebouw of one of his favourite works, Mahler's Titan symphony, replacing Klaus Tennstedt as conductor of the NDR Orchestra, Kiril Kondrashin died at the age of 67. The Russian conductor, born on 12 January 1914, studied at the Tchaikovsky Conservatory in Moscow. His conducting career began in Leningrad at the Little Opera, after which he was given the direction of the Bolshoi Theatre in Moscow in 1943. In the 1970s tighter links were forged between Kondrashin and Western Europe. In 1975 be became permanent guest conductor of the Concertgebouw Orchestra in Amsterdam. Four years later he was appointed its permanent conductor, alongside Bernard Haitink. Had his death not intervened, in 1982 Kondrashin would have succeeded Kubelik as principal director of the symphony orchestra of the Bayerische Rundfunk.

Koussevitsky

Serge Koussevitsky made his début with the Berlin Philharmonic in 1908 with an entirely Russian programme. The next year he set up a music publishing company in Berlin, with an emphasis on contemporary Russian music. Shortly thereafter he returned to Russia where, thanks to his father-in-law's generosity, he could found his own orchestra, giving popular concerts in the large cities and taking the music of Beethoven, Bach and contemporary Russian composers to the country on a boat rebuilt into a concert hall, which he sailed along the Volga. From 1917 to 1920 he was music director of the court orchestra in Leningrad, after which he emigrated via Berlin to Paris where he founded the Concerts Symphoniques Koussevitsky, which gave performances of much contemporary work. In 1924 he was chosen by the Boston Symphony Orchestra as successor to Pierre Monteux, a position he retained until 1949. Not only did Koussevitsky champion the cause of modern music by performing a great deal of it with every orchestra he conducted – he gave first performances of Honegger, Prokofiev, Stravinsky, Copland, Barber, Gershwin and others – but he also commissioned a great many works. In 1931, for example, on the occasion of the Boston Symphony's fiftieth anniversary, he commissioned Stravinsky's *Symphony of Psalms*, Prokofiev's Fourth Symphony, Honegger's Third Symphony, Hindemith's *Concert Music for Strings and Brass* and Respighi's *Metamorphoses*. The Koussevitsky Foundation, founded in 1942, also commissioned such important compositions as Stravinsky's *Ode*, Bartók's *Concerto for Orchestra* and Schoenberg's *A Survivor from Warsaw*.

The Russian conductor Serge Koussevitsky played a role of great importance in the art world. He was born on 26 July 1874 near Moscow and died on 4 June 1951 in Boston.

He began his career as a double-bass player, but after hearing Artur Nikisch he decided to take up conducting. Following studies at the Hochschule für Musik in Berlin and early conducting experiences in Berlin, Vienna, London and Paris, his dream became reality when he married Olga Uschkoff, daughter of a wealthy landowner who gave his son-in-law his own symphony orchestra.

Kubelik

The time Kubelik spent at the Conservatory was of very great importance for his formation as a conductor. Throughout these five years he was part of the Conservatory's orchestra in various capacities: member of the first violin section, first-chair violist and finally, leader of the entire orchestra. Here Kubelik learned the value of good teamwork between orchestra and conductor. He thus became a conductor who attempts to work with his orchestra in a spirit of friendly and harmonious cooperation rather than one of coercion and forceful dominance, an attitude he has maintained from his first appearance as conductor with the national theatre of Brno (1936–41). From 1941 to 1948 he was conductor of the Czech Philharmonic, after which his international career began with important posts such as principal conductor of the Chicago Symphony Orchestra (1950–53), music director of the Royal Opera House, Covent Garden (1955–58), conductor of the symphony orchestra of the Bavarian Radio (1961–79), and music director of the Metropolitan Opera in New York (1973–74). Kubelik's repertory is extremely varied, including nearly everything from Mozart to Schoenberg, with a special affection for the works of Dvořák, Janáček and Mahler. His interpretations are charged with an impulsive spontaneity and fiery temperament.

Rafael Kubelik, born in 1914, grew up in an extremely musical family. His father Jan Kubelik, from whom Rafael professes to have learned a great deal, was a celebrated violinist. In the Kubelik household, music-making was intense. All seven children studied the piano, two also studied the violin, and another, singing. From 1928 to 1933 Rafael Kubelik studied violin, piano, conducting and composition at the Conservatory in Prague. He marked the taking of his final diplomas at that institution with the composition of a Fantasie for violin and orchestra, the playing of a Paganini violin concerto and the conducting of Dvořák's overture Othello. After a year as accompanist to his father, he began his conducting career.

Leppard

Raymond Leppard made his conducting début in 1952 in London's Wigmore Hall. in 1959 he conducted for the first time at Covent Garden and three years later at Glyndebourne. From 1973 to 1980 Leppard was principal conductor of the BBC Northern Symphony. His most significant symphonic activities, however, have been with the English Chamber Orchestra since 1963. With this ensemble he has been able to explore to his heart's content his areas of special interest, early Baroque music and

contemporary compositions. He has earned respect for his critical editions of the operas of Monteverdi, Cesti and Cavalli, and for numerous recordings, including Handel's Concerti a due cori, as well as for conducting the world première of Nicholas Maw's *The Ring of the Moon* in 1970.

Raymond Leppard, British conductor, harpsichordist and musicologist, was born in London on 11 August 1927. He studied at Cambridge University from 1948 to 1952, eventually joining the faculty of Trinity College as Fellow and University Lecturer in Music (1957–67).

Maazel

To avoid being for ever branded as a prodigy, from 1946 to 1950 Lorin Maazel attended the University of Pittsburgh, studying mathematics, languages and philosophy. During this period he remained busily involved with music: he was leader and assistant conductor of the Pittsburgh Symphony Orchestra and founded the Fine Arts Quartet, in which he played first violin. In 1953 he went to Rome in order to study Baroque music, and in that year made his European début, thus launching his adult conducting career, still without an orchestra or musical organization of his own, but with countless invitations from all over the world. He became both the youngest and the first American to conduct at the Bayreuth Festival in 1960. He has been principal conductor of the Deutsche Oper in Berlin (1956–71) and of the Radio Symphony Orchestra of Berlin (1965–75), as well as music director of the Cleveland Orchestra (1972). Lorin Maazel is principal conductor of the Orchestre National of France and beginning with the 1982/83 season, of the Vienna State Opera. Lorin Maazel still appears as a violinist and

his conducting repertory is extremely varied, including music ranging from Bach through Tchaikovsky to Schoenberg. 'I don't want to have anything to do with specializing in particular compositions. I believe the interpretation of any piece whatsoever can benefit from the experiences one has gained from the entirety of the musical repertoire.' His performances are characterized by a balance between heart and intellect, an analytical clarity and a brilliant feeling for orchestral sound.

Lorin Maazel was a child prodigy. This American violinist and conductor, born in Neuilly-sur-Seine near Paris on 6 March 1930, not only played the violin at the age of five and the piano two years later, but conducted his school orchestra at the age of eight. His performance with the University of Idaho Orchestra of Schubert's *Unfinished* was so successful, the following year he was invited by Stokowski to direct the Los Angeles Philharmonic, and two years later, by Toscanini to conduct a concert with the NBC Symphony Orchestra.

Marriner

In the years Marriner spent with the London Symphony Orchestra, he formed first the Virtuoso String Trio and, in 1959, the Academy of St Martin-in-the-Fields. He is still the artistic director of this ensemble. In 1969 he was appointed conductor of the Los Angeles Chamber Orchestra. From 1971 to 1973 he directed the Northern Sinfonia in Newcastle, and from 1975 to 1979 he assumed André Previn's responsibilities for the concert series in the Elizabeth Hall of the Greater London Council for the South Bank Summer Music. In 1978 he was appointed director and conductor of the Minnesota Orchestra. Marriner has won his greatest fame as director of the Academy of St Martin-in-the-Fields. Putting to use his experience as an ensemble violinist, he has moulded an orchestra of extreme refinement and polish.

Neville Marriner, born in Lincoln, England, on 15 April 1924, was obliged to interrupt his studies at the Royal College of Music during the Second World War. Having fulfilled his military duties, he again took up his music studies, including a year at the Paris Conservatoire. After teaching music for a year at Eton College (1947–48), he devoted himself to musical performance as second violinist with the Martin String Quartet and as co-founder of the Jacobean Ensemble, specializing in the interpretation of seventeenth- and eighteenth-century music. He taught violin at the Royal College of Music from 1949 until 1959, at the same time taking lessons in conducting from Pierre Monteux during the latter's summer courses in Maine. From 1952 onwards he was violinist with the Philharmonia Orchestra and during 1956–68 leader of the second violins with the London Symphony Orchestra.

Mehta

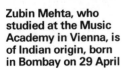

The son of a violinist and founder of the symphony orchestra in Bombay, Mehta was familiar with music-making by the age of seven. He played both the violin and the piano. After pursuing a course of medical studies, he decided in 1954 to devote himself full-time to music. In that year he began his studies in Vienna, in particular receiving instruction in conducting from Hans Swarowsky. Later he attended the summer courses given in Siena by Carlo Zecchi and Alco Galliera and also studied at the Berkshire Music Centre in Tanglewood, USA with Eleazar de Carvalho. In 1958, after winning first prize in the Liverpool International Conducting Competition, he was appointed assistant conductor of the Royal Liverpool Philharmonic. The following year his replacement of the ailing Eugene Ormandy with the Vienna Philharmonic was an outstanding success. In 1960 a similar opportunity came his way when he was called upon to substitute for Igor Markevitch with the Montreal Symphony Orchestra. He was associated with this orchestra until 1967. In 1962 he received the additional appointment of permanent conductor of the Los Angeles Philharmonic. Under his direction both orchestras developed remarkably. In 1969 Mehta was named chief conductor and musical advisor of the Israel Philharmonic Orchestra. Since 1978 he combines these functions with the music directorship of the New York Philharmonic Orchestra. In his performances Mehta, in his own words, seeks to find 'a mid-point between the clarification of structure and the expression of content, without being a purely emotional musician'. Harold Schonberg of the *New York Times* gave the following description: 'Mehta is a Romantic through and through, and he draws from his orchestra an especially rich sound. His beat is a pleasure for an orchestral player . . . There is something Toscanini-like about it.'

Zubin Mehta, who studied at the Music Academy in Vienna, is of Indian origin, born in Bombay on 29 April 1936. As a musician, however, he feels himself to be thoroughly Viennese, one who can conduct a performance of Die Fledermaus with immense pleasure.

Mengelberg

Mengelberg's sovereignty with the Concertgebouw Orchestra came to an abrupt, though not unexpected, end in 1945, due to the attitude he maintained during the Second World War. During the half century that the Concertgebouw Orchestra, then still called the Orchestra of the NV Het Concertgebouw, was in his control, he built it into one of Europe's most important orchestras, with the consequence that The Netherlands' capital Amsterdam in turn became one of the foremost international music centres. Thanks to Mengelberg's prestige nearly every prominent European musician came to Amsterdam at one time or another, both performers and composers, including Mahler, Richard Strauss, Debussy and Ravel. His approach to conducting was described by Concertgebouw member Jo

Hekster in these terms: 'He was without any doubt a very great conductor. Could he ever create an atmosphere during a concert! But he was also a very one-sided musician. The Romantics, yes. But he really should have stayed away from the French and from Mozart. His division of rehearsal time was also far from ideal. He could spend two hours on a single page . . . Before a concert Mengelberg would look everyone in the orchestra straight in the eye. He stared at you, sometimes for several seconds. Whether the audience was waiting or not. A magical look.' Mengelberg won world renown for his Mahler interpretations. The great Mahler festival of 1920 has never been equalled in the history of its concert performances.

The Dutch conductor Willem Mengelberg (1871–1951) was born in Utrecht, the son of German parents. He took his first music lessons in his birthplace, completing

his education at the conservatory in Cologne. There he made rapid progress as a pianist, conductor and composer. At the age of twenty he already occupied the

post of 'Städtischer Musikdirektor' in Lucerne. Four years later he was appointed principal conductor of the Amsterdam Concertgebouw, a position he would

retain for nearly half a century.

Munch

In addition to conducting, Munch also wrote a book *Je suis chef d'orchestre* (1954) which gives a clear picture of his style of working with an orchestra. He was not an advocate of detailed rehearsal, measure by measure. Such 'disciplining', as he called it, acts as a block to true music-making. 'I myself played in an orchestra for a long time and know from experience not only what makes a rehearsal pleasurable but more important, what makes one boring and dull, so that attention strays continually

to the clock and the moment of freedom.' Munch was a conductor of heightened temperament, sometimes so swept away by his passion of the moment that he spontaneously did things in quite another way than he had during rehearsals. He did not hesitate to make changes in scores, but always with an eye to the composer's intentions.

Son of an organist, violinist, choir director and teacher at the local conservatory, Charles Munch (1891–1968) may have seemed destined to enter musical life. But this was not the case. At the age of twenty-one he left his birthplace of Strasbourg for medical

studies in Paris. But the violin lessons he received there gradually gained the upper hand. In 1919 he set himself up as a violin teacher in Strasbourg, where from 1920 to 1926 he was also leader of the local orchestra. In the seven years which followed he played

under Furtwängler in the Gewandhaus Orchestra in Leipzig. He himself then began conducting in Paris, with the Lamoureux Orchestra, the Philharmonic Orchestra of Paris and the orchestra of the Conservatory. Munch remained in Paris for fifteen years, then

went to Boston as successor to Koussevitsky. Until 1962 he was principal director of the Boston Symphony Orchestra, at which time he returned to Paris where, together with Serge Baudo, he founded the Orchestre de Paris.

Muti

Riccardo Muti's large and varied repertoire extends from Mozart to such twentieth-century composers as Petrassi, Ligeti and Dallapiccola. The freshness of his approach and his scrupulousness in regard to the printed notes are striking. He was one of the first conductors to make use of the recent Bärenreiter edition of the Mozart symphonies, which expunges from the scores 'corrections' and additions made by previous editors. He takes great pains to revive proper articulation and phrasing. In preparing for a performance, he says he first studies the score at his desk, then

works with it at the piano, before finally, and away from the piano, adding the last refinements. Due to his Italian background, Muti emphasizes singing lines in music. 'Every part in the score should sing, not only the melody and then nothing. Toscanini always said that every note in the score is not a second actor, but is a first actor.' The three past conductors he admires most are Bruno Walter, Toscanini and Wilhelm Furtwängler. He himself combines Toscanini's precision with Furtwängler's feeling for monumental structure.

Riccardo Muti, born in Naples on 28 July 1941, began his musical studies at the age of eight, with lessons in piano and violin. He continued hs study at the Conservatories of Naples and Milan in the areas of composition and conducting. While in

Milan, he also took courses in literature and philosophy at the local university. In 1967 he won first prize in the international Guido Cantelli conducting competition and this immediately resulted in a number of important offers. First music director of the

Teatro Communale (1968) and the Maggio Musicale Fiorentino (1969), both in Florence, he was appointed in 1973 to the position of principal director of the New Philharmonia Orchestra in London, succeeding Otto Klemperer, and in 1980 he was named

successor to Eugene Ormandy with the Philadelphia Orchestra. As an opera conductor he has worked in all the principal opera centres of Europe and at the Salzburg and Edinburgh festivals. He is a much sought-after guest conductor, making frequent

appearances with the RAI Orchestra and the Vienna Philharmonic among others.

Ormandy

At the age of five Ormandy was sent by his father to the music academy of his birthplace. Four years later be became a pupil of the great violinist Hubay and studied composition, counterpoint and playing from score with Zoltán Kodály and Leo Weiner. In 1917, having at the age of eighteen won honours in every field, he was appointed to a teaching position at the Royal Academy of Budapest. In 1921 he left for a concert tour of America, but once there, penniless and championed by no-one, he was obliged to make do with a job in the cinema orchestra of the Capitol Theater in New York. This, however, gave birth to his future career, for in 1924 he became conductor of the ensemble. His superior conducting talents were soon discovered and in 1931 he was appointed conductor of the Minneapolis Symphony

Orchestra. His appointment with the Philadelphia Orchestra followed. Ormandy is regarded as a first-rate conductor with great technical expertise and an extremely colourful approach to music. Some critics find the richness of orchestral sound he produces excessive, too obviously calculated for brilliant effects. Others value precisely this richness, particularly the warmth and polish of the strings. 'I conduct the way I do because I was a violinist. Toscanini always played the cello while he conducted; Koussevitsky, the double-bass; and Stokowski, the organ. Conductors who have been pianists almost always make sharper, stricter movements and this can be heard from the orchestra.' He made numerous recordings, most of which testify to his preference for late Romanticism, Impressionism and early contemporary music.

Born in Budapest on 18 November 1899, Eugene Ormandy, who took American citizenship in 1927,

made his reputation mainly in the New World, as head of the Philadelphia Orchestra for more than forty

years (1938–1980).

Ozawa

Ozawa, who avoids interviews, did tell the British press some years ago in Tokyo: 'It was incredible that the Boston Symphony Orchestra should ask me to become its music director. It is a very traditional orchestra and I am not a traditional musician. Coming from Japan, which has no history or tradition of performing Western music, I am at a distinct disadvantage. I still must learn so much music. But this disadvantage also has its benefits. As my great teacher Professor Saito said to me, I have no bad habits and can choose from the emotional world of Latin, German, French or Russian music.' This lack of tradition has become the

subject of various opinions. Richard Dyer wrote in the *Boston Globe* in 1978, 'Ozawa knows how to forge a direct link between orchestra, music and audience. His body is a brilliant medium of communication . . . Ozawa possesses a vital feeling for instrumental colour, he knows how to concentrate an orchestra and keep it alert . . . But his work also displays moments of surprising tastelessness. More serious, for such breaches of taste are relatively rare, is Ozawa's continual inability to penetrate beyond the direct link between orchestra, music and audience . . . Too much is superficial.'

Forced to abandon his piano studies as a result of a hand injury sustained during a rugby match, the Japanese Seiji Ozawa, born in Hoten in 1935, devoted himself to composition and conducting. He took

his training at the Toho Music School in Tokyo, continuing his studies in Europe from 1959 onwards. He won first prize in the international conducting competition in Besançon and in 1960,

the Koussevitsky Prize. He was assistant to Herbert von Karajan and to Leonard Bernstein, who in 1961 asked Ozawa to accompany him and the New York Philharmonic on a tour of Japan in that year.

After several years of guest conducting, he was appointed music director of the Ravinia Festival of the Chicago Symphony Orchestra (1964–68), principal conductor of the Toronto Symphony Orchestra (1965–69)

and director of the San Francisco Symphony Orchestra (1970–76). Ozawa has been associated with the Boston Symphony Orchestra since 1970.

Previn

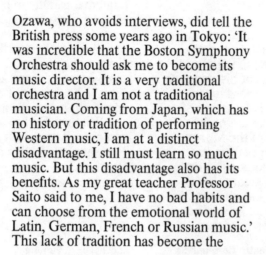

Newly settled in Los Angeles, Previn studied with Castelnuovo-Tedesco, the classical composer who had himself fled the Nazi regime. He then launched a career as jazz-pianist and film orchestrator. In 1951, while in the Forces, he studied conducting with Pierre Monteux and after several years began a new career as concert pianist and conductor. He made his conducting début in 1963 with the St Louis Symphony Orchestra. Four years later he became principal conductor of the Houston Symphony Orchestra (1967–70). In 1965 he made recordings with the London Symphony Orchestra, whose principal conductor he later was for a period of ten years (1969–79). He was finally appointed 'Conductor Emeritus' by this orchestra. In 1975 Previn was made chief conductor of

the Pittsburgh Symphony Orchestra. Alongside his many activities in the field of classical music, Previn has not shrunk from serving the popular muse as pianist, arranger, conductor and composer. He has made recordings of his own jazz music, among them *A Different Kind of Blues*, to which the violinist Itzhak Perlman also contributed. As a conductor Previn has a strict preference for music with nationalistic or strongly coloured features; the abstract symphonic repertoire is not his long suit. In this respect it is not surprising that his recordings with the London Symphony Orchestra of Vaughan Williams' symphonies and music by William Walton and Rachmaninov have been very highly regarded.

André Previn, American conductor, pianist and composer, is, no doubt due to his Christian name, frequently thought to be of French origin. Actually he was born in Berlin on 6 April

1929 as Andreas Ludwig Priwin, son of German parents of Russian-Jewish descent. In any event André Previn, who as a child studied piano at the Berlin Hoschscule für Musik and the Paris

Conservatoire, is a true American.

Escaping the Nazi regime, the Previn family emigrated to the USA in 1939, where André's uncle was music director at

Hollywood's Universal Studios.

Rostropovich

Rostropovich made his conducting début in 1968 with Tchaikovsky's *Eugene Onegin* at the Bolshoi Theatre in Moscow. His wife, Galina Vishnevskaya, whom he also regularly accompanies at the piano, sang the role of Tatjana. He made his conducting début in Western Europe with the same work, also with the Bolshoi Theatre, in Paris from December 1969 to January 1970. A recording of the opera was also made at this time. Following his appointment as music director of the National Symphony Orchestra of Washington DC in 1977, he became permanent guest conductor of the London Symphony Orchestra, with which he has made a number of recordings, notably of the Tchaikovsky symphonies.

Rostropovich has an instinctive feeling for the intentions of the composer. This is to be heard in performances of contemporary music as well as of the traditional repertoire.

Mstislav Rostropovich, born in 1927, received his first music lessons from his parents. His mother was a concert pianist, his father, a cellist of note, pupil of Casals and teacher at the Gnesin Institute in Moscow where he studied with Shostakovich, among others. Having completed his studies with the highest honours, in the late 1940s he took prizes in cello competitions in Moscow, Prague and Budapest. In 1956 he became a professor at the Moscow Conservatory and in 1975 received an honorary doctorate in music from Cambridge Univeristy.

Rozhdestvensky

When Rozhdestvensky completed his studies at the conservatory, he was already a highly regarded conductor both inside and outside Russia. He was conductor and chief conductor of the Bolshoi Theatre in the periods 1951–61 and 1964–70. In 1961 he was named artistic director and principal conductor for life of the Symphony Orchestra of the Russian Radio. In Western Europe he made a name not only as guest conductor with most of the front-ranking orchestras but also as director of the Stockholm Philharmonic Orchestra (appointed in 1974) and as chief director of the BBC Symphony Orchestra (appointed in 1978). Equipped with a brilliant and supple technique, Rozhdestvensky offers a clear portrayal of the structure of a composition as well as of its emotional content. His performances, a combination of analysis, intuition and apparent spontaneity, frequently bring undiscovered aspects of a composition to the fore. Alongside an interest in the younger generation of Russian composers, Rozhdestvensky also shows an affinity for the classics. The recent revival of interest in the symphonies of Prokofiev is largely due to his efforts.

Gennadi Rozhdestvensky was born in Moscow on 4 May 1931. He received his first instruction in music at the Moscow State Conservatory from his father Nikolai Anosov (conducting) and from Lev Oborin (piano). While still at the conservatory he made his conducting début, having taken part in 1951 in a conducting competition at Moscow's Bolshoi Theatre and been immediately thereafter appointed student conductor there. Studying during the day at the conservatory and working in the theatre in the evening, he became acquainted not only with the ballet and theatre world in its smallest details but also with the conditions necessary for becoming a first-rate conductor.

Sanderling

Shortly after Kurt Sanderling took up residence in Moscow in 1936 he was appointed conductor of the Moscow Radio Symphony Orchestra. He remained there until 1941, at which time he was named conductor of the orchestra in Leningrad, initially along with Mravinsky. In the twenty years of his direction of this orchestra he brought it to a peak of international fame. In 1960 Sanderling returned to Germany, where he was appointed conductor of the Symphony Orchestra of East Berlin. From 1964 to 1967 he was also principal conductor of the Dresden Staatskapelle. Sanderling is a much sought-after guest conductor, with successful appearances at festivals in Prague, Vienna, Salzburg and Warsaw to his credit.

His large repertory consistently shows an instinctive feeling for form and a great attention to detail. He has a particular affection for the music of Mahler, Prokofiev, Shostakovich, Sibelius and Tchaikovsky.

The German conductor Kurt Sanderling was born in Arys in East Prussia on 19 September 1912. In 1931 he became a coach with the State Opera of Berlin until, in 1936, he was obliged to flee Germany for political reasons. This obligatory emigration **launched him upon his eminent career.**

Sawallisch

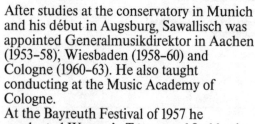

After studies at the conservatory in Munich and his début in Augsburg, Sawallisch was appointed Generalmusikdirektor in Aachen (1953–58), Wiesbaden (1958–60) and Cologne (1960–63). He also taught conducting at the Music Academy of Cologne.

At the Bayreuth Festival of 1957 he conducted Wagner's *Tristan und Isolde*, the youngest artist to have been invited to conduct in the festival's history up to that time. In 1960 he was appointed principal conductor of the Vienna Symphony Orchestra, a post he held from 1961 onwards, simultaneously with that of chief conductor of the Hamburg Philharmonic. In 1971 he was named general music director of the Bavarian State Opera in Munich. Sawallisch also regularly appears as a pianist, usually in the role of accompanist, as, for example, in the integral recording of Schubert's secular music for more than one voice, but also as a concerto soloist, often conducting from the keyboard.

Sawallisch's interpretations are characterized by an extreme faithfulness to the score, resulting in the correction of many 'traditional' inaccuracies, and by an aesthetic approach coupled with a certain reticence in respect of over-emotional expression.

When, as a child, the German conductor Wolfgang Sawallisch, born on 26 August 1926 in Munich, first heard Humperdinck's opera Hansel und Gretel, **he knew that he was destined for a conducting career. Chance dictated that the first opera he was** to conduct, in Augsburg in 1947, was in fact Hansel und Gretel. **His success was so great that many concert and** **opera invitations followed.**

Solti

As musical director at the Frankfurt Opera from 1952–61, Solti won international fame as one of the greatest interpreters of Wagner, and he went next to London's Royal Opera House (1961–71), where his efforts transformed Covent Garden into a world-class company and earned him a knighthood in 1971. He has been musical Director of the Chicago Symphony Orchestra since 1969, a close and cherished association.

Solti remains young and vigorous at seventy, bringing a unique freshness, insight and excitement to all his performances. He is well aware of the dangers of performing familiar works from the standard repertory too often. For example, when he recorded his widely-acclaimed performance of Mahler's Second Symphony for Decca, he had not looked at the score for eight years, feeling that only in this way can an interpreter approach such well-known music with fresh perception.

Several colourful incidents mark the career of Sir Georg Solti, British conductor of Hungarian birth, born in Budapest on 21 October 1912. On the evening of his début with the Budapest Opera, 12 March 1938, news came that Hitler's troops had invaded Vienna and spread quickly through the theatre where the performance was taking place. By the time the opera, Figaro, was over, hardly any of the audience was left. Nazi injunctions made it impossible for Solti to continue working in Hungary and he went to Switzerland where, forbidden to seek employment, he made an intensive study of the piano. At the end of the war when Germany was occupied by the Allied Forces, Solti was invited by the American authorities to assume direction of the Bavarian State Opera in Munich, at the age of thirty-four and with scarcely any conducting experience behind him.

Stokowski

Stokowski was a controversial musical phenomenon. On the one hand, he added to his prestige by continually championing new works, which he often himself premièred. Schoenberg and Varèse, for example, owe him a great deal. On the other hand, he considered it perfectly normal to perform compositions from the eighteenth or nineteenth centuries in arrangements which often differed enormously from the originals. Add to this that Stokowski did not hesitate to publicly reprimand an ill-behaved audience, that he changed the disposition of the orchestra on the platform and that he was known to give instructions to the strings by imitating their movements, and it is clear that Stokowski produced considerable perplexity in the average concert-goer. Stokowski also worked in films, most notably in his collaboration with Walt Disney in *Fantasia*. At the advanced age of ninety-five, Stokowski was still energetically at work, giving concerts and making recordings.

Leopold Stokowski (1882–1977), a London-born American of Polish-Irish origin, studied at The Queen's College, Oxford, and at the Royal College in London. After a period as organist at St James in Piccadilly, he pursued further studies in Paris, Munich and New York. He received his first important appointment as conductor of the Cincinnati Symphony Orchestra. In 1912 he was also given the direction of the Philadelphia Orchestra. In his thirty years with the latter, he transformed it into a world-famous ensemble.

Svetlanov

Svetlanov began his conducting career in 1953 while still a student at the Moscow Conservatory, taking the direction of the Radio Orchestra in the same city. In 1955 he was appointed assistant director of the Bolshoi Theatre, becoming its principal conductor in 1962. Although Svetlanov concentrated mainly on opera during this period, he did not neglect the concert repertory. His reputation as a conductor of symphonic works was, however, not established until 1965 when he was made chief director of the USSR State Symphony Orchestra. His repertory contains both classics and moderns, with particular emphasis on symphonists from his own country, Miaskovsky, Shostakovich, Prokofiev and Khatchaturian. International acclaim was accorded to him for his recordings of Tchaikovsky's symphonies.

The Russian conductor, composer and pianist Yevgeny Svetlanov, born 6 September 1928, comes from a family of theatre people. His mother was a member of a pantomime group and his father was a soloist with the Bolshoi Theatre. This proved decisive for his future career. At the age of seven he played a small part in an opera and made occasional appearances with the pantomime theatre. He breathed deeply and gladly of this theatrical atmosphere, which later worked greatly to his advantage as an opera conductor.

Szell

When in 1946 Szell was invited to assume the direction of the Cleveland Orchestra, he declared himself willing only on the condition that he be given *carte blanche* on every level. And during his years with the orchestra, until his death in 1970, Szell was indeed given free rein. This allowed him to mould the Cleveland Orchestra into one of the finest orchestral ensembles in the world.

Szell, whose interpretations have been characterized by some as both self-indulgent and unimaginative, has won particular respect for his extraordinary professionalism. He conducted everything from memory, even accompaniments in concertos. More than any other conductor, he knew the peculiarities of each instrument and could give not only bowing suggestions but advice to wind instrumentalists on the proper use of keys, valves and reeds.

Hungarian conductors who have pursued a career in the West have, without exception, earned great admiration and respect: Solti, Richter, Nikisch and Dorati, for example. This list must also include George Szell, an American conductor of Hungarian origin, born in Budapest on 7 June 1897. He grew up in Vienna, studying composition with Foerster and Reger, and piano with Richard Robert. At the age of eleven he made his piano début, playing his own compositions. Five years later he conducted the Vienna Symphony Orchestra. Shortly thereafter he made his début in Berlin, in the role of pianist, composer and conductor. In 1915 Richard Strauss engaged him for the Berlin State Opera. For twelve years he was director of the German Opera and of the Prague Philharmonia. He then left the continent, going first to Britain, where he conducted the Scottish Orchestra from 1937 to 1939. Finally settling in America, he conducted various orchestras, though his name will for ever be associated with the Cleveland Orchestra.

Tennstedt

Following studies at the Leipzig Conservatory (piano, violin and theory), Klaus Tennstedt was in 1948 appointed conductor of the Municipal Theatre in Halle. Later he was given the direction of the opera house in Dresden and of the Schwerin Orchestra, all the while being frequently invited throughout Eastern Europe as a guest conductor. Since his defection, which obliged him to leave behind family, friends and acquaintances, Tennstedt has kept silent as to his experiences in East Germany.

Before coming to the opera in Kiel, he spent a year in Sweden working with the Stora Theatre in Gothenburg and with the Swedish Radio Symphony Orchestra. In Kiel he was heard by the manager of the Toronto Symphony Orchestra, who immediately invited him to appear as guest conductor. Through the intervention of an American impresario, this in turn led to an extremely successful guest appearance in Boston. In the succeeding years all the important American orchestras clamoured for his direction, and after his 'second début' in Western Europe in London in 1976, he began travelling the world. His permanent association since 1979 has been with the Orchestra of the North German Radio.

Tennstedt considers it a priceless advantage to have worked for years as an orchestral string-player. 'This makes it possible for me to draw out a string sound which many conductors, those coming to the profession via the piano for example, would find difficult. String-players trust me and follow my directions much more easily.'

Recording companies regard Tennstedt as a new kind of conducting phenomenon, offering 'an ideal possibility to maintain contact with various musical genres'. An excellent conductor in the studio, he pays special attention to difficulties, in order to realize every detail to perfection. He has earned a great reputation as an interpreter of Bruckner and Mahler.

Klaus Tennstedt, born 6 June 1926, led a busy conducting career from 1948 until 1971. But as this took place entirely on the eastern side of the Iron Curtain, little was known of him until he came to the West in 1971 and took over the opera orchestra in Kiel. In a very short time his career blossomed to an extraordinary degree.

Toscanini

Toscanini, much sought after and widely admired throughout the world, worked principally at La Scala in Milan and in New York. He was chief conductor of La Scala from 1898 to 1903, 1906 to 1908 and 1921 to 1929. From 1908 to 1915 he conducted at the Metropolitan Opera House in New York, and in 1928 he assumed the direction of the New York Philharmonic, remaining with this orchestra until 1936. In 1937 the NBC Symphony Orchestra, also in New York, was founded especially for him; he remained at its head until 1954.

Despite his extreme reserve in matters of movement and bearing, Toscanini was a very vital and imperious conductor. It was his firm resolve to perform each work as perfectly as possible with a great respect for the composer's own intentions. In a time when conductors regularly tampered with scores (Mengelberg springs to mind), Toscanini took a position which served as an example for all later conductors. For him it was not the interpreter, no matter how beautifully he made music, but the composer who came first. His striving for perfect interpretation often brought him into conflict with soloists who had achieved musical stardom. He never gave an inch. In 1935 he said, 'I will never conduct for the gramophone!' Fortunately however a number of recordings were made and these are now widely available.

The son of a tailor, Arturo Toscanini was born on 25 March 1867 in Busseto, near Parma. Nearly ninety years later, on 16 January 1957, he died, the most celebrated conductor of the twentieth century. At an early age Toscanini gave evidence of exceptional musical talent. At the age of nine he was admitted to the Conservatory of Parma, leaving it nine years later in 1885 as a cellist 'cum laude'. The following year he joined the orchestra of the Italian opera in Buenos Aires. His conducting career was soon under way. One evening he was asked to replace the conductor for a performance of Verdi's Aida, and to everyone's astonishment he performed the task faultlessly – from memory.

Walter

At Gustav Mahler's suggestion, Bruno Walter dropped his surname of Schlesinger upon taking Austrian citizenship in 1911. At that time he had been conducting alongside Mahler for ten years at the Hofoper in Vienna. From 1914 to 1922 he was General Music Director in Munich, followed by two years devoted entirely to guest conducting, after which, between 1924 and 1931, he directed the German opera performances at Covent Garden in London. During these years he appeared in various capacities in Germany, but in 1933 the political climate impelled him to again return to Austria. Subsequently he took up residence in Paris, changing his nationality to French. In 1939 he resettled in the United States where he made numerous guest appearances with leading orchestras, the Los Angeles Symphony Orchestra, the NBC Symphony Orchestra, the New York Philharmonic – where he was musical advisor from 1947 to 1949 – and the Philadelphia Orchestra. From 1948 onwards Walter also appeared regularly with all major European orchestras. He made a name as an exceptional interpreter of Mozart and Mahler, and in his autobiography *Theme with Variations* gives a direct insight into his conducting methods. He had learned from Mahler that small movements are sufficient to produce enormous results and that the degree of expressiveness achieved has nothing whatsoever to do with the breadth or vehemence of gesture. This accorded perfectly with Walter's reserved nature, as did his manner of conducting rehearsals. He did not coerce his players, but brought them gently over to his point of view. In this way he achieved an astonishing orchestral unity, with a warm sound and noble Romantic expression.

Bruno Walter's assertion, 'I hate reticence in art, but in life I love it', might have been the motto of this German conductor, who was born in Berlin on 15 September 1876 and died in Beverly Hills on 17 February 1962. For over half a century he belonged in the front-rank of conductors, while continually demonstrating a great reserve, even shyness in his private life.

10

A guide to the great orchestras

Academy of St Martin-in-the-Fields

The extraordinary success of the Academy of St Martin-in-the-Fields is a triumph both for the group's unquestioned excellence and for the recording industry. In 1958 the twelve founder members (eleven string players and a harpsichordist) made their debut in the London church from which they took their name. Their aim was to promote music of the late Baroque period, performed without a conductor in the spirit of chamber music. Neville Marriner, a violinist in the London Symphony Orchestra, was chosen as leader. His job was to direct with 'nods and smiles' (as one member put it), while playing first violin. Early concerts attracted almost no attention, but a trial tape interested one record company enough to take a risk with this unusual ensemble. In 1961 A Recital by the Academy of St Martin-in-the-Fields was released. According to The Gramophone, the Academy played on this record 'with more sense of style than all the other chamber orchestras in Europe put together'.

From then on the orchestra's history has been more a tale of the recording studio than of the concert hall. By 1980 they had made nearly 250 recordings. At the top of the chart was Vivaldi's The Seasons, which had sold about three-quarters of a million copies. In twenty years the membership had expanded to include winds, brass and percussion, and the repertoire to include a wide range of works, from the Albinoni and Corelli of their early days, to Schoenberg, Britten and Rodrigo. Their bread and butter of recording is Bach, Handel and Mozart.

In order to catch up with their reputation on record, the Academy has made many international tours in recent years. Neville Marriner ceased to play with the orchestra in 1975, but he frequently returned to conduct those pieces that could not easily be played without full-time direction. His place as leader was assumed by Iona Brown, a long-time member, who continued to direct from the string section in the orchestra's traditional repertoire.

During its brief, intense existence, the Academy's idealistic commitment to clarity, authenticity and ensemble playing has been surprisingly little affected by the glamour of its reputation.

Rostropovich conducting
the Berlin Philharmonic
Orchestra.

Berlin Philharmonic Orchestra

The Berlin Philharmonic was formed in 1882
when more than fifty musicians broke away
from the orchestra of Benjamin Bilse to form
their own self-governing body. They found a
concert hall in a former roller skating rink
(renamed the Philharmonie) and teetered on
the verge of financial collapse for several
years, despite the immediate support of
Brahms and the violinist Joseph Joachim.
Artistic security, at least, was ensured when
Hans von Bülow became the first permanent
conductor in 1887. A mercurial and deeply
serious musician (who once performed
Beethoven's Ninth Symphony twice in an
evening), von Bülow had no patience with the
ephemeral. 'I will no longer promote bad
music', he announced during his first season at
Berlin, and proceeded to concentrate on the
symphonies of Beethoven and Brahms. He
stayed with the orchestra only five years but
established a precedent of virtuoso
performance that has remained a hallmark of
the Berlin Philharmonic.
Artur Nikisch, von Bülow's successor,
became permanent conductor in 1895. He
was a man of enormous charm, who directed
the orchestra with apparent ease.
Tchaikovsky, whose music Nikisch frequently
programmed, once said of him, 'He doesn't
conduct, rather it seems as if he indulges in a
mysterious magic'. Nikisch favoured romantic
composers. Beethoven, Liszt and Brahms
received regular performances as did the
contemporaries Richard Strauss and Anton
Bruckner. Throughout these years Strauss was
a frequent guest conductor.

There was no possibility of finding an exact
replacement for Artur Nikisch when he died
suddenly in 1922, but in Wilhelm Furtwängler
the orchestra chose an inspiring successor.
Furtwängler was a man for whom the
interpretation of great music was a sacred
experience. His priest-like devotion to the
works of Beethoven, Brahms and Bruckner
could turn the old roller skating rink, where
the orchestra still played, into a cathedral of
music. His intensely personal interpretations
were occasionally criticized by foreigners but
rarely by Berliners themselves. Perhaps it was
Furtwängler's other-worldly reverence for
music that enabled him to remain in Germany
during the Second World War, when the only
Jewish face in the Philharmonie was the
plaster bust of Mendelssohn, mysteriously
neglected by the Nazis.
The Philharmonie in ruins and Furtwängler in
temporary disgrace, the orchestra struggled
on with only a six-week interruption at the fall
of Berlin in 1945. Furtywängler returned from
1947 until his death in 1954, when the
orchestra, a democratic organization with a
fascination for musical dictators, selected
Herbert von Karajan as its next permanent
conductor. A man of enormous personal
power, von Karajan has made the orchestra so
much his own that he has referred to it as an
extension of his arm. He conducts with his
eyes closed and aspires to recreate exactly the
composer's intentions, but despite these
self-effacing gestures, no modern conductor
more completely dominates an orchestral
performance.
Since 1963 the Berlin Philharmonic has
played in the round at a new Philharmonie, a
building known to some as the 'Circus
Karajani'.

BBC Symphony Orchestra

The BBC Symphony Orchestra is the senior of many orchestras under the auspices of the British Broadcasting Corporation. Unlike other symphony orchestras, it does not run itself, but has external management; while this might put a 'them and us' between the management and the players, it does mean that the musicians have a secure salary and paid holidays, which many other orchestral players might envy.

The orchestra was founded in 1930 by Adrian Boult; its original purpose was not solely to act as a radio orchestra, but it sprang into being as a result of the possibility of the Queen's Hall promenade concerts being dissolved. Since then, the BBC has taken over sponsorship of the world-renowned 'proms' now held at the Royal Albert Hall, although they still bear the name of their originator, Sir Henry Wood. It is not an exaggeration to say that the last night of the promenade season is one of the world's most extraordinary musical events. For many years, Sir Malcolm Sargent was associated with the 'proms' and the succes of these events has tended to obscure the fact that the BBCSO is a busy working orchestra with a heavy schedule of broadcast concerts throughout the year.

Sir Henry Wood.

Boston Symphony Orchestra

In the spring of 1881 Major Henry Lee Higginson, a wealthy businessman and music lover, announced the formation of 'a full and permanent orchestra, offering the best music at low prices'. That October, under the direction of George Henschel, the Boston Symphony Orchestra made its debut. Sixty local musicians were employed to play twenty concerts, including works by the contemporary composers Dvořák, Wagner and Brahms. Under Henschel and subsequent conductors – Wilhelm Gericke (1884-89 and 1898-1906), Arthur Nikisch (1889-93), Emil Pauer (1893-98) and Max Fiedler (1908-12) the BSO grew and prospered. It was the first American orchestra to employ a full-time manager, the first to make a recording (1917) and the first to consult an accoustical engineer in the design of the magnificent Symphony Hall, which opened in 1900. Writing in 1908, Gustav Mahler described the BSO as 'an orchestra of the first rank'. Difficulties arose, however, during the First World War, when a wave of anti-German hysteria swept the United States. Karl Muck, who successfully conducted the orchestra from 1906-8, suffered cruelly from this witch-hunt during his second spell in Boston (1912-18). He was interned as an enemy alien in Georgia in 1918.

Troubles continued under Pierre Monteux (1919-24), when the BSO lost thirty of its members in an union despute, but by the time Serge Koussevitsky arrived on the scene in 1924 it had fully regained its reputation.

A wealthy Russian emigré, Koussevitsky was a musical despot who bullied the orchestra into some of its greatest performances. 'You are my children', he explained, as if to justify his unfatherly behaviour. He continued the practice of feeding conservative Bostonians a steady diet of new music, including works by Ravel, Hindemith, Milhaud, Britten and many contempory American composers. Bartóks Concerto for Orchestra and Stravinsky's Symphony of Psalms were among many pieces commissioned especially for the orchestra. Koussevitsky also established a summer season for the orchestra at Tanglewood in the hills of western Massachusetts. He remained with the BSO for twenty-five years, adored by Bostonians, feard by his musicians.

Charles Munch succeeded Koussevitsky in 1949. Genial and beloved, he loosened the disciplinary reins, occasionally allowing the orchestra to slip into an uncharacteristic laxness, but urging it back to unparalleled brilliance with the music of Debussy, Berlioz and Ravel. A severe seven years under Erich Leinsdorf, beginning 1962, restored the ancien régime of Koussevitsky, but did little for morale in the liberal 1960s. Leinsdorf's successor, William Steinberg, was dogged by illness and remained only three years, but the orchestra re-established a congenial stability when the young and ebullient Seiji Ozawa became Musical Director in 1972.

Under Ozawa the BSO remains one of the greatest and busiest orchestras of the world, giving well over 200 concerts a year and making numerous recordings. In the late spring many of its members let down their hair for series of light concerts with the Boston Pops Orchestra before the summer season at Tanglewood.

Chicago Symphony Orchestra

Briefly it became the Theodore Thomas Orchestra, but in 1912 assumed its present name. Stock may not be remembered as a great interpreter, but he prepared the ground in which a great orchestra could flourish, establishing a civic orchestra for the training of young musicians and introducing a summer season at the Ravinia Festival north of the city. He also encouraged the performance of new music, including premières of works by Stravinsky, Kodály, Milhaud, Prokofiev and Walton. Désiré Defauw (1943–47), Artur Rodzinski (1947–48) and Rafael Kubelik (1950–53) succeeded Stock. Then, under Fritz Reiner (1953–63), the orchestra became recognized as one of the finest in America. A series of brilliant recordings (many still available) persuaded even sceptical Europe of this fact. It may have been during these years that the orchestra also became known as the loudest in the world. Jean Martinon (1963–68) did not mantain this momentum, but under the long tenure of Sir Georg Solti (from 1969) the orchestra has combined flawless technique with magnificent sound, playing with what André Previn calls 'ceaseless brilliance'. There is little that is romantic about the city of Chicago, yet its orchestra has made at least two conductors think of love. Sir Georg Solti calls his long association with the Chicago Symphony Orchestra 'a love-filled marriage', while for Carlo Maria Giulini, a frequent guest conductor, it has provided a 'twenty-four year love affair'. It was founded by Theodore Thomas in 1891 and at first called simply the Chicago Orchestra. Thomas, a pioneer of American orchestral music, stayed with the orchestra until his death in 1905. From 1905 to 1942 the orchestra played under Frederick Stock, like Thomas a German-born American.

Giulini has long been a popular guest conductor in Chicago.

Concertgebouw Orchestra

Although 'Concertgebouw' means 'concert hall' the orchestra which bears this name was founded in 1883, some years before the concert hall itself was built. The Society's first concerts were given under the baton of Willem Kes, from 1888 to 1895, when he was succeeded by Willem Mengelberg. For well nigh fifty years, under Mengelberg's direction, the orchestra maintained an international reputation for its spectacular staging of large-scale works. As a friend of Mahler, Mengelberg was mainly responsible for introducing the latter's music to an international audience. In 1903, Mahler visited Amsterdam to conduct his first and second symphonies, and the second and fourth in the following year. Further visists were made in 1906 and 1909 to perform the fifth and seventh symphonies. In 1920, Mengelberg celebrated his silver jubilee with the orchestra by giving a Mahler festival at which all of Mahler's works were played. Unhappily, in 1941, Mengelberg expressed his approval of the Nazi invasion, and at the end of the war he was forbidden to practise his profession for five years. Mengelberg retired to, and died in, Switzerland.

From 1945 the Concertgebouw's conductor was Eduard van Beinum, joined by Bernard Haitink in 1959. The latter is now regarded as one of the finest exponents of Mahler's music.

A photo from the archives of the Concertgebouw during the reign of Eduard van Beinum, showing a recording being made.

Cleveland Orchestra

In December 1918, fifty-seven local musicians played a concert to raise funds for St Ann's church in Cleveland. To everyone's surprise, this pick-up group was encouraged to give a further twenty-seven concerts that season. As the Cleveland Orchestra it has continued to this day. Nicolai Sokolov, a Russian-born violinist, was the first conductor. He was the discovery of Mrs Adella Prentice Hughes, the orchestra's first manager and principal benefactor, known locally as the 'Mother of the Cleveland Symphony'. Sokolov remained for fifteen years, during which time the orchestra moved (or squeezed, as some conductors complain) into Severance Hall, its permanent home since 1931. Two distinguished Europeans, Artur Rodzinski (1933– 43) and Erich Leinsdorf (1943–46) succeeded Sokolov, but the emergence of Cleveland as an internationally famous orchestra was solely the work of George Szell (1946–70). Under Szell's precise and stern direction the orchestra achieved an astonishing clarity and uniformity of sound, ideally suited to the classic repertory. The American conductor James Levine, for six years Szell's assistant, thought the orchestra at times 'too dry, almost without breath', but Szell, not known for his humour, once wittily defended his balanced and controlled interpretations of the classics. 'I cannot pour chocolate sauce over asparagus,' he said. In 1972 Lorin Maazel, who had first conducted the orchestra as a thirteen-year-old prodigy in 1943, returned as Szell's successor. Christoph von Dohnányi became musical director on Maazel's departure in 1982.

Like many American orchestras, the Cleveland Orchestra plays throughout the year. During the summers since 1968 it has moved to the wide open spaces of the nearby Blossom Music Center, where it can entertain audiences of over 18,000.

Israel Philharmonic Orchestra

Few cities have had such an eager audience for symphonic music as Tel Aviv in the 1930s. On the eve of its first concert, in December 1936, tickets for the Palestine Symphony Orchestra (as the Israel Philharmonic was known until 1948) were selling on the black market for £1 apiece, and afterwards the applause lasted for more than half an hour. Arturo Toscanini, who had amazingly managed to control his temper throughout the rehearsals, announced that Palestine had one of the best orchestras in the world. His claim was prophetic rather than strictly accurate, for this 'orchestra of concertmasters' assembled by the violinist Bronislaw Huberman, came from many different musical cultures and took several years to achieve a homogeneous sound of its own. The first decade imposed difficulties quite apart from these musical ones. On tour in remote parts of the new country, orchestra members were obliged to erect their own makeshift stages, while during the war the depleted orchestra, often without a conductor, played before half-empty houses and in allied army bases. The worst of these struggles ended in 1945 when the Italian conductor Bernadino Molinari bullied the orchestra into a higher standard than it had known for years. Since then the Israel Philharmonic has gradually assumed a place as one of the best and busiest of the world's orchestras. The international popularity of Zubin Mehta, who was appointed Music Adviser in 1969, has ensured many recordings and international tours.

For the beleaguered state of Israel the Philharmonic has assumed an extra-musical importance as an ambassador of good-will. 'No diplomatic mission sent abroad,' said Prime Minister Golda Meier after one successful mission, 'could have accomplished what the orchestra's tour produced for our country.'

Right: Seiji Ozawa, director of the Boston Symphony Orchestra since 1970.

Overleaf: Bernard Haitink conducting Beethoven's ninth symphony in the Amsterdam Concertgebouw.

Leipzig Gewandhaus Orchestra

Founded in 1743, the Leipzig Gewandhaus probably has prior claim to being the oldest orchestra in the world. It's name is derived from the Hall of the Guild of Cloth Merchants, where some of its earliest concerts were given, in the period 1778-1884. Its first conductor, Johann Friedrich Doles, was a pupil of Bach, and Bach himself played at those early concerts. Later conductors have been Mendelssohn (from 1835 to 1843) and more latterly, Wilhelm Furtwängler and Bruno Walter.

Leningrad Philharmonic Orchestra

St Petersburg was the centre of musical life in nineteenth-century Russia. Even the turmoil of revolution and a world war could not break the traditions of music-making in the old Imperial City. The court orchestra, established in 1882, weathered these social storms and survived three name changes to emerge in 1921 as the Leningrad Philharmonic Orchestra. On the eve of this final metamorphosis, as the Petrograd State Orchestra, it was conducted by Serge Koussevitsky (1917–20). He was followed by Emil Cooper (1921–23), Nikolai Malko (1926–29), Alexander Gauk (1930–33) and Fritz Stiedry (1934–37). Then, in 1938, Yevgeni Mravinsky won a national competition and became the Philharmonic's principal conductor, a position he has continued to hold for more than forty years. Over this long period he has shared his duties with many outstanding younger men, most notably the German conductor Kurt Sanderling from 1941 to 1960. Under Mravinsky the orchestra successfully persuaded sceptical western audiences that Soviet music was worth an airing. A long and fruitful relationship with Dmitri Shostakovich resulted in premières of his symphonies number five, six, eight, nine and ten, but it was left to the Radio Orchestra, the Philharmonic's sister ensemble, to first perform his Seventh Symphony (1942) in beleaguered Leningrad. The Philharmonic itself, like a wise general, had retired to Siberia for the duration of the war.

As might be expected, the Leningrad Philharmonic excels in the music of Tchaikovsky. 'They played with a conviction born of absolute belief in the work,' wrote a critic in the *Sunday Times* after hearing Mravinsky conduct the fifth symphony. Despite a new name and a Soviet repertory, the Leningrad Philharmonic can still recall its Tsarist origins in the court of St Petersburg.

Above: Bruno Walter.
Below right: Dmitri Shostakovich.

Left: Leonard Bernstein, honorary conductor for life of the New York Philharmonic Orchestra since 1969.

Sir Thomas Beecham

London Philharmonic Orchestra

In 1931 Sir Thomas Beecham discussed with Sir Robert Mayer the possibility of forming a new orchestra, and was assured of engagements with many of the country's leading musical societies, including the Royal Choral Society and the Royal Philharmonic Society. The germ of an idea became a reality when the wealthy industrialist Samuel Courtauld advanced £ 30,000 to fund the new venture. Assembled in 1932, some 106 of the country's finest musicians were guaranteed more than 70 concerts annually, and a season with Covent Garden. Its début was on 7 October 1932 at Queen's Hall (destroyed by bombing during the war). Critics hailed the performance as a triumph, and under the baton of Sir Thomas Beecham the orchestra dominated the London musical scene. But financial difficulties lay ahead, and at the beginning of the war, Beecham had to tell the orchestra that they were on their won. For a fortnight, the orchestra was technically disbanded and went into liquidation, but reformed under a self-governing committee and became a touring orchestra, travelling the country under constant that of enemy air attack. At the end of the war, Beecham was invited to be the orchestra's conductor once again, but he declined and formed another orchestra of his won, the Royal Philharmonic. The orchestra suffered yet another setback when Walter Legge founded the Philharmonia, taking away many of the orchestra's best players. However, by engaging such eminent conductors as Furtwängler, and newcomers such as Georg Solti, Leonard Bernstein and Bernard Haitink, the orchestra were able to regain their former eminence.

London Symphony Orchestra

According to its own contemporary programme notes, the London Symphony Orchestra was 'second to none in Europe' at its first concert in June 1904. There may have been some truth in this extravagant claim, for the new group consisted of some of London's best musicians, who had broken away from Henry Wood's Queen's Hall Orchestra over a dispute about the use of deputies. Emulating the orchestras of Berlin and Vienna, the LSO established itself as a musical republic, a limited company with directors chosen solely from within the orchestra and every member a shareholder, to be paid by the concert rather than by the season.

This unusual venture was an immediate success. The orchestra chose as its first Principal Conductor the eminent Wagnerian Hans Richter. His successors included Arthur Nikisch, Albert Coates, Sir Hamilton Harty and Josef Krips.

Exposed to most of this century's great conductors and many composer/conductors, from Elgar to Boulez, the orchestra has a tradition of adaptability in both style and repertoire.

Crises among directors or members themselves have often affected the quality of performance of this volatile orchestra. Administrative wrangling in 1929, 1955 (when a number of principals resigned) and 1964 resulted in relatively inferior performances, but each time the men of the LSO emerged from these musical doldrums

with renewed *esprit de corps*. (The orchestra now, as in 1904, is comprised almost exclusively of men. Its democracy is of the Grecian variety.)

A look at the LSO's recent history gives some idea of the lively existence this musical republic leads. In 1961 eighty-six year old Pierre Monteux optimistically signed a twenty-five year renewable contract with the orchestra. His benign but undisciplined rule ended with his death in 1964, whereupon the directors chose the Hungarian Istvan Kertesz. Here was a man of sterner stuff, who alienated the administration with unacceptable demands for greater control. Meanwhile the orchestra had lost both its secretary and its chairman (the principal horn, Barry Tuckwell) in an unsettling spell of boardroom infighting. Kertesz left in 1968 to be succeeded by the young American André Previn. The decade ended with a particularly fruitful series of concerts conducted by Pierre Boulez.

The seventies were relatively sunny, with Previn proving such a successful choice that he remained for an unprecedented eleven years. This was a properous period, rich in broadcasting and recording sessions, which are the life-line for modern orchestras. In 1982 the LSO, now under the direction of Claudio Abbado, moved into its first permanent home, the modern Barbican Centre in the City of London.

The LSO may be thought lucky to have a history at all. In 1912, just before leaving for their first American tour, members of the orchestra were annoyed to discover that plans had been changed and that they were to sail on the White Star liner *Baltic* rather than on the grandest ship of the day: *S.S. Titanic*.

André Previn

Los Angeles Philharmonic Orchestra

The Los Angeles Philharmonic was the brainchild of William Andrews Clark, a music-loving millionaire. In 1919, with an initial grant of one million dollars, Clark transformed the old Los Angeles Symphony Orchestra into the Philharmonic, greatly expanding its concert schedule and increasing its membership to ninety-four. Walter Rothwell, formerly an assistant to Gustav Mahler, was the first conductor, remaining with the orchestra until 1927. He was succeeded by Georg Schnéevoigt (1927–29), Artur Rodzinski (1929–33), Otto Klemperer (1933–39), Alfred Wallenstein (1943–56) and Eduard van Beinum (1956–58). Even under these eminent Europeans the Philharmonic failed to achieve the reputation of its patrician rivals in the east – Boston, Cleveland, New York and Philadelphia. When Zubin Mehta, then only twenty-five, became principal conductor in 1962 the Philharmonic's fortunes began to turn. Mehta remained for sixteen years, leaving his successor, Carlo Maria Giulini, with an orchestra widely regarded as one of the best in the world. Yearly national and international tours continue to confirm this reputation. The Philharmonic is known as a relaxed and friendly orchestra, unlikely to call a new conductor 'maestro' for more than a few rehearsals. Since 1964 it has played for the winter season in the Music Center of the Dorothy Chandler Pavilion. In the summer it moves outside to the vast Hollywood Bowl.

Zubin Mehta.

New York Philharmonic Orchestra

The oldest orchestra in the United States had an unpromising youth. In December 1842 the newly-formed New York Philharmonic Society gave its first concert – Beethoven's fifth symphony followed by an uneven medley of shorter compositions by Hummel, Weber, Rossini and Mozart – with three conductors sharing the evening's responsibilities. For many years the orchestra plodded on in this benign manner, giving no more than six annual concerts, finding conductors from among the musicians themselves and sharing the profits at the end of the season. By the time Theodore Thomas took charge in 1877, one musical journal had already dismissed the Philharmonic as 'antiquated and old fogyish.' Thomas and his successor Anton Seidl (1891–98) had great personal followings, and transformed an evening with the Philharmonic (in Carnegie Hall from 1892) into a glamorous social occasion. This metamorphosis was not a moment too soon. New Yorkers had already begun to look elsewhere for their orchestral music, especially to the New York Symphony, founded in 1878. In the early years of the century the success of the Philharmonic again began to wane. Gustav Mahler's two stormy seasons as conductor (1901–11) did nothing for either the orchestra's music or its morale. But a bequest of nearly a million dollars in 1911 from Joseph Pulitzer (on the condition that the organization be restructured) gave the Philharmonic new life. Josef Stransky was the conductor from 1911–23, during which period the Philharmonic and the Symphony merged to form the Philharmonic-Symphony Orchestra (though it has continued to be called by its first name). During the 1930s, several distinguished Europeans, including

Willem Mengelberg (1921–30) and
Wilhelm Furtwängler (1925–27) shared the
conducting, but the glory of that decade
was stolen by Arturo Toscanini (1927–33),
who terrified his musicians, while
entrancing New York audiences.
John Barbirolli (1937–40) understandably
failed to recreate the fierce exuberance of
Toscanini's rule. Subsequent conductors,
however, have maintained the
Philharmonic's position as one of
America's great orchestras. Artur
Rodzinski (1942–47) and Dmitri
Mitropoulos (1949–58) were followed by
Leonard Bernstein (1958–69), whose sound
musicianship, combined with a sure
instinct for showbiz, found an enthusiastic
following on national television. In 1962 he
and the orchestra moved into Philharmonic
Hall in the new Lincoln Center. His
successor, the composer Pierre Boulez
(1971–77), startled audiences with an
uncompromisingly contemporary
repertoire, but the popular Zubin Mehta
(from 1978), has since reintroduced a more
familiar musical path.

New York Philharmonic
Orchestra.

Orchestre de Paris

The creation of a major symphony orchestra was a bold and extravagant gesture in 1967, but the founders of l'Orchestre de Paris had confidence in their unwieldy infant. Here was

an orchestra for all seasons. Funded by the City of Paris and the central government, it would compare in quality with the long-established orchestras of Berlin, Philadelphia and London, re-establishing the reputation of French music-making that had been in decline since the war. It also aimed to educate the common Frenchman with regular concerts in the provinces and the neglected suburbs of Paris. As for the repertoire, 'They will play Mozart, Dutilleux, Brahms, Schoenberg alongside one another', said the Minister for Music at a press conference prior to the orhestra's debut. Charles Munch, then seventy-six years old, was the natural choice as Principal Conductor, a position he shared with another Frenchman, Serge Baudo. Munch auditioned all 400 candidates and formed an orchestra with a brightness of sound and suppleness of technique that critics frequently describe as 'characteristically French'. 'When it comes to French music…it has to be played by the French', said Munch. He died while on tour with the orchestra less than a year after the inaugural concert, since when the baton has passed into foreign hands – Herbert von Karajan, Sir Georg Solti and, in 1975, Daniel Barenboim.

In its short life L'Orchestre de Paris has made many recordings and tours, featuring an eclectic repertoire with a strong French accent. Barenboim, a conductor with little previous affinity for French music, has become something of a specialist in the works of Berlioz and, true to Munch's dictum, the orchestra receives the highest praise for its national repertoire. When it strays far beyond this musical boundary it is occasionally accused of sounding insecure, as if, like a wine, it were still in need of maturing.

Daniel Barenboim.

Philadelphia Orchestra

Stung by the prestige of orchestras in Boston and New York, music-loving Philadelphians asked the visiting German conductor Fritz Scheel to create an orchestra in 1900. The success of this new venture may have surprised a few of even its most enthusiastic founders. In 1902 The New York Times spoke of the Philadelphia Orchestra's 'uncommon excellence', and two years later Richard Strauss declared it 'wunderschön'. The popular Scheel suffered a mental breakdown and died in 1907. His place was taken by Karl Pohlig, a fellow countryman with what was called 'a difficult disposition', who remained in an atmosphere of gathering animosity for five years.

Leopold Stokowski, conductor of the Cincinnati Symphony Orchestra, became Pohlig's successor. His debut in 1912 gave no indication of what was to follow. A critic at his first concert was impressed by this 'boyish' and 'thoroughly businesslike' young man, but Stokowski was also opinionated, temperamental and extremely eccentric. Over the next twenty-three years he became the most controversial personality in Philadelphia and his orchestra among the best in the world. He continually experimented in attempts to create better balance and greater sonority. He moved the second violins from the right of the stage to the position they generally occupy today – just beside the firsts on the left. He also abolished uniform bowing in order to establish the silky legato for which the orchestra grew famous. Claiming that Philadelphia 'must not be provincial but become universal', he assaulted his audiences with world and American premieres: Schoenberg, de Falla, Shostakovich, Stravinsky, Webern and ten sold-out performances of Mahler's Symphony of a Thousand. When his audiences coughed obtrusively he lectured them from the podium for their 'disagree able and disgusting noises'. Under Stokowski the orchestra became familiar to non-concert-goers from its radio broadcasts and the sound-tracks of three Hollywood films, including Walt Disney's controversial Fantasia.

Eugene Ormandy, the young Hungarian who shared conducting duties for five years before taking over entirely in 1941, had the great advantage of being unlike Stokowksi in every way except his ability to make the orchestra play beautifully. He was reserved but gracious towards the public; polite and firm with his musicians. His choice of music was what one grateful reviewer called 'progressive rather than radical'. Far from declining, the standard of the orchestra soared. Virgil Thomson, praising its 'flexibility' and 'sensitivity' in 1952, declared that the Philadelphia Orchestra under Ormandy was 'better...than any other orchestra has ever been'. Ormandy, a man not given to extravagant claims, became so

identified with his orchestra that he could say in all modesty, 'The Philadelphia sound, it's me'. It remained so until his retirement in 1980, when the awesome responsibility of succeeding Stokowski and Ormandy fell to Riccardo Muti.

Riccardo Muti.

Philharmonia Orchestra

The Philharmonia Orchestra was founded after the war by Walter Legge, primarily for producing recordings of the highest quality; although the repertoire was, some might have thought, all-embracing, there was no disputing the exceptional quality of the orchestra, many of whose players (such as its first horn player, Dennis Brain) were soloists in their own right. Among its conductors have been Otto Klemperer, Guido Cantelli, and Herbert van Karajan. Eventually, Legge rescinded his management of the orchestra to its members.

Pittsburgh Symphony Orchestra

In 1895 the Art Society of Pittsburgh established a symphony orchestra that rapidly became recognized as one of the finest in America. Although it attracted Victor Herbert and Emil Paur as conductors, with Richard Strauss and Edward Elgar among its eminent guests, the project foundered in 1910. It was not until 1926 that the present Pittsburgh Symphony Orchestra emerged to take its place. The new organization, consisting mainly of local musicians, was slow to regain the reputation of its predecessor, but in 1937 Otto Klemperer, Eugene Goossens, Georges Enesco and Fritz Reiner, among others, shared a season of conducting, giving the orchestra a shakedown that marked the beginning of Pittsburgh's musical renaissance. Reiner became permanent conductor the next year, remaining until 1948. The young Lorin Maazel, though not yet twenty, moved from the violin section to the podium as apprentice conductor on Reiner's departure, but it was William Steinberg who was appointed next permanent conductor. From 1952 Steinberg established the Pittsburgh Symphony as a sound, if not particularly adventurous, ensemble. André Previn, who succeeded Steinberg in 1976, admitted that the orchestra had become 'a bit sloppy' and embarked upon an energetic programme of recordings and tours, expanding the repertory to include works of the eighteenth and twentieth centuries that had previously been neglected. A festival of English music in 1982 was characteristic of Previn's innovative programming.

Since 1971 the orchestra has played in Heinz Hall, a converted cinema. Its season of over 200 concerts includes annual visits to New York and Washington, and an ambitious schedule of television appearances.

Lorin Maazel.

Royal Philharmonic Orchestra

After the Second World War Sir Thomas Beecham returned from his concert tours in Australia, Canada, and the USA. He was invited to return to his old orchestra, the London Philharmonic, but declined, preferring to employ an orchestra rather than be its employee, Consequently, in 1947 he formed the Royal Philharmonic Orchestra, which under his baton, also became associated with the annual Glyndebourne opera season in Sussex. The orchestra tours frequently, making regular visits to the USA. The orchestra has made several experiments with the repertoire, often performing pieces associated with the realms of light music, or jazz or pop genre. In recent years, one of the leading names associated with the orchestra has been Antal Dorati.

Rotterdam Philharmonic Orchestra

Rotterdam began to be one of Holland's most important musical centres in the nineteenth century. The Philharmonic Orchestra was founded in 1918, and was housed at the Doele. Sadly, during the war the concert hall was destroyed, and the orchestra's entire collection of scores and instruments with it. The new home, De Doelen, opened in 1966; the orchestra has since received international acclaim on its world-wide tours.

Sydney Symphony Orchestra

The Sydney Symphony Orchestra began life in the studios of the Australian Broadcasting Commission in 1937. Its core of forty-five musicians formed the A.B.C. Symphony Orchestra, but for eight concerts a year, joined by twenty-five or more part-time professionals, they emerged on the concert platform as the Sydney Symphony Orchestra. In 1946, subsidies from the state government and the Sydney City Council enabled the orchestra to become a full-time, full-size enterprise. Eugene

Goossens, the first resident conductor, was impressed enough with the young orchestra's playing (and his own conducting) to claim that he would make it one of the ten best in the world. He left the orchestra in 1957 as Sir Eugene, having made some progress towards this grandiose goal. Subsequent permanent conductors have included Nicolai Malko (1957), the black American Dean Dixon (1962), Willem van Otterloo (1972) and Sir Charles Mackerras (1983). This last appointment represents a homecoming for Mackerras, who began his career at the age of nineteen as the orchestra's principal oboist.

The Czech Philharmonic Orchestra

For the first few years of its life (1894–1901) the Czech Philharmonic was the orchestra of the Prague National Opera. It only became an independent organization when the opera management dismissed its musicians *en masse* for daring to go on strike. Vilém Zemánek was the conductor from 1903–18. He was succeeded by the great Václav Talich, whose combination of inspiration and painstaking discipline made the Philharmonic one of Europe's most esteemed orchestras. Many works by Janáček, Suk and Novák first became known to western audiences through the tours of Talich and his orchestra between the wars. In 1941 the young Rafael Kubelik, who had frequently appeared with the orchestra during the 1930s, was appointed

permanent conductor. He left his homeland in voluntary exile when the communists became political (and cultural) masters of Czechoslovakia in 1948. Karel Ančerl conducted the Philharmonic from 1950–68, maintaining the internationally high standards of his predecessors while championing a predominantly national repertory. He left Czechoslovakia in the wake of the political disturbances of 1968, taking up residence in Canada.
Under Václav Neumann the Czech Philharmonic has continued to enjoy a high reputation. Its frequent international tours and many recordings make it the most familiar and admired of Eastern European orchestras.

Vienna Symphony Orchestra

In the years following the death of Beethoven it became increasingly evident that Vienna did not have an orchestra capable of playing his symphonies. This need was filled in 1842 by the establishment of the Vienna Philharmonic, a self-governing body of professional musicians. The conductor was Otto Nicolai, musical director of the Court Opera. His musicians were all familiar faces, members of his own opera orchestra who had moved from the pit to the concert platform. In its first years the Philharmonic performed infrequently, but already by 1845 had impressed Hector Berlioz with its 'outstanding technical skill' and 'meticulous accuracy of instrumental tuning'. The Revolution of 1848 very nearly put an end to the enterprise, but under Karl Eckert and Felix Dessoff the orchestra struggled to its feet. In 1870 the Philharmonic moved into its own concert hall, the Grosser Musikvereinsaal. In this splendid auditorium were heard for the first time the symphonies number two and three of Brahms and numbers three and eight of that controversial modernist Anton Bruckner. Hans Richter was principal conductor during this golden period. His long reign extended from 1875 to 1898,

when Gustav Mahler stepped in for three unhappy years. From 1908 until 1927 Felix Weingartner was principal conductor, maintaining the Philharmonic's remarkable standards throughout the First World War and organizing a triumphant tour of South America in 1922. A succession of glamorous guest conductors appeared during the darkening 1930s: Richard Strauss, Bruno Walter, Otto Klemperer, Toscanini and Furtwängler. The latter remained to direct the orchestra during the German occupation, a decision which obliged him to undergo the ignominy of de-Nazification by the Americans after the war. The Philharmonic itself did not meet with such disdain but stepped out of the rubble of Vienna, once again into the forefront of the world's orchestras. Under recent conductors, including Claudio Abbado (1971–77) and Karl Böhm, the Philharmonic has maintained its reputation and fierce pride. 'We are the successors of artists who learned their craft with Beethoven', boasted Richard Strauss for the orchestra in 1923. Sixty years later the Vienna Philharmonic still lives up to this grand heritage.

Sir Georg Solti conducting the Vienna Philharmonic Orchestra.

Vienna Philharmonic Orchestra

Such is the fame of the Vienna Philharmonic Orchestra, that its hard-working younger sister is little-known outside Austria. The Vienna Symphony Orchestra was founded as the Wiener Konzertverein in 1900. Ferdinand Löwe, its permanent conductor until 1924, championed the music of his former teacher, Anton Bruckner, whose ninth symphony received its posthumous première in 1903. Subsequent first performances have included Ravel's Piano Concerto for the left hand, Boris Blacher's Requiem and, in the opera pit under Karl Böhm, the Viennese premières of Alban Berg's *Lulu* and Richard Strauss's *Daphne*. In 1921 the Konzertverein incorporated another local orchestra and changed its name to the Wiener Sinfonie-Orchester. Twelve years later it became the Wiener Symphoniker, the name by which it is still known. During these early years it attracted the world's most distinguished musicians as guest conductors: Gustav Mahler, Bruno Walter, Richard Strauss, Arnold Schoenberg and Wilhelm Furtwängler. Despite this galaxy of great names, the Vienna Symphony Orchestra had come close to financial ruin when it was adopted as Vienna's principal radio orchestra in 1934. Sponsorship from the City of Vienna and the Austrian Ministry of Education in 1938 further assured its future.

Since the war the orchestra has been closely associated with a number of eminent conductors, among them Herbert von Karajan, Otto Klemperer, Karl Böhm and Ernest Ansermet. The longest-serving principal conductor has been Wolfgang Sawallisch (1960–70). With a season of approximately 120 concerts in the city, frequent broadcasts and annual tours of the provinces, the Vienna Symphony Orchestra is an essential part of Austria's cultural life, while remaining one of the least known of the world's outstanding orchestras.

Herbert von Karajan.

11

Discographies

Rotterdam Philharmonic Orchestra.

C. P. E. Bach

AAM	Academy of Ancient Music
ASMF	Academy of St Martin-in-the-Fields
BournS	Bournemouth Sinfonietta
BPO	Berlin Philharmonic Orchestra
BSO	Boston Symphony Orchestra
CA	Collegium Aureum
ClevO	Cleveland Orchestra
CO	Concertgebouw Orchestra
CologneCO	Cologne Chamber Orchestra
ColSO	Columbia Symphony Orchestra
CSO	Chicago Symphony Orchestra
CzPhO	Czech Philharmonic Orchestra
DetroitSO	Detroit Symphony Orchestra
DSO	Dresden State Orchestra
EastmanR	Eastman Rochester Symphony Orchestra
EC	English Concert
ECO	English Chamber Orchestra
Ens13	Ensemble 13 Baden-Baden
l'EsArm	l'Estro Armonico
FLisztCO	Franz Liszt Chamber Orchestra
IPO	Israel Philharmonic Orchestra
LACO	Los Angeles Chamber Orchestra
LAPO	Los Angeles Philharmonic Orchestra
LPO	London Philharmonic Orchestra
LSO	London Symphony Orchestra
MunichBO	Munich Bach Orchestra
NatPO	National Philharmonic Orchestra
NBCSO	NBC Symphony Orchestra
NCO	Netherlands Chamber Orchestra
NewPhil	New Philharmonia Orchestra
NYPO	New York Philharmonic Orchestra
OdP	Orchestre de Paris
ONF	Orchestre National de France
ORTF	Orchestre Radio Télévision Français
Phil	Philharmonia Orchestra
PO	Philadelphia Orchestra
PolishCO	Polish Chamber Orchestra
PragueCO	Prague Chamber Orchestra
ROTPO	Rotterdam Philharmonic Orchestra
RPO	Royal Philharmonic Orchestra
RSOCologne	Radio Symphony Orchestra of Cologne
RSOPoland	Radio Symphony Orchestra of Poland
RSOMoscow	Radio Symphony Orchestra of Moscow
SOBR	Symphony Orchestra of the Bavarian Radio
SRomande	Orchestre de la Suisse Romande
St.LouisS	St. Louis Symphony Orchestra
VPO	Vienna Philharmonic Orchestra

6 Sinfonias, Wq 182

The six Hamburg symphonies for strings by Carl Philipp Emanuel, Johann Sebastian's second son, have gradually taken a firm place in the standard repertory since the Collegium Aureum first recorded them with original instruments in 1973. The main drawback of this disc, initially released in Great Britain on BASF, is that only four of the six, nos. 2–5, are given. This is also the failing of the most recent recording on Telefunken with the Hungarian Franz Liszt Chamber Orchestra (1–3+5). The Hungarians do however have the advantage of the very best recording technique, Telefunken's digital DMM – Direct Metal Mastering – system. The virtue of completeness is shared by recordings made by two London groups, the Academy of Ancient Music directed by Hogwood (three sides, the fourth with Wq 174+176 with winds) and The English Concert directed by Pinnock (two sides). In both recordings the fanciful compositional style emerges clearly, thanks to a vital pointed approach, with Pinnock leaning slightly more in the direction of eighteenth-century elegance.

EC/Pinnock, Archiv 2533349
CA/Maier, EMI 065/99691
AAM/Hogwood, DSLO 0557/8

4 Sinfonias, Wq 183

The four symphonies Wq 183, published in Hamburg in 1780, are no less original or characteristic of C.P.E. Bach's emotionally expressive style with its frequent surprising twists, than the six Wq 182. Oddly enough, however, they have aroused less interest with specialists of the period than those of Wq 182. They are written for winds and strings and are the last symphonies Carl Philipp Emanuel published. Taking into consideration that at this time Mozart was composing his violin concertos, serenades, divertimentos and cassations, it is striking to note the lack of balanced classical construction in these symphonies, where the unexpected seems rather to be the norm. From a historical standpoint the recording with Richter and his Münchener Bach Orchestra is interesting, despite a somewhat overly literal, one-sidedly rhythmic approach. The recording by the English Chamber Orchestra under the direction of Leppard from 1969, re-released in 1981, is livelier, the sound-coloration of strings and winds playing against each other like organ registers. A good alternative is the Schwann recording.

MBO/Richter, Archiv 2547026
ECO/Leppard, Phil 9502013
CologneCO/Müller Brühl, Schwann VMS 2044

J. C. Bach

Sinfonias

In 1982, to commemorate the two-hundredth anniversary of the death of Johann Christian Bach, Philips issued a box of 5 discs containing virtually all the symphonies of this youngest son of Johann Sebastian. These are the 6 Sinfonias opus 3, the 6 Sinfonias opus 6, opus 8 nos. 2, 3 and 4, opus 9 nos 1, 2 and 3, plus the overture La Calamità. A considerable number of works, but not quite complete. Charles Sanford Terry, Johann Christian's biographer, lists a large number of symphonies which have remained in manuscript. In addition there are many works denominated overtures (and actually used as the introductions to operas) which, in matters of structure, form perfect three-movement symphonies. He may lack the originality of his half-brother Carl Philipp, but surpasses him in structural balance and melodic invention. The Philips box is a collection of older recordings from 1970, 1976 and 1978. Opus 3 is played by Marriner's Academy, the remainder by the Netherlands Chamber Orchestra under the direction of David Zinman. Both ensembles are known for the quality of their performances.

ASMF/Marriner, Phil 6768336
NCO/Zinman, Phil 6768336

Balakirev

Symphonies nos. 1 and 2

The only recording of both, still underrated symphonies is on the not easily obtainable Ariola label. Yevgeny Svetlanov conducts an enthusiastic and meticulous USSR Symphony Orchestra, though the sound produced by the brass section is rather rough. The clarity of the recording of Svetlanov's lively interpretations leaves a great deal to be desired. The true lover of Balakirev will find this disc worth the outlay, as it also contains the symphonic poems Russia and Tamar as well as the Overture on Three Russian Songs. The first symphony is also available in mono on a 1980 reissue which Herbert von Karajan made in 1950 with the Philharmonia Orchestra (HMV XLP 60001). Anyone who values monaural recording will find this an interpretation filled with sparkle and passion.

USSRSO/Svetlanov, Ariola 300045-440

Beethoven

Symphony no. 1 in C, opus 21

Beethoven's first two symphonies have been coupled on one disc by both Marriner and Karajan. The big difference between them is that Karajan works with a large nineteenth-century Romantic orchestra, whereas Marriner opts for orchestral forces similar to those of Mozart's day. Karajan thus tips Beethoven's earlier symphonies in the weightier direction of the later ones. Marriner, with greater historical accuracy, places the symphonies in the world of the Classics (Haydn and Mozart). The lightness of the chamber orchestra does not prevent Marriner from finding sufficient robustness to bring out dramatic contrasts without relying on mannerisms. Karajan on the other hand, in his inflated yet very exciting recording, does just that by now and then drawing certain instruments into the foreground. Furtwängler and Bernstein couple the first with the fourth symphony. Bernstein's electric reading is clearly influenced by the presence of an audience.

BPO/Karajan, DG 2535301
VPO/Furtwängler, EMI 027-00806
VPO/Bernstein, DG 2531308
ASMF/Marriner, Phil 6527074

Symphony no. 2 in D, opus 36

Beethoven's second symphony on record is often coupled with one or more of his overtures. This is the case with Bernstein's live recording with the Vienna Philharmonic; here, Die Geschöpfe des Prometheus. (More could have been included; the playing-time is very short.) It is a lively performance which generously compensates for occasional inaccuracies of ensemble due to public performance. Another frequent coupling is that of the second symphony with the first. For the recordings by Karajan and Marriner, see the entry for the first symphony. Less usual, but no less sensible, is the coupling of the second and fourth symphonies. Kubelik's recording of these two for DG, taken from a complete set of the nine symphonies, is excellent. The second symphony is played by a luminous-sounding Concertgebouw Orchestra. The orchestra for the fourth symphony is the Israel Philharmonic Orchestra.

CO/Kubelik, DG 2544145
VPO/Bernstein, DG 2531309

Symphony no. 3 in E flat major, opus 55 – Eroica

Maier with the Collegium Aureum strives for an authentic performing style. Anyone wanting to hear an Eroica as a massive monument of early nineteenth-century symphonic art is bound to feel the lack of a certain tension. If however one can free oneself of expectations bred by late nineteenth-century performing practices calling for Beethoven's opus 55 to be played as forcefully as possible and at full volume, one will be attracted by the power which emanates from the transparent ensemble sound of Maier's Collegium. The horns have more bite than in traditional recordings, and this has a very suggestive effect, certainly against the thinner, more rarified sound of the strings, which avoid the use of excessive vibrato. Karajan's interpretation is completely different. He aims at the fullest possible sound, taking advantage of technical possibilities to bring forward certain instruments or instrumental groups in the total sound-picture. The contrasts which the score offers are heightened to the extreme, giving Karajan's Eroica interpretation enormous dramatic presence.

BPO/Karajan, DG 2531103
CA/Maier, HMV 065-99629
NBC/Toscanini, RCA VL 46012

Symphony no. 4 in B flat major, opus 60

In recent years chamber orchestras, previously favouring the baroque, rococo or early classical periods and some work from early Romanticism, have discovered that Beethoven's symphonies offer fresh territory. Chamber performances offer certain advantages, precision worthy of soloists, rhythmic sharpness and, especially, transparency of sound. These characteristics apply not only to the recording by the English Chamber Orchestra under the direction of Tilson Thomas, who offers a very detailed, analytical interpretation of the work, but also to Marriner's disc with the Academy. Both are excellent digital recordings; the Marriner is also available on Compact Disc. With the recordings by Karajan and Haitink we enter the traditional world of large orchestra and rich sound. For the latter Karajan is matchless, always brilliant and exciting, even in the extremely rapid finale. Haitink's reading, coupled with Leonora no. 3, is noticeably fresher and lighter, the coloration finely shaded yet providing ample contrast.
ECO/Tilson Thomas, CBS 37209
BPO/Karajan, DG 2531 104
LPO/Haitink, Phil 9500 258
ASMF/Marriner, Phil CD410044.2

Symphony no. 5 in C minor, opus 67

Compact Disc's ability to strengthen the forceful elements of a recording and interpretation while mercilessly pin-pointing weaknesses is amply demonstrated by the three recordings released on Compact Disc. In Maazel's with the Vienna Philharmonic, coupling Beethoven's fifth with Schubert's 'Unfinished', the overall sound is incredibly dense, whereas the sound of the violins is reproduced with appalling thinness. Compact Disc does however carry the day when allied to high quality digital engineering, as shown by Ashkenazy's recording for Decca. In this demonstration of the technological capabilities of the laser, the supple, rhythmically assured and dramatically intense reading comes through with flying colours. Ashkenazy's interpretation is also available on LP, the technical quality being equally excellent. A good alternative on Compact Disc is Giulini's reading with the Los Angeles Philharmonic Orchestra, which possesses greater sonority and nobility of expression.

VPO/Kleiber, DG 2530516
LAPO/Giulini, DG 2532049 (CD)
PHILH/Ashkenazy, Decca SXDL 7540 (CD 400060-2)
VPO/Maazel, CBS CD 36711
NYPO/Mehta, CBS 76969

Symphony no. 6 in F major, opus 68 – 'Pastoral'

Beethoven's 'Pastoral' symphony exists in a number of older recordings of outstanding quality, now available in relatively inexpensive reissues. In the first place, the soberly published series of 'Great Performances' from CBS contains the famous interpretation by Bruno Walter with the Columbia Symphony Orchestra. The performance radiates warmth and the recorded sound, dating from the 1960s, is excellent by modern standards. Jochum's recording for Philips is slightly more recent, dating from the end of that decade. His interpretation, with the Concertgebouw Orchestra playing with great clarity, is somewhat reserved; the geniality of the landscape receives more emphasis than the tumultuousness of the storm. Ashkenazy's performance, available on both LP and Compact Disc, demonstrates the same excellent technical features and artistic qualities that make his interpretation of the fifth a welcome addition to any Beethoven collection.

Phil/Ashkenazy, Decca SXDL 7570 (CD 410003-2)
VPO/Böhm, DG 2530142
ColSO/Walter, CBS 60107
CO/Jochum, Phil 8833183

Symphony no. 7 in A major, opus 92

Beethoven's seventh symphony has been nicknamed the Dance Symphony and this dance-like character seems extremely appropriate for performance with chamber forces. The Collegium Aureum, playing on authentic instruments, give a lively interpretation with certain features reminiscent of solo concertizing.
Drama is however evident in the beautifully broad and sonorous recording from the Chicago Symphony Orchestra under the direction of Giulini. It is a performance in the traditional mould, but of unparalleled clarity. As an Italian, Giulini gives the themes a lyrical bel canto songfulness. Kubelik, with his own orchestra of the Bavarian Radio, produces a relaxed and lyrical seventh with a warm spontaneous sound. Karajan in his recording emphasizes the dramatic qualities of the work rather than its dance-like character. This he has to some extent in common with Toscanini, although the latter, even in the most highly charged sections, maintains the rhythmic spring of the dance.

SOBR/Kubelik, DG 2544043
BPO/Karajan, DG 2531107
NBCSO/Toscanini, RCA VL 46001
CA/Maier, EMI 067-99872
CSO/Giulini, EMI 037-02165

Symphony no. 8 in F, opus 93

Beethoven's 'little' eighth symphony is coupled by various conductors, including Bernstein and Karajan, with the ninth, the Choral Symphony. In such double albums the main stress is of course laid on the ninth symphony. Both Karajan and Bernstein give electrifying performances of great character. Bernstein offers a sympathetic reading of the eighth symphony, an outpouring of great joy. Karajan tends more to emphasize the brilliant virtuosity of the orchestra. Solti's performance, coupled less characteristically with the first symphony, is broader and more concentrated.

BPO/Karajan, DG 2707109
VPO/Bernstein, DG 2707124
CSO/Solti, Decca SXL 6760

Berlioz

Bernstein

Berwald

Symphony no. 9 in D minor, opus 125 – Choral

After an excellent recording in 1962 of Beethoven's ninth symphony, a recording which is still available, in 1972 Karajan made a new one with the Berlin Philharmonic. This second performance, is more imposing for the tightness of concentration with which the entire composition is charged, with an exciting finale as the high point. The recorded balance unfortunately leaves something to be desired. Bernstein's recording with the Vienna Philharmonic was made during a public performance and is good in every respect, although the chorus is somewhat muted due to the exigencies of live performance. The recording from the Concertgebouw Orchestra under the direction of Haitink was also made before an audience, but the atmosphere of a live occasion is scarcely discernible. This is likewise the case with Bernstein. He draws strength from the tension arising on such an occasion, whereas it is precisely tension which seems to be lacking in Haitink's interpretation. Böhm, who recorded the Choral Symphony a number of times, gave a powerful new reading shortly before his death, choosing slow tempos which make the most of the work's breadth.

VPO/Böhm, DG 2741009
CO/Haitink, Phil 6769067

Symphonies nos. 1–9

The discography of Beethoven's nine symphonies is tremendous. Since the first integral issue in 1927 there have been more than fifty editions of the complete symphonies, from Hans von Bülow on Edison cylinders to Kurt Sanderling's digital recording of 1982. Jochum, Karajan and Bernstein have each more than once felt themselves called to record the entire set. In his last two integral recordings, with the Concertgebouw (Philips) and the London Symphony Orchestra (EMI), Jochum's work is solidly professional. Each symphony is approached clearly and in detail, sharpening mutual points of contrast. Bernstein replaced his CBS studio recording with the New York Philharmonic, taken from public performances. The engineers were obliged to make certain concessions to reduce noise from the audience, but results are good. The last of Karajan's three integral recordings, dating from 1977, is a monument to perfection, the strings given some prominence in order to accentuate Karajan's characteristic flexibility of attack and phrasing.

Phil/Klemperer, EMI 181-50187/94
VPO/Bernstein, DG 2740216
BPO/Karajan, DG 740172
LSO/Jochum, EMI 137-53490/7

Symphonie fantastique, opus 14

The performances by Mehta and Maazel, both with an American orchestra, are surprising. Maazel, with the Cleveland Orchestra, underlines Berlioz's extravagant imagination with a great display of virtuosity. He chooses tempos which are quicker than is customary.
Maazel seems to have let himself be guided by Gounod's remark that with Berlioz all feelings and impressions are expressed as strongly as possible in a kind of delirium.
Mehta's interpretation with the New York Philharmonic is less wayward, though what he gains in control of the huge structure, he loses in sparkle and effervescence. This digital recording has also appeared on Compact Disc. The older, much prized reissue of Karajan's performance is not convincing in every respect. The recording by Colin Davis with the Concertgebouw stands out, especially in the two final movements, by reason of its freshness and rhythmic precision.

NYPO/Mehta, Decca SXDL 7512 (CD 400046-2)
BPO/Karajan, DG 2543534
CO/Davis, Phil 6500774
ClevO/Maazel, CBS 76652

Symphonies

Probably no conductor is better equipped to conduct Bernstein's three symphonies, Jeremiah, The Age of Anxiety and Kaddish, than the composer himself. Having made earlier recordings of the symphonies with the New York Philharmonic Orchestra, he returned to this material in 1978 with the Israel Philharmonic Orchestra. The execution of the Israelis is less perfect and homogeneous than that of the New Yorkers, yet thanks to Bernstein's passionate dramatic conducting, the warmth of his own compositional voice is excellently captured. The fine soloists are mezzo soprano Christa Ludwig in the Jeremiah Symphony, pianist Lukas Foss in The Age of Anxiety and soprano Montserrat Caballé in the Symphony no. 3, Kaddish. In the last symphony Bernstein uses his definitive revised version in which the recitation is given to a male voice rather than the female voice of the earlier version. The recordings with the New York Philharmonic are outdated. Those with the Israel Philharmonic are available individually as well as together as a boxed set (DG 2709177)

IPO/Bernstein, DG 2530968 (No. 1)
IPO/Bernstein, DG 2530969 (No. 2)
IPO/Bernstein, DG 2530970 (No. 3)

4 Symphonies

The symphonies of Sweden's Franz Berwald, as well as many of his other orchestral compositions, are works of great originality, powerful imagination and invigorating freshness. All the significant orchestral music, performed by the Royal Philharmonic Orchestra under the direction of Ulf Björlin, has been assembled in a 4-disc boxed set, which also includes the less penetrating concertos for violin and for piano. As fate would have it, the performances of these solo works are more appealing than those of the symphonies. Melodic contours in the symphonies remain vague, and Björlin lacks vision as to the originality of the four symphonies' structural aspects. But there is little alternative. The recordings by Ehrling with the London Symphony Orchestra of the third symphony (La Singulière) and by Dorati with the Stockholm Symphony Orchestra of no. 2 (Capricieuse) are no longer generally available.

RPO/Björlin, HMV SLS 5096

Bizet

Borodin

Boyce

Brahms

Symphony in C

The best performances of Bizet's undramatic music have been put on disc by non-French conductors. The only French conductor to give an acceptable interpretation of the symphony in C is Martinon with the orchestra of the ORTF (DG Privilege 2535 238). The disc is attractive because of its inclusion of La Jolie fille de Perth in addition to the customary coupling of Jeux d'enfants. The recording is however far less transparent than that by Haitink with the Concertgebouw Orchestra. Haitink's reading is broader and more generous than others, but the imprint of his personality makes for a performance of convincing naturalness. The CBS disc with Bernstein also contains Dukas's Sorcerer's Apprentice and Prokofiev's first symphony. Bernstein stresses the symphony's liveliness, casting a magic spell with brilliant virtuosity. Ozawa's interpretation is remarkably exact as regards the rhythmic profile and the sound-relationships. The Orchestre National de France reacts with alertness and subtlety, giving the symphony an appropriate transparency and playfulness.

ONF/Ozawa, EMI 067-43339
CO/Haitink, Phil 9500443
NYPO/Bernstein, CBS 60112

3 Symphonies

Varviso with the Orchestre de la Suisse Romande couples the second symphony with Tchaikovsky's Francesca da Rimini (Contour CC 7533), Benzi, with Rimsky-Korsakov's Tsar Saltan (Opera Orchestra of Monte Carlo/Philips 6570 105) and Tjeknavorian and the National Philharmonic Orchestra, with other works by Borodin; the Polovtsian Dances, Prince Igor, In the Steppes of Central Asia and the nocturne from the second string quartet in Gerhard's celebrated orchestration (RCA RL 25225). Originally Tjeknavorian's recording of the second symphony was part of a boxed set containing all three of Borodin's symphonies. (This is still available in the USA.) Now nos. 1 and 3 have been issued on a separate disc. The recordings are technically excellent and the National Philharmonic Orchestra play well, but Tjeknavorian's interpretations lack personality. In this respect the recordings of the complete set by Andrew Davis are far to be preferred by reason of his vital, imaginative, concentrated approach. But the recording technique and the sound quality of the Orchestra of Toronto do not come up to those of the RCA version.

TorontoS/ADavis, CBS 79214
NPO/Tjeknavorian, RCA RL 25322

Symphonies nos. 1–8

Although various well-known ensembles have included one or another of Boyce's symphonies in recorded programmes (symphony no. 1: English Concert/Pinnock, Archiv 2533 423; symphony no. 4: English Chamber Orchestra/Garcia, CBS 76719; symphonies nos. 4, 5, 8: Lucerne Festival Strings/Baumgartner, Archiv 2547 054), there are only two integral recordings of the eight symphonies. both are of excellent quality, technically as well as artistically. Thomas with the Bournemouth Sinfonietta and Marriner with his Academy offer interpretations which allow plenty of space for the melodiousness of the slow movements, nicely contrasted with the lively thrust of the fast ones. By and large Thomas's choice of tempos is more audacious than Marriner's, but there is little to choose between them.

BournS/Thomas, CRD 1056
ASMF/Marriner, Argo ZRG 874

Symphony no. 1 in C minor, opus 68

Together with the fourth, Johannes Brahms's first symphony was Furtwängler's favourite and he recorded it no less than six times. the only easily obtainable recording is that of 1947, in mono of course, with the Vienna Philharmonic. His approach is unmistakably Beethovenian. Karajan also puts the first at the top of his list of Brahms's symphonies. In the complete cycle he places it last, thereby emphasizing its importance. The quality of the recording is debatable, but certainly not the quality of Karajan's vision. In mid-1983 a reading by Bernstein with the Vienna Philharmonic appeared on Compact Disc, continuing the tradition of live recordings with this orchestra. The version by Giulini is available both on Compact Disc and an LP. Giulini does not keep strictly to Brahms's tempo indications in the finale; the extreme slowness of this movement produces a sobering effect. The nobility of all that precedes it is enhanced by the excellent digital recording.

VPO/Bernstein, DG CD410 081-2
LAPO/Giulini, DG 2532056; CD410 023-2
BPO/Karajan, DG 2531 131
VPO/Furtwängler, EMI 027-01145

Symphony no. 2 in D major, opus 73

Haitink with the Concertgebouw Orchestra gives a confident and very moving performance of Brahms's second symphony. Every detail is in place; the clarinet's nostalgic outcries throughout the symphony, the liveliness of the scherzo, the fiery finale, all are captured with exact precision. The logic of the overall structure always remains in the foreground. Giulini, who rightly takes the first movement's exposition repeat, leaving no room, contrary to Haitink, for a coupling, is less convincing. In his digital version, also available on Compact Disc, the winds overpower the strings. This produces a certain aggression which contrasts oddly with the measured tempos Giulini chooses. The sound of the Compact Disc is noticeably more transparent than that of the LP. In direct opposition to Giulini, Karajan selects a remarkably quick tempo for the finale, taxing even the excellent instrumentalists of the Berlin Philharmonic. The recording has great immediacy, disclosing not only the superior qualities of the orchestra but also Karajan's dynamic personality.

VPO/Bernstein, DG CD410 082-2
LAPO/Giulini, DG 2532041
BPO/Karajan, DG 2531132
CO/Haitink, Phil 6500375

Symphony no. 3 in F major, opus 90

All that holds true for Haitink's visionary approach to Brahms's second symphony applies equally to his reading of the third. It is a compulsive interpretation, giving a natural coherence to the heroic nature of the first movement, the rolling character of the second, the melancholy of the third and the fury of the finale. With a certain austerity, Klemperer also keeps the symphony's overall structure in the foreground. He chooses extremely slow tempos and secures a richness of sound which combine to clarify his comprehensive view of form.
Karajan omits the first movement's exposition repeat, not without damage to the equilibrium of the work as a whole. Where Karajan is unsurpassable is in his ability to depict Brahms as a composer whose fascinating handling of the orchestra creates magnificent sound-pictures, from an almost inaudible pianissimo to a thundering fortissimo. Bernstein's electrifying performance with the Vienna Philharmonic, made during a public performance, has been issued on a splendid Compact Disc.

VPO/Bernstein, DG CD410 083-2
BPO/Karajan, DG 2531133
Phil/Klemperer, EMI SXLP 30255
CO/Haitink, Phil 6500 155

Symphony no. 4 in E minor, opus 98

Giulini gives us one of the most thoroughgoing visions of the fourth symphony, now broad and meditative, now radiantly transparent. Kleiber's vision is also all-embracing, assigning his attention to detail to a position of secondary importance. It is a highly personal interpretation which sometimes seems to offer the first taste of, in Brahms's own words, 'these cherries that will never grow sweet'. Strings come up as fresh as paint and winds strike the ear as never before. The high quality of the digital recording further enhances these characteristics. In his search for ever greater perfection of orchestral sound, Karajan and the Berlin Philharmonic rerecorded the symphony in 1978, supplanting the earlier release, also for DG, of 1964. In addition to these two there is an excellent medium-priced recording with the Philharmonia Orchestra (HMV SXLP 30503), whose quality is scarcely inferior to either of those with the Berlin Philharmonic.

VPO/Bernstein, DG CD410 084-2
VPO/Kleiber, DG 2532003
BPO/Karajan, DG 2531134
NYPO/Mehta, CBS 79949
CSO/Giulini, EMI 037-02083

Symphonies nos. 1–4

Brahms's symphonies harbour so many secrets that perhaps only the very greatest conductors can penetrate them. Many of the 43 integral recordings made in the course of the history of the gramophone have proved disappointing; an individual symphony can be successful, but the four together generally lack the necessary differentiation. Even Klemperer's integral recording suffers in this regard, despite many brilliant moments. In Karajan's integral recording of 1978 however each symphony is given its own individuality, enhanced by the extremely refined sound of the Berlin Philharmonic. Engineering techniques, on the other hand, do not always bring about improvements compared to the 1964 issue. Solti achieves a completely acceptable balance between brilliantly Romantic music-making and a profoundly conceived control of form. Of Bernstein's 1983 interpretation on Compact Disc it can be said that the tension of a live appearance is clearly to be felt.

BPO/Karajan, DG 2740193
Phil/Klemperer, EMI 137-50034
VPO/Bernstein, DG 2741023
CSO/Solti, Decca S151D4

Simple Symphony, opus 4
Sinfonia de Requiem, opus 20
Spring Symphony, opus 44

In the Simple Symphony I Musici play flawlessly and with great beauty of tone. Despite the light, transparent timbre, however, there is a certain lack of clarity. And of course the performance by the English Chamber Orchestra under the composer's direction remains a gem for the collector. Previn's 1973 recording with the St Louis Symphony Orchestra of the Sinfonia de Requiem furnished proof that this conductor could interpret Britten's music with great precision and inspiration. This is one of the first recordings Previn made as a conductor of the symphonic repertory. Even more convincing evidence of Previn's affinity for Britten was supplied six years later when he recorded the Spring Symphony with the London Symphony Orchestra. As heart of the composition Previn emphasizes Auden's poem 'Out on the lawn I lie in bed'. The recording is richly atmospheric and technically first-class.

LSO/Previn, HMV ASD 3650
St LouisSO/Previn, CBS 61167
I Musici, Phil 6570181
ECO/Britten, Decca SXL 6405

Symphony no. 0 in D minor

A certain atmosphere of mystery hangs over this symphony, which has come down to us in a manuscript of 1869. This must represent a second draft, for the official first symphony (initially no. 2), composed between 1865 and 1866, is much more advanced and personal. The 'nought' was probably written in 1864. It was later withdrawn by Bruckner with the comment, 'Of no value, only an experiment'. Not all conductors have taken Bruckner at his word. The first recording was made, in mono, by the Dutchman Henk Spruit for the American label Concert Hall. The most recent recording is from Barenboim with the Chicago Symphony Orchestra. A good recording with excellent orchestral playing, but not always sufficiently penetrating to bring out the composition's noble seriousness. Haitink's eloquent reading approaches this nobility more closely.

CSO/Barenboim, DG 2531319
CO/Haitink, Phil LY 802724

Symphony No. 1 in C minor

There are two versions of this symphony, both included in the most commonly used Gesamtausgaben, that of Haas and that of Nowak. The first version, called the Linzer Fassung, is preferred by most conductors. This edition provides the work with a youthful recklessness and élan. The 'Wiener Fassung' of a quarter-century later (1890–1891) came into being when in 1887 Hermann Levi raised objections to a large part of Bruckner's symphonic output. Bruckner improved a great number of compositional/ technical errors, but at the cost of freshness and spontaneity. This Wiener Fassung, included in the Nowak edition, is seldom performed. There is only one gramophone recording of this version that by the Radio Symphony Orchestra of Cologne under the direction of Günter Wand. Haitink, Jochum and Karajan use the Linzer Fassung in the Nowak edition. All four are very well recorded. Wand's insights form a natural complement to the others but seem incomplete with a 'Linzer' alternative.

DSO/Jochum, EMI 063-03716
BPO/Karajan, DG 2532062
RSOCologne/Wand, HMV 065-99937
CO/Haitink, Phil 6527142

Symphony no. 2 in C minor

The second symphony also exists in two versions, but the differences are slighter. When Bruckner gave the symphony, on which he had worked assiduously from 1871 to 1877, to his friend, the composer Herbeck, the latter suggested a number of small corrections. The most significant change involved modifications in the orchestration. Bruckner had composed a sublime horn solo for the close of the adagio, but this seemed technically unplayable at the time. Bruckner replaced the horn with a clarinet, doing a certain violence to the unique poetry of the passage. Nowadays this passage presents no problems and there is no reason to avoid the original version. Giulini and Jochum maintain the later cuts and use the clarinet solo. Haitink uses the original version, including the horn solo, though he does omit the repeats in the trio, basing his performance on the Nowak edition. Barenboim, Wand and Karajan opt for the Haas edition, which represents a synthesis of the two versions.

DSO/Jochum, EMI 063-43097
BPO/Karajan, DG 2532063
VPO/Giulini, EMI 063-02633
RSOCologne/Wand, HMV 065-99938
CO/Haitink, Phil LY 802912

Symphony no. 3 in D minor

This is the famous 'Wagner symphony'. Bruckner dedicated it to the composer of Tristan and quoted the opera at several points, leading to a misunderstanding of many years' duration. The first version of the symphony dates from the end of 1872 to 31 December 1873 and remained unpublished before the Nowak edition of 1977. No recording of this version has been made to date. In 1876 Bruckner began a second version. This was again revised in 1877–78. In 1889 Bruckner undertook a third version. The version which Haitink made for Philips was until recently the only one to make extensive use of the 1877–78 vesion; it is an older recording (1964) and since then Haitink has developed remarkably. Karajan and Jochum use the Nowak edition of Bruckner's 1888–96 version, which has recently been the subject of much debate. Karajan's reading is one of great intensity with great dynamic contrasts. Jochum's recording with the Symphony Orchestra of the Bavarian Radio is atmospheric, but his recent recording with the Dresden Orchestra has greater transparency.

DSO/Jochum, EMI 063-03598
BPO/Karajan, DG 2532007
SOBR/Jochum, DG 2535265

Symphony no. 4 in E flat major – Romantic

There are, world-wide, more than twenty-five recordings of this most popular of Bruckner's symphonies, which itself exists in several versions. The first version of 1874 was little known before its publication by Nowak in 1975. In 1878 Bruckner gave the first three movements the form in which we now know them and in 1880 he wrote a new finale. Generally this is how the Romantic is now performed: the first three movements of 1878 with the finale of 1880. Klemperer, Böhm, Haitink and Solti keep to the Nowak edition, which contains a few yet later corrections by the composer. Karajan uses the 1880 version in Haas's edition. Through an excellent choice of tempos Solti keeps the clarity of the musical structure firmly in view, even in the longest sections. Haitink's recording, somewhat older and reissued, possesses an unforced naturalness. Günter Wand holds his own in this company, certainly in regard to his grasp of the symphonic structure.

PhilO/Klemperer, EMI 037-00593
BPO/Karajan, DG 2530674
CSO/Solti, Decca SXDL 7538 (CD410550-2)
CO/Haitink, Phil 6527101 (LY 835385)
RSOCologne/Wand, HMV 065-99738

Symphony no. 5 in B flat major

Bruckner's colossal fifth, so complex for the listener and full of problems for the performers, at least offers the simplicity of a single version. Bruckner worked on it from 1875 to 1878. the four most recent recordings – by Barenboim, Karajan, Wand and Solti – are all of a very high quality. Barenboim, whose recording is perhaps the best engineered (DG 2070113), achieves the radiant spirituality also manifested by Jochum and the Symphony Orchestra of the Bavarian Radio (DG 2707020) and again with the Concertgebouw Orchestra (Phil 6700 028). Karajan, producing a broad and almost sumptuous sound, with one of the best recordings ever given to his excellent orchestra, remains nonetheless earthbound. Günter Wand, with a less prestigious ensemble at his disposal, presents a modern synthesis of these extremes. Solti's electrifying interpretation underlines the score's many contrasts.

BPO/Karajan, DG 2707101
CSO/Solti, Decca D221D2
RSOCologne/Wand, HMV 153-9967071

Symphony no. 6 in A major

Shorter than either of its neighbours, the fifth and the seventh, and less immediately imposing, the sixth symphony was underrated for a long time and less frequently performed. Joseph Keilberth, nearly twenty-five years ago, was the first to regard the symphony highly enough to record it. The most significant interpretational problem is the choice of the two tempos in the first movement, a problem which eludes many conductors. Günter Wand seems to have found the best solution; he gives the triplets a 6/4 count with a slight accelerando. Barenboim, Karajan, despite other positive qualities, and Solti, despite imposing sound and some marvellous moments, do not measure up to Wand in regard to tempo and rhythm. Haitink's realization comes closest, except for a somewhat prosaic adagio.

BPO/Karajan, DG 2531295
NPhilO/Klemperer, HMV SXLP 30448
Dresden/Jochum, EMI 063 03958
CO/Haitink, Phil 6500164
RSOCologne/Wand, HMV 065-99672

Symphony no. 7 in E major

Five years before he made his DG recordings, Karajan recorded Bruckner's Seventh with the same orchestra, the Berlin Philharmonic, for HMV (1973). It was an excellent recording, both technically and artistically. Yet the DG version is richer in sound and evidences Karajan's tighter grasp of the monumental structure of the work. Haitink has also recorded the symphony twice. The 1980 recording (Phil 6769 028) shows Haitink's growth in terms of the depth of interpretation compared to the 1967 reading (Phil 6833 253). Both the opening allegro and the adagio have gained atmospherically. Jochum with the Dresden Staatskapelle presents a more monumental Bruckner than he did with the Berlin Philharmonic in 1967 (DG 2726 054). Haitink, Karajan and Solti couple the symphony with Wagner's Siegfried Idyll.

BPO/Karajan, DG 2707102
CO/Haitink, Phil 6769028
Dresden/Jochum, EMi 157-03776/7
RSOCologne/Wand, HMV 153-99877/8
VPO/Solti, Decca SET 323

Symphony no. 8 in C minor

The first version of the eighth symphony, 1884–87, was not published until 1973 (by Nowak) and never performed before that time. In this version the tripled woodwind section is used only in the finale and the first movement ends with a fortissimo coda. There are no recordings of this version. In 1890 Bruckner changed this coda to a tragically despondent pianissimo concluding section. This second version appeared in a Nowak edition in 1959. After the war Haas published an edition of the eighth, taking the essentials from the 1890 version and restoring several sections from the first. The Haas edition is preferred by most conductors. Jochum uses Nowak's; Haitink, Karajan, Barenboim and Wand use Haas's. Jochum's aggressive approach in the consistent use of Nowak is revelatory. Haitink is the most neutral, while Barenboim exposes a certain volatility in the score, a flickering passion that contrasts with the work's basically sober mood.

CSO/Barenboim, DG 2741007
BPO/Karajan, DG 2707085
Dresden/Jochum, EMI 157-034023
RSOCologne/Wand, HMV 153-99853
CO/Haitink, Phil 6769080

Symphony no. 9 in D minor

Furtwängler's rendering of this unfinished symphony remains an ideal within the realm of Bruckner interpretation. In spite of less satisfactory sound than in the recordings of the seventh and eighth, this is a high point in Furtwängler's discography. For those less interested in historical recordings, there exist a great number of issues of exceptionally high quality. Jochum with the Dresden Staatskapelle provides a gripping version. Karajan's reading is enormously refined, here and there exhibiting a Wagnerian character. Barenboim, in his first great sortie into this composer's music, gives a very moving adagio, but fails to give the scherzo sufficient vehemence. Giulini's reading is relaxed with sound quality of a supernatural character. Günther Wand's excellent performance suffers only from the fact that the first two movements occupy a single side, with unfavourable consequences for the dynamic level. Haitink's reliable insights are also available on Compact Disc.

BPO/Karajan, DG 2530828
CO/Haitink, Phil 6514191 (CD10039-2)
Dresden/Jochum, EMI 063-43197
RSO Cologne/Wand, HMV 065-99804
LPO/Tennstedt, EMI 165-43434/5

Complete symphonies

In addition to Jochum's widely known set with the Berlin Philharmonic, issued in September 1972 (DG 2720047) and re-released in 1976 with the addition of the Te Deum (DG 2740136), we now have this conductor's most recent insights in a new complete recording. This time Jochum sticks more closely to the printed score, indulging his previous penchant for wayward crescendos, accelerandos and ritardandos only very infrequently. He faithfully follows the Nowak edition. Haitink's and Barenboim's choice of editions is very nearly the same. Both include no. 0 in their integral sets, contrary to Jochum and Karajan. Barenboim displays a certain kinship to Jochum in his application of occasional dymanic and rhythmical effects which are not in the score. Haitink, continuing the tradition of van Beinum and the Concertgebouw Orchestra, comes closer to Furtwängler's purity of musical expression. DG's collection of four, seven, eight and nine provides a magnificent document of Furtwängler's art as a symphonic conductor.

CO/Haitink, Phil 67702
CSO/Barenboim, DG 2740253
BPO/Karajan, DG 2740264
Dresden/Jochum, EMI 127-54232/44
VPO-BPO/Furtwängler, DG 2740201

Carter

Symphony of Three Orchestras

Elliott Carter, born in 1908, is one of the most fascinating composers to come out of the United States. His symphony clearly shows his preference for complex atonal polyphony. According to the composer, it is not intended that each and every detail in the constantly shifting sound-patterns should be clearly perceived. The symphony is written for three orchestral groups, each playing four of the composition's twelve movements. In this way the movements are superimposed one on top of another. The emotions aroused by the work are entirely personal and dependent on each individual listener. Pierre Boulez with the New York Philharmonic gives a vivid and fascinating interpretation. The disc also contains another substantial composition by Carter, A Mirror on which to Dwell, on texts by Elisabeth Bishop (which are unfortunately not included).

NYPO/Boulez, CBS 76812

Chausson

Symphony in B flat major, opus 20

Paray's performance of this attractive symphony, recorded with the Detroit Symphony Orchestra in 1960, is still worth acquiring. The sound-spectrum is not ideal, but the interpretation has a marvellous drive which affirms the place of this symphony, beside Franck's, as a pinnacle of French symphonic art in the last half of the nineteenth century. The disc also includes Chabrier's Suite Pastorale. In 1981 Plasson with the Capitole Orchestra made a good alternative recording, vividly played and better engineered. The coupling is Chausson's Soir de Fête, opus 32.

CapitoleO/Plasson, EMI 069-14096
DetroitSO/Paray, Mercury SRI 75029

Cherubini

Sinfonia in D

Cherubini wrote his only symphony after becoming acquainted with Beethoven's music. In 1805 he went to Vienna and his vocal music had a great influence on Beethoven. His instrumental compositions display a cantabile style and this gives the symphony its greatest charm. But Cherubini does not attain the magnitude of his great contemporary. There is a historical recording of this symphony directed by Toscanini, which reflects not only the cantabile element but also the firm formal structure. The recording by Placanik with the Prague Chamber Orchestra, coupled with the overture Medea, is artistically sound but the pressing leaves much to be desired. An interesting issue is the one by Gerard Schwarz and the Los Angeles Chamber Orchestra, which also includes two early works by Rossini, the Sinfonia al conventello and the Grand Ouverture. The ensemble plays excellently and the fine recording captures their full richness of sound.

LAPO/Schwarz, Nonesuch D79023
NBC/Toscanini, RCA 26.41311
PragueCO/Placnik, Supr 11100568

Clementi

4 Symphonies

Muzio Clementi was long considered merely a composer of pedagogical piano pieces whose most important activity lay in the field of music publishing. Forced to live and work in the shadow of the great Viennese Classicists, only recently has he won the attention of musicologists who are now showing interest in his weightier compositions. Thanks to the tireless investigations and reconstructions of Pietro Spada, Clementi's four symphonies have been made ready for performance. The third symphony, nicknamed the Great National Symphony, is noteworthy for the inclusion in the third movement of 'God Save the King', subjected to a variety of variation and contrapuntal techniques. The performances by the Philharmonia Orchestra under the direction of Claudio Scimone are lively and alert, with lovely sound. The pressing and recording are both good.

PHO/Scimone, Erato STU 71174

Copland

Dance Symphony, Short Symphony, Symphony no. 3

The recordings Copland made in 1969 of his Dance Symphony and the second Short Symphony, as well as his 1979 recording of his third symphony, are of special interest as the performances are in the hands of the composer himself and thus give authoritative insight into his intentions. But they are also exceptionally gripping. On both discs he draws magnificent playing from the orchestra, the London Symphony Orchestra in the first two symphonies and the Philharmonia Orchestra in the third symphony. In the Dance Symphony and the Short Symphony, energetic and full of originality, Copland achieves a remorseless drive, in composition as well as in performance, reminiscent of Stravinsky. The performance of the Dance Symphony by the Detroit Symphony Orchestra under the direction of Antal Dorati is at once milder and fruitier. Bernstein and the New York Philharmonic Orchestra give a performance of the third symphony on CBS 61681 which is even more vital than that of the composer himself.

LSO/Copland, CBS 61997
DetroitSO/Dorati, Decca SXDL 17547
PhilO/Copland, CBS 61869

Dvořák

Symphonies nos. 1–5

Aside from issues of his complete symphonies, Dvořák's first five symphonies are available on separate discs in performances by Kertesz and the London Symphony Orchestra. Only the first (Supraphon 1110 2728) and the fifth (Supraphon 110 1333) have received the attention of Vaclav Neumann and the Czech Philharmonic Orchestra. Kertesz's version of the first symphony is preferable to Neumann's, who makes several cuts in this, the longest of Dvořák's symphonies. In terms of dramatic expression, however, there is little to choose between the two versions. Kertesz takes the slow movements, especially in the second symphony, rather quickly, bringing out their freshness and clarity. Neumann brings out the expression of the slow movements beautifully and gives the quicker sections a certain impetuousness.

CzPhO/Neumann, Ariola XR 87574K (from Supraphon, see above)
LSO/Kertesz, Decca JB 110-114

Symphony no. 6 in D major, opus 60

Dvořák's sixth symphony in many respects shows the influence Brahms's second symphony exerted on the Bohemian master. Both the thematic and formal structure of the first movement are permeated by a Brahmsian glow. Kubelik somewhat underplays this Brahmsian element, placing Classical seriousness and proportion in the shadow of Dvořák's own Romantic drive. Vaclav Neumann emphasizes the alternation between the control of form, which Dvořák learned from Brahms, and the impulse towards emotional expression, more closely approaching the composition's individuality. The recording by Andrew Davis is very direct but rather uninspired. Digital mastering provides excellently balanced sound but underscores the lack of dramatic power.

CzPhO/Neumann, Ariola XH 86550K (Supr 11101834)
BP/Kubelik, DG 253425
PhilO/ADavis, CBS 36708

Symphony no. 7 in D minor, opus 70

Kertesz's reading of the symphony in D minor still stands as the ideal model for this work in the gramophone repertory. This was the first symphony which Kertesz and the London Symphony Orchestra recorded in his complete survey of the symphonies. This perhaps explains why his performance of the seventh is somewhat lacking in the spontaneous open-heartedness that characterizes his interpretations of the other symphonies. If greater tension is preferred, a good choice is Colin Davis with the Concertgebouw Orchestra in a performance both warm and exciting. Giulini brings out the composition's lyrical strength in his expressive reading, played with great precision by the London Philharmonic Orchestra.

LSO/Kertesz, Decca JB 116
CO/Davis, Phil 9500132
LPO/Giulini, EMI 063-02830

Symphony no. 8 in G major, opus 88

There are digital recordings of Dvořák's eighth symphony from Maazel and the Viennese (DG 2532034) and from Marriner and the Minnesota Orchestra. Maazel has the advantage of a top-ranking orchestra, whereas the Minnesota Orchestra does not quite reach the level of quality the work requires. But where Maazel reveals virtually nothing new in the score, Marriner on the contrary expresses a personal vision and gives it form most convincingly. The recording by Colin Davis and the Concertgebouw Orchestra is excellent, candid and direct with lively orchestral playing. Kubelik's version shares these expressive qualities but the engineering furnishes a less brilliant sound. Giulini and the Chicago Symphony Orchestra approach the score with a greater calm, rhythmically precise and broadly phrased to suggest a feeling of tranquillity.

BPO/Kubelik, DG 2535397
CSO/Giulini, DG 2531046
Minnesota/Marriner, Phil 6514050
CO/Davis, Phil 9500317
CzPhilo/Neumann, Ariola K87775K (Supr 11101203)

Symphony no. 9 in E minor, opus 95 – From the New World

So strong is the attraction of this symphony that the three existing digital LP recordings were released on Compact Disc within several months of their introduction. Two with the Vienna Philharmonic, conducted by Maazel and Kondrashin, and one from Levine and the Chicago Symphony Orchestra. Levine gives the work an aggressive character which allows too little room for the score's moments of relaxation. Kondrashin's reading is noticeably milder. The LP lacks definition, which makes Kondrashin's performance seem underpowered, but on CD Kondrashin draws from the orchestra an extremely warm sound that adds an extra dimension to the liveliness and realism of the interpretation. This controlled reading forms a strong contrast to Maazel's much more dramatic approach with the same orchestra. Kubelik's recording, tense and alert on the one hand, lyrically supple on the other, is an excellent alternative.

UPO/Kondrashin, Decca SXDL 7510 (CD400 047-2)
BPO/Kubelik, DG 2543513
UPO/Maazel, DG 2532 079 (CD410 032-2)
CSO/Levine, RCA RL 14248 (CDRCD 14552)
NPhO/Muti, CBS 76817

Elgar

Symphony no. 1 A flat major, opus 55
Symphony no. 2 in E flat major, opus 63

Franck

Symphony in D minor

Glazunov

Symphonies nos. 3, 4 and 5

Gounod

Symphony no. 1 in D major
Symphony no. 2 in B flat major

Complete symphonies

The integral recording of the nine symphonies which Deutsche Grammophon issued in 1983 consists of recordings Kubelik made with the Berlin Philharmonic in 1973. Kubelik's approach is extremely Romantic. He does not hesitate to adjust tempos not marked in the score to insist on such and such a point or to heighten contrasts. Much greater faithfulness to the score is shown by Vaclav Neumann with the London Symphony Orchestra. But the Berlin Philharmonic plays sumptuously as usual, though with slightly less sheen under Kubelik, and the choice of that recording is justified. The DG release distributes the nine symphonies over nine records, with a symphony complete on each disc. This does result in two very short sides containing scarcely twelve minutes of music. Decca takes only seven sides, making this recording considerably less expensive.

LSO/Kertesz, Decca D6D7
CzPhO/Neumann, Ariola XR 87118K (Supraphon 111016248)
BPC/Kubelik, DG 2740237

There exist more than ten recordings of each of the two symphonies. James Loughran, drawing splendid sound from the Hallé Orchestra, takes a somewhat reserved view of Elgar's symphonies. for those unfamiliar with Elgar's music, this has the disadvantage of providing an only moderately analytical presentation of the works. (The first movement of the second symphony, for example, contains twelve themes!) But if an analytical view is not wanted and it is wished to simply enjoy Elgar's lovely music a good choice is Vernon Handley and the London Philharmonic (CFP 40331 and CFP 40350), whose performance is much more expressive and emotional than Loughran's. A pupil of Boult, Handley works in the same tradition. And of course the Barbirolli performances are collectors' items.

Hallé/Loughran, ASV ALPHB 201
PhilO/Barbirolli (no. 1), HMV SXLP 30268
LPO/Boult (no. 1), HMV ASD 3330
Hallé/Barbirolli (no. 2), HMV SXLP 30287
LPO/Boult (no. 2), HMV ASD 3266

Kondrashin's recording of Franck's D minor symphony with the Orchestra of the Bavarian Radio is one of the last he made. The orchestra plays accurately and well, but, particularly in the woodwind and brass sections, produces a vigorous timbre that is quite un-French. The symphony sounds much earthier than is usual from a Beecham or a Maazel. It is a live recording, as is also the very French interpretation from Bernstein and the Orchestre National de France. Bernstein extracts every last ounce of emotion from the score. Maazel's reading is equally emotional and finely shaded, moving right along in the slow movement, at no disadvantage to the work's poetic content.

ONF/Bernstein, DG CD 400070-2
SOBR/Kondrashin, Phil 6514119
ClevO/Maazel, Decca SXL 6823
PhO/Muti, EMi 067-43230

Glazunov, with eight symphonies to his credit and one in preparation, was highly regarded as a symphonist in his own country and time, but little of that prestige now remains. With considerable difficulty recordings can be obtained of his third, fourth and fifth symphonies, though of less than optimal quality technically and artistically. The recording of the third symphony by Fedoseyev and the Moscow Radio Symphony Orchestra is the most accessible, the only criticism of the orchestral playing being that to Western ears the brass do sound quite raw and grating. This holds true of the recording by the same orchestra of the fifth symphony directed by Ivanov, and of the USSR State Orchestra in the fourth. All the issues were originally Russian Melodia's and the sound-quality leaves a great deal to be desired.

Moscow RSO/Fedoseyev, HMV/Mel ASD 3993
USSR SO/Rachlin, DG/Mel 2530613
Moscow RSO/Kondrashin, DG/Mel 2530509

Although Plasson's insights into Gounod's symphonies are not negligable, it is a pity that there is no competition at this time. The Capitole Orchestra of Toulouse means, but does not always sound, well and cannot maintain the same high standards as its conductor – who sets this music on a par with Bizet's symphony, giving it an unmistakably Schubertian colouring.

Capitole/Plasson, HMV 069-16334

Haydn

Morzin Symphonies

After the complete recording by Antal Dorati and the Philharmonia Hungarica of all Haydn's symphonies, there seemed still to be room for new interpretations. Derek Solomons offers the earliest of this Classical master's more than 100 symphonies, arranged chronologically in the order established by Robbins Landon. Haydn composed these symphonies while in the service of Count Morzin before going on to Esterház. The two albums contain symphonies nos. 1–5, 10, 11, 15, 18, 32–34 and 37. L'Estro Armonico plays on authentic instruments tuned to a lower pitch. The small forces produce surprising results. Derek Solomons takes all the repeats. This ensemble has also recorded symphonies nos. 35, 38, 39, 49, 58 and 59 for CBS.

L'EsArm/Solomons,
Saga Haydn 1
l'EsArm/Solomons,
Saga Haydn 2
l'EsArm/Solomons,
CBS D3-37861

The Tageszeiten Symphonies
no. 6 Le Matin
no. 7 Le Midi
no. 8 Le Soir

The orchestra which Joseph Haydn had at his disposal when he came to Esterház in 1761 consisted of three violins, a cello and a double-bass. Wind players were recruited as necessary from the military band. Haydn enlarged the orchestra and with the Tageszeiten Symphonies, the first he wrote for his new employer, he attempted to show off the expanded ensemble to good advantage. The Capella Clementina directed by Helmut Müller-Brühl benefit from the use of historic instruments, producing a sound of extreme clarity and striking differences of coloration from the various instrumental groups. Anyone interested in a more traditional orchestral sound could hardly do better than Marriner and the Academy of St Martin-in-the-Fields, with wonderful solo playing by Iona Brown in Le Matin and by Kenneth Sillito and Malcolm Latchem in Le Midi and Le Soir.

ASMF/Marriner, Phil 6514076
Clementina/Müller-Brühl, Schwann VMS 2085

6 Paris Symphonies, nos. 82–87

Haydn wrote the six Paris Symphonies, which include the poplar L'Ours (no. 82 in C), La Poule (no. 83 in G minor) and La Reine (no. 85 in B flat), for the 'Concert de la Loge olympique', with forty violins and ten double-basses: an unusually large orchestra for the time. Stylistic purists therefore have no cause in this instance to criticize Herbert von Karajan's use of the large Berlin Philharmonic Orchestra. Marriner is a fraction livelier with greater attention to clarity, though oddly enough his speeds are slower than the uncommonly quick tempos Karajan chooses. The Marriner box consists of older analogue recordings together with some new digitals and the various discs are available separately. A more authentic performance of L'Ours and La Poule comes from Collegium Aureum whose smaller forces play on period instruments. Dorati's performance of L'Ours is also still available. A safe recommendation for music lovers is Furtwängler's coupling of Haydn's no. 88 with Mozart's no. 39.

ASMF/Marriner, Phil 6725012
BPO/Karajan, DG 2741005
PhilHugarica/Dorati, Decca HDNH 35–40
CA, EMI 065-99762
BPO/Furtwängler, DG 2535825

12 London Symphonies, nos. 93–104

There are at least a dozen integral recordings of the twelve London Symphonies, including the ninth instalment in Dorati's complete series. Particular high points are no. 98 in D major and no. 94, the Surprise. Not everything in Dorati's collection is 100 per cent successful, but the same can be said for the recordings of Haydn's last twelve symphonies by Karajan and the Berlin Philharmonic Orchestra and by Colin Davis and the Concertgebouw Orchestra. Karajan gives Haydn a heavy, almost Romantically rich orchestral sound, whereas Davis keeps his numerous players more within Classical bounds, finding an ideal mid-point between easy-going naturalness and pure virtuosity. He carefully observes all of the repeats Haydn calls for. Many excellent recordings exist of individual symphonies from among the twelve.

BPO/Karajan, DG 2741015
CO/Davis, Phil 6725010
PhilHungarica/Dorati, Decca HDNJ 41–46

Surprise and Drum Roll Symphonies, nos. 94 and 103

Recent digital recordings have been made of Haydn's Drum Roll, coupled with the London Symphony no. 104, and Surprise, coupled with the Symphony no. 93 in D major, by Herbert von Karajan and the Berlin Philharmonic. Both have also been released on Compact Disc. Anyone preferring more traditional interpretations and requiring less technical sophistication can safely go for Beecham's coupling of the Drum Roll with Symphony no. 104 (HMV SXLP 30257) and for either Szell's or Furtwängler's approach are well served by the Collegium Aureum, playing without conductor on old instruments. The ensemble produces a surprisingly rich sound, enhanced by the spacious acoustic of Schloss Kirchheim where the recording was made.

BPO/Karajan, DG CD410 517-2
RPO/Beecham, HMV SXLP 30257
CA, HMV 065-99873
VPO/Furtwängler, EMI 027-00906
ClevO/Szell, CBS 61908

Symphony no. 101 in D major – The Clock
Symphony no. 102 in B flat major

Davis's interpretation with the Concertgebouw Orchestra comes from the complete set of the London Symphonies. The orchestra, considerably larger than any at Haydn's disposition, produces quite a full sound, but with enough freshness and attention to detail to be convincing. Beecham's recordings, made before the appearance of the critical editions by Robbins Landon, contain a number of small textual differences. But both discs offer great purity of conception and fullness of tone. Davis is the more exact in matters of detail, Beecham's phrasing more natural.

CO/Davis, Phil 9500 679
RPO/Beecham, HMV SXLP 30265

Hindemith

Mathis der Maler
Symphony

The outstanding quality of Karajan's performance of this opera-symphony with the Berlin Philharmonic is the richness of the orchestral sound. This may seem a superfluous comment as Karajan always strives for perfection in terms of orchestral sonority, but in Mathis der Maler he achieves this with abundant naturalness, free of mannerisms, producing an overall sound of superb refinement and transparency within which every detail and shade of nuance is firmly in place. His atmospheric and dramatic vision far outstrips the interpretation by the composer himself. Karajan's coupling is Bartók's Music for Strings, Percussion and Celesta. **Hindemith** offers a performance of his own Metmorphoses on themes by Weber, another work of symphonic nature.

BPO/Hindemith, DG 2535820
BPO/Karajan, EMI 063-00547 also: HMV SCLP 30536

Honegger

Complete symphonies

Within the totality of Honegger's symphonic output, which shows him to have developed as a symphonist in a highly individual manner, the second and third occupy a special place. Both are written according to his motivic procedure of small chromatic alterations. In the second the motivic cell is extremely small, containing only three notes. A thoroughgoingly pessimistic mood prevails in both works, written as they were during the Second World War. Karajan's unbeatable performance of nos. 2 and 3, with the Berlin Philharmonic on top form, is unrestrained and highly poetic. All five symphonies have been recorded by Plasson with the Toulouse Capitole Orchestra and Baudo with the Czech Philharmonic. Both give readings of sufficient power to do justice to Honegger's distinctive symphonies.

BPO/Karajan, DG 2543805
CzPhO/Baudo, Supr 1101741/3
Capitole/Plasson, EMI 167 16327/9

Ives

Symphonies 1–3

Although various recordings of Ives's symphonies have appeared – this great pioneer of new American music has received the attention of Stokowski, Bernstein and Ormandy, among others – no truly reliable survey of his total symphonic output exists. Conductors have always felt themselves obliged to alter the scores considerably, often in order to reduce the difficulty of certain passages. Now the first steps towards a pure approach to Ives have been taken by the young American conductor Michael Tilson Thomas who has recorded symphonies nos. 2 and 3 with the Concertgebouw Orchestra. He presents an Ives of great character, more American than ever before. His greatest merit is that he is entirely faithful to Ives's own scores, respecting the composer's intentions and realizing them with unimpeachable integrity. Ormandy's collection is not recommendable for the reasons given, but it is complete.

CO/Tilson Thomas, CBS 37300
CO/Tilson Thomas, CBS 37823
PO/Ormandy, CBS 77424

Liszt

Dante **Symphony**
Faust **Symphony**

Both Liszt's monumental Faust Symphony and the 'Symphonie zu Dantes Divina Commedia', which he dedicated to Wagner, have been charged by many music critics with ungainliness and a lack of structural balance. Nothing could be further from the truth. The works' highly individual structures arise from the composer's attempt to translate the extravagantly Romantic concepts of his day into a personal exposition of feelings centred around a single underlying theme, in the Dante Symphony, for example, the Italian poet's descriptions of Hell and Purgatory (Heaven was omitted at Wagner's suggestion). A conductor must be fully in agreement with this extremely individualistic music in order to bring out its coherence. Lopez-Cobos, in his performance of the Dante **Symphony**, does not quite manage this.

BSO/Bernstein, DG 2707 100
SRomande/Lopez-Cobos, Decca SXDL 75

Lutoslawski Mahler

Symphonies nos. 1 and 2

Wergo's 'Studio-Reihe neuer Musik', recording subsidiary of the music publisher Schott, has built up a considerable repertory of contemporary music from various countries, with an emphasis on Germany and Eastern Europe. The series includes a disc containing Lutoslawski's first and second symphonies which gives an interesting picture of the composer's development, as the first dates from 1941–47 when Lutoslawski was writing in the manner of Szymanowski, and the second from 1966–67 after he had ventured for a time into twelve-tone writing, then returned to more traditional techniques but with the addition of aleatory elements. The performances by the Polish Radio Symphony Orchestra under the direction of Jan Krenz and the Sud West Funk under the direction of Ernest Bour are excellent. A more comprehensive view of Lutoslawski's compositional ventures is provided by the 6-record set which includes in addition to the two symphonies such other important orchestral works as Mi-Parti and the Symphonic Variations.

Krenz/Bour, Wergo
WER 6044
RSOPoland/Jablonski,
EMI 165-03231/6

Complete Symphonies

There currently exist five integral recordings of Mahler's complete symphonies, by Abravanel, Bernstein, Haitink, Kubelik and Solti. None of these includes the tenth symphony in the performing version by Deryck Cooke and Solti does not give even the adagio which Mahler did himself complete. Five more integral recordings are underway, by Abbado, Levine, Mehta, Tennstedt and Neumann. The performances by Abravanel and the Utah Symphony, not widely known in Europe, are somewhat uneven (seven and eight are very fine) but attractive by reason of their moderate price. The most homogeneous and consistently commendable realization is Haitink's with the Concertgebouw Orchestra. Aside from good readings of the first and fourth symphonies, Kubelik's interpretations seem pallid and somewhat lax.

Utah/Abravanel,
Musidisc CRC 18
NYPO en LSO/
Bernstein, CBS GM 15
CO/Haitink, Phil 6768
021
SOBR/Kubelik, DG
2720 090

Symphony no. 1 in D major – Titan

The first recording of Mahler's Titan symphony on Compact Disc, with Claudio Abbado and the Chicago Symphony Orchestra, is not likely to displace the front-runners among the thirty-five recordings already available. Technically it is the best version imaginable, with an extremely wide dynamic spectrum and beautifully detailed transparency. The orchestra play marvellously and Abbado gives a radiant performance, which nonetheless does not penetrate beyond the surface of the musical content. Haitink with the Concertgebouw Orchestra is much to be preferred in either his older or his more recent recording (included in the complete set), giving a thoroughly considered reading without spectacular showiness and thus reaching to the heart of Mahler's idiom. Tennstedt is more reserved, keeping strictly to the indications in the score at the cost of a loss of freedom and naturalness in respect to phrasing. A good alternative to the Abbado, also still available on LP (DG 2532020), is the no less spectacular version by Levine.

CSO/Abbado, DG
CD400033-2
CO/Haitink, Phil
6500342
LPO/Tennstedt, EMI
063-0398
LSO/Levine, RCA ARL
10894
ColSO/Walter, CBS
60128

Symphony no. 2 – Resurrection

The irreplaceable historical versions by Bruno Walter (CBS 77271) and Klemperer are rivalled by Bernard Haitink's definitive reading. Elly Ameling, Aafje Heynis and the Concertgebouw Orchestra are all on top form. Abbado's very controlled interpretation remains rather earthbound, missing an inner glow despite a well-structured, very well-recorded performance. Tennstedt presents a determined Mahler, allowing insufficient room for the nervous tension contained in the work. Solti provides many spectacular moments, especially in the breathtaking fire of the brass in the final movement, but provides ample contrast with a lightly played and elegant andante and scherzo. This recording is also available on Compact Disc.

CSO/Solti, Decca D
229 D 2
CO/Klemperer, EMI
163 00570/71
CO/Haitink, Phil
677008
CSO/Abbado, DG
2707094
LPO/Tennstedt, EMI
157-43141/42

Symphony no. 3 in D minor

This recording, taken from the complete set, is one of Bernard Haitink's finest. His vision is truly pantheistic, delineating with razor-sharp precision the complexly interwoven portrayal of all the spirits, alive and dead, peopling the earth. The approach is perhaps somewhat cerebral but allows for sufficient expression. Forrester's solo work is excellent. Tennstedt's approach is similar, his slower tempos giving the wildness of certain sections greater freedom. The fifth movement's 'Bimm-Bamm' is sung with great freshness by the Southend Boys' Chorus. Abbado's performance, like many of his Mahler interpretations, is spectacular but never overdone. James Levine, who received an award for his recording, brings out the score's drama with sound of particular clarity.

VPO/Abbado, DG
2741010
CO/Haitink, Phil
6747435
CSO/Levine, RCA RLO
1757
CSO/Levine, EMI
15703835/6

Symphony no. 4 in G major

The number of worthwhile recordings from among the many versions of Mahler's fourth symphony is so large a short list of recommendations is bound to be arbitrary. Bruno Walter's unparalleled liveliness contrasts with Szell's extreme attention to detail (both on CBS). Kubelik gives a sensitive, stylish interpretation. Both Karajan and Klemperer seem unable to come to terms with the 'smallness' of this symphony – without trombones or tubas – producing a sound of unwarranted heaviness. Haitink and Abbado on the other hand are extremely successful in realizing a chamber music atmosphere in which the symphony's melancholy, naive detachment and touches of sarcasm are all superbly captured. In 1983 Tennstedt added his open, transparent, unmannered reading to the catalogue. His performance has the unsentimental directness of a fairy tale, with tempos that seem just right and an agreeable concern for detail. The London Philharmonic Orchestra produces a sound at once mild and clear.

VPO/Abbado, DG 2530966
BPO/Karajan, DG 2531205
ClevO/Szell, CBS 60124
LPO/Tennstedt, HMV ASD 4344

Symphony no. 5 in C sharp minor

Nearly half of the some twenty-five recordings of this symphony were made after 1974, this recent popularity no doubt owing to Visconti's film Death in Venice with its wholesale use of the adagietto. Haitink again provides an excellent interpretation, one of the best in his integral recording of all Mahler's symphonies, though he shows less similarity to Bruno Walter than in the other most successful recordings in this series. The symphony is coupled with the opening adagio from the unfinished tenth symphony. Tennstedt, with the same coupling, gives excellent performances which combine an intelligent approach with radiant expression. Levine furnishes an irresistibly involving interpretation of the Trauermarsch and the rondo-finale but his extremely slow reading of the adagietto is disappointing. Claudio Abbado's good but not especially spontaneous performance is coupled with the Rückert Songs.

CSO/Abbado, DG 2707 128
SOBR/Kubelik, DG 2543535
CO/Haitink, Phil 6700048
EMI 15703440/41
PhilO/Levine, RCA RLD 2905

Symphony no. 6 in A minor

Structurally the most classical of Mahler's symphonies, this is also the most tragic in terms of content; and finding an appropriate balance between these two elements poses the work's greatest interpretational problem. Karajan produces an excellent sense of proportion by surrounding the biting melancholy of the andante with a finely nuanced account of the alternating light and shade of the outer movements. Haitink achieves similar results, combining supreme control of the score with an eloquent expression of Mahler's darkest thoughts. Whereas Haitink remains strictly faithful to the score, Kubelik allows himself a great deal of freedom in matters of tempo and dynamics, though always with impressive consequences. Abbado, quite beautifully stressing the work's melodious aspects, gives a highly controlled performance, diametrically opposed to Levine's brilliantly cogent reading.

CSO/Abbado, DG 2707117
BPO/Karajan, DG 2707106
CO/Haitink, Phil 67100034
SOBR/Kubelik, DG 2726065
LSO/Levine, RCA RLO 3213

Symphony no. 7 in E minor

With this least known and most mysterious of Mahler's symphonies, Solti and in particular Bernstein give the best performances in their integral sets. Solti is especially imaginative in the middle movements, lively in the scherzo and seductively magical in the Night Music. Haitink's reading is precise and assured but does not achieve the geniality of his best Mahler performances. In the quick movements Tennstedt is the most convincing, and the same could almost be said for Kubelik's moderately priced recording, which somewhat misses the atmosphere of the Night Music, but presents the outer movements with great point and elasticity.

SOBR/Kubelik, DG 2726066
CO/Haitink, Phil 6700036
LPO/Tennstedt, EMI 157-43008/9
CSO/Solti, Decca 390124
NYPO/Bernstein, CBS 77284

Symphony no. 8 in E flat major – Symphony of a Thousand

Three first-class recordings exist of Mahler's most colossal symphony, by Solti, Ozawa and Gielen. The last gives a totally unexpected picture of the work by reason of a choice of extremely fast tempos, cutting eight minutes off the work in comparison to the quickest of the other versions and infusing the reading with enormous tension. Unfortunately the team of soloists is weakened by the contribution of tenor Mallory Walker. The quality of the recording is slightly less good than that of Solti's and noticeably inferior to Ozawa's, whose digital issue is also available on Compact Disc (Philips CD410607-2). The Boston Symphony and Chorus perform excellently in a mild warm acoustic and Ozawa's soloists are each of them superb. Kubelik's recording, which forms a reasonable alternative, also offers the adagio of the tenth symphony.

CSO/Solti, Decca SET 534/5
SOBR/Kubelik, DG 2726053
LSO/Bernstein, CBS 77234
BSO/Ozawa, Phil 6769069
Frankfurt/Gielen, CBS 79238

Martinů

Mendelssohn

Symphony no. 9 in D major

In the category of historical recordings two versions by Bruno Walter exist, made at a distance of twenty years and both admirable for all their many differences. In 1936, under the threat of fascism, Walter gave a fiery dramatic performance (EMI 151 53824/25) and later, with the Columbia Orchestra, a ripely meditative interpretation (CBS E 4). Present-day recordings of the ninth symphony are dominated by Giulini's, a reading of matchless beauty, and Karajan's, giving one of the finest performances of his recording career, crisply humourous in the middle movements, rich and charged with expressivity in the outer ones. Tennstedt's approach is similar, though it provides a lessening of tension: Kubelik is somewhat reserved, nevertheless achieving in the finale a splendid sense of serenity. By comparison with any of these, Levine's reading seems undernourished. Solti's version is also available on Compact Disc (CD410012).

BPO/Karajan, DG
2707125
CSO/Giulini, DG
2707097
LPO/Tennstedt, EMI
153-0617/8
PO/Levine, RCA RLO
3461
CSO/Solti, Decca D
274D2

Symphony no. 10 in F sharp major

Anyone wishing to hear only the adagio of the tenth symphony, the only movement completed by Mahler, will as a rule find it coupled with the fifth symphony. Recent recordings have been made by Simon Rattle and James Levine of the entire work in the performing version prepared by the musicologist Deryck Cooke. Ormandy's older recording of this version has become outdated by Cooke's discovery of further documentation in the meantime. Both Rattle and Levine offer with their lively interpretations a passionate argument for the viability of his completed version. Rattle penetrates further into the score's essentials; Levine brings the Philadelphia Orchestra to a greater level of refinement.

BournS/Rattle, EMI
157-07347/48
PO/Levine, RCA RL
03726
PO/Ormandy, CBS
61447

Symphonies nos. 1–6

Martinů's symphonies occupy a firm place in the repertory of the Czech Philharmonic Orchestra and its conductor Vaclav Neumann. This can be clearly heard in the 4-disc set of the six symphonies (where space was left over for the attractive Inventions of 1934) as orchestra and conductor show themselves to be thoroughly familiar with the musical idiom of their countryman. The orchestra play excellently, though this does not always come through well in a recording that suffers from a lack of definition. Neumann is extremely attentive to the melodic contours but could do more in matters of colour and expression. The discs making up the set are also available individually.

CzechPO/Neumann,
Supr 14103071/74

Early symphonies

At the age of twelve Felix Mendelssohn wrote a dozen small-scale symphonies for strings. Although earlier influences are unmistakable, these early works possess a number of individual features. The excellent strings of the Polish Chamber Orchestra under the direction of Jerzy Maksymiuk give a highly polished view of nos. 2, 3, 5 and 6, perfectly disciplined but somewhat lacking in excitement. Greater inspiration informs performances of the sixth, seventh and tenth symphonies by members of Ensemble 13 Baden-Baden, who more commonly specialize in twentieth-century music.

PolishCO/Maksymiuk,
EMI 067-43034
Ens 13/Reichert, EMI
065-99823

Symphony no. 1 in C minor, opus 11 Symphony no. 2 in B flat major, opus 52 – Lobgesang

Mendelssohn's second symphony, the Lobgesang for soloists, chorus and orchestra, does not belong to the most frequently recorded of this composer's works. In addition to Sawallisch and Karajan, the Italian Riccardo Chailly reproduces the inner voices with very exact definition, showing great care to bring out the warmth of the cantabile lines in sound of uncommon transparency. The young conductor's performance eclipses even those of his illustrious precedessors. The coupling of the Scottish symphony shows the same attentiveness to detail within the spaciousness of the larger lines. The advantage of the recordings by Sawallisch and Karajan is that they both offer the first symphony coupled with the second, but Sawallisch's interpretation is insufficiently inspired to bring to life the weaker pages in Mendelssohn's scores. Haitink, whose coupling is the Italian symphony, gives honest forthright readings, somewhat lacking in colour.

NewPhil/Sawallisch,
Phil 6768030
LPO/Haitink, Phil 9500
708
LSO/Chailly, Phil
6769042
BPO/Karajan, DG
2721107

Messiaen

Symphony no. 3 in A minor, opus 56 – Scottish

Chailly's inviting warmth of sound and aesthetic refinement are qualities which are also present in the versions by Haitink and Muti. Both couple the symphony with the overture Calm Sea and Prosperous Voyage. Muti, contrary to Haitink, gives the exposition repeat, which argues for his structural insight. Yet Haitink's performance is more profoundly symphonic in atmosphere. Bernstein, whose coupling is the Hebrides overture, provides a sympathetic view of the work, though the tempos in the slower sections are a bit too broad to be totally convincing, and the frequent mannerisms rob some of Mendelssohn's freshness. Marriner, whose disc contains both the Scottish and the Italian, greatly benefits from the lighter timbre produced by his chamber-sized orchestra. He reveals, in Schumann's words, 'a Mozart of the nineteenth century'. His choice of tempo for the adagio is nonetheless on the slow side.

CO/Haitink, Phil 9500535
ASMF/Marriner, ARGO ZRG 926
NPO/Muti, EMI 063 02731
IPO/Bernstein, DG 2531256
LSO/Chailly, Phil 6769042

Symphony no. 4 in A major, opus 90 – Italian

Haitink's careful and rich-sounding version of the Italian symphony needs more liveliness and sparkle to be fully convincing. Bernstein provides this spark in a recording made during a public performance. The over-expressiveness which marred his reading of the Scottish here presents no problem and with his choice of rapid tempos he achieves remarkable spontaneity. Like Bernstein, Leppard couples the Italian with the fifth symphony. The rhythmic vitality and clean timbre of his chamber forces afford an agreeable lightness of touch which, combined with Leppard's close attention to detail, make for a performance of great stylishness and charm. Tennstedt's reading, coupled with Schumann's fourth symphony, is also lively and stylish, though he lacks flair when compared to Bernstein or Leppard.

IPO/Bernstein, DG 2531097
ECO/Leppard, Erato STLL 71264
BPO/Tennstedt, EMI 067-03904

Symphony no. 5 in D minor, opus 107 – Reformation

Bernstein's and Leppard's qualities have been sufficiently discussed in treating the fourth symphony, the Italian, while Haitink's interpretation of the Reformation symphony displays the same advantages of rich sonorousness and symphonic grandeur, yet wanting in fire and presenting a fifth symphony of undue heaviness. Muti hovers just this side of over-expressiveness, producing a Mendelssohn interpretation of great liveliness and authenticity. The vivace of the second movement's allegro vivace might perhaps have been taken a shade more literally, but the music tolerates Muti's more danceable tempo well. The reverse side of the disc contains a finely detailed version of Schumann's first symphony.

LPO/Haitink, Phil 9500713
PO/Muti, EMI 063-03640

Complete symphonies

Those wishing to include Mendelssohn's complete symphonies in their collection are advised to choose from among the various recordings which are separately available. Two integral sets do exist but neither is entirely satisfactory. Sawallisch's recordings of the symphonies, spread over two double albums and dating from the late 1960s, are too inflexible and linear to distil adequate charm. They however have the attraction of being moderately priced. Karajan, on the other hand, offers such highly charged interpretations, particularly of the first three symphonies, that the necessary lightness of touch is missing.

BPO/Karajan, DG 2740128
NewPhil/Sawallisch, Phil 6768030
NewPhil/Sawallisch, Phil 6768031

Turangalîla symphony

The title of this symphony is a Sanskrit word composed of 'Turanga', meaning Time and rhythmic movement, and 'Lîla', meaning Divine Play and also Love. Together they suggest the powers that govern life, creation and dissolution, birth and death. The symphony is the aural realization of Messiaen's vision of the Tristan and Isolde legend, taking love as the fundamental element of human existence, inspiring both life and death. The presence of love is expressed most frequently by the Ondes Martenot, an electronic instrument of highly individual character, capable of producing a large range of sounds, from the quietest, almost flute-like pianissimo to the most piercing fortissimo. Previn gives an extremely vivid interpretation of the work, full of colour and mystery. The richly varied orchestral palette is marvellously reproduced by a superb recording. Previn is at his most convincing in the expansive energetic sections.

LSO/Previn, EMI 165-02974/5

Mozart

Symphonies 1-21

The numbering is that of the old collected edition of Breitkopf & Härtel, and conforms to that of Köchel's catalogue. These are the symphonies between K 16 and K 135, written in the years 1764-72. Böhm's recording of the first 24 which he made in 1972 is serious and at times a little austere. Marriner, who also recorded the so-called numbers after 41 (discovered after the appearance of Breitkopf's catalogue but belonging to Mozart's earlier works) gives stylish, lively interpretations in which the polished sound of the chamber orchestra is captivating. Hogwood and the Academy of Ancient Music have produced a number of albums containg these symphonies together with some written later in Salzburg. They are all excellent recordings, and the 'authentic' sound of the Academy is most persuasive.

ASMF/Marriner,
Phil 6747374
BPO/Böhm,
DG 2740109
AAM/Hogwood
Oiseau D 167 D 3
AAM/Hogwood
Oiseau D 168 D 3
AAM/Hogwood
Oiseau D 169 D 3

Symphony no. 31 in D, K 297 – Paris

Some records from the complete recording of Mozart's symphonies by the Academy of Ancient Music conducted by Hogwood and Schröder are available separately, such as the Paris together with the symphony no. 40 in a energic and authentic interpretation. Playing in an authentic style but not using authentic instruments, the Concertgebouw Orchestra conducted by Harnoncourt gives a refreshing and direct performance. Although a large symphony orchestra the Concertgebouw plays very lightly. In colour it is a match with the RIAS Sinfonietta. Kuhn gives a characterful and Italianate performance. Coupled with this work Kuhn gives no. 21, and Harnoncourt no. 33.

CO/Harnoncourt,
Tel. AZ 6.42817
RIAS/Kuhn,
EMI 067-99884

Symphony no. 35 in D, K 385 – Haffner
Symphony no. 36 in C, K 425 – Linz

Both Karajan and Böhm couple the Haffner symphony with the symphony no. 32 in G major. the others couple as above. Both Böhm's and Karajan's accounts are reliable, if not what we now think of as properly Mozartean. The Collegium Aureum, on authentic instruments and conducted by Franz-Josef Maier, choose on the whole slower tempos to allow the music to sing. The result is at times a little monotonous. the Czech Philharmonic, with marvellously disciplined playing and a shimmering timbre, give a festive account of the Haffner and a sharply pointed Linz. A good alternative is Harnoncourt with the Concertgebouw Orchestra on Telefunken AZ 6 42703.

BPO/Böhm,
DG 2535358
BPO/Karajan,
DG 2531136
Czech PO/Koster,
Supr 11102608
AAM/Hogwood,
Oiseau DSLO 6594212
CA/Maier,
EMI 065 99903

Symphonies 22-41

Mozart wrote these symphonies after 1773 in Salzburg, Paris, Linz and Vienna.
They are listed as KV 162 – 551. To these belong also the Paris, Linz, Haffner, Prague nd Jupiter. Marriner's interpretation has great style, and the orchestral playing is smooth and elegant. The numbers 35 and 40 are recorded with original instruments. In the sphere of authentic performance and the use of the old instruments, Hogwood's Academy stands on a higher plane. Not only does Hogwood include well-known symphonies, but also compositions constructed like symphonies and adapted from such compositions as the overture Il re Pastore, the Haffner Serenade and the Post-horn Serenade. The use of a harpsichord as a basso-continuo is finely handled. Musicologist Neal Zaslaw supervised the project and produced the excellent documentation that accompanies each record.

BPO/Böhm,
DG 2740110
ASMF/Marriner,
Phil 6769043
AAM/Hogwood,
Oiseau D 170 D 3
AAM/Hogwood,
Oiseau D 171 D
AAM/Hogwood,
Oiseau D 172 D4

Symphony no. 40 in G minor, K 550

The 'Great' G minor symphony retains its place as the most popular of the composer's works in this form. Accordingly the piece has been well served in the gramophone catalogues, and choice is not easy. Benjamin Britten was a musician with an especial affinity for Mozart's music, and a recording he made with the English Chamber Orchestra is to be highly recommended. Karajan has also made some outstanding versions of this great work. Perhaps the finest of these, coupled with no. 39, is with the Berlin Philharmonic on HMV. The rhythm has an exquisite poise throughout, and the orchestra's marvellous playing is no less marvellously recorded. Sir Colin Davis, in a similar coupling, has also produced an account of high quality with the London Symphony Orchestra that is light, fresh and vigorous.

ECO/Britten,
Decca JB 107
BP/Karajan,
HMV SXLP 30527
LSO/Davis,
Phil Fest 6570 143

Nielsen

Prokofiev

Rachmaninov

Symphony no. 41, K 551 – Jupiter

Levine and the Chicago orchestra give a clean, exemplary performance, with sensitive shading and intelligent tempi. But he makes it into something of a large scale work, which somewhat reduces the classical elegance. His reading of the symphony no. 40 in G minor takes a similar view.
The way Telefunken cut their records means that Harnoncourt's version takes up two sides. Paradoxically, Harnoncourt is often much more Romantic than other less 'authentic' conductors, and infuses his performance with an unexpected tenderness. Maier, who directs the Collegium Aureum from the harpsichord, gives a strong and rhythmically lively account. Colin Davis's interpretation with the Dresden State Orchestra is available on CD. The recording quality is of a high standard throughout.

CSO/Levine, RCA RCD 14413
CO/Harnoncourt, TEL.AZ6.42846
CA/Maier, EMI 065 99673
DSO/Davis, Phil CD 410046-2

Symphonies nos. 1–16

Despite unorthodox harmonies that involve more daring modulations than any attempted by Mahler, Sibelius or even Shostakovich, Nielsen's transitional passages retain a clear logic, which brings his symphonies within the scope of the average music-lover reared on a more classical tradition.
No conductor knows Nielsen's scores better than Ole Schmidt, whose meticulous attention to detail enables the players to do full justice to the composer's intentions without sacrificing any of the music's essential vitality. Previn's interpretation of the first symphony is altogether more relaxed. It is coupled with the Prelude to Act II of Saul & David. Karajan, on the other hand, gives a very sensitive account of Nielsen's best-known symphony, no. 4 – the Inextinguishable; but it must be admitted that the somewhat woolly string section tends to obscure the finer points of the woodwind playing.

LSO/Schmidt, Unicorn KPM 7001/7006
LSO/Previn, RCA GL 42872
BPO/Karajan, DG 2532 029

Symphony no. 1, opus 25 – Classical

On a recital-disc with, amongst others, **Mozart's** Eine Kleine Nachtmusik and **Grieg's** Holberg Suite, **Herbert von Karajan** directs Prokofiev's Classical **Symphony. This is not brilliant programming, but more intended to show off Karajan's extremely polished craftsmanship. Previn gives this first symphony, and the seventh, much more vitality and warmth. The digital version from Solti released in Sept. 1983, but still on ordinary LP, with the suite from the ballet** Romeo and Juliet **as an addition is also available on CD. Karajans' collective record is also recorded on CD.**

BPO/Karajan, DG 2532031
LSO/Previn, EMI 065-03342
CSO/Solti, Decca SXDL 7588

Symphony no. 5 in B flat major, opus 100

Bernstein obviously feels very much at home with this symphony, demonstrating his mastery of music written on such a monumental scale. His dramatic account lends a strong tension to the music. Karajan remains meticulously faithful to the score, and his performance seems perhaps a little stilted. Both Previn and Maazel are excellent alternatives. Bernstein is also available on CD.

BP/Karajan, DG 139040
IPO/Bernstein, CBS 35877
IPO/Bernstein, CBS CD 35877
LSO/Previn, HMV SCLP 30315
ClevO/Maazel, Decca SXL 6875

Complete symphonies

Previn's recordings date from respectively 1973, 1975 and 1977, but technically they are so exemplary that they meet with the most demanding requirements, especially as great extra technical care has been taken with the new pressing. Previn's interpretation of Rachmaninov is highly idiomatic. The music is given warm expression, the orchestral sound an almost melancholic sonority. The Intermezzo and the dance from Aleko form a pleasant addition to the recordings, issued on three discs.
Edo de Waart's interpretation contains less melancholy, but his recordings have a well-proportioned symphonic depth. The Rotterdam Philharmonic Orchestra plays excellently, and in turn is recorded well by Philips.

ROTPO/de Waart, Phil 6768148
LSO/Previn, EMI 153 53893/5

Rimsky-Korsakov

Saint-Saëns

Symphony no. 1 in D minor, opus 13

Ormandy's recording of Rachmaninov's first symphony was the first stereo recording of this work and it still remains one of the strongest renderings (CBS 61991). There is also a version by Ashkenazy, that compares well with his account of Rachmaninov's second symphony. Edo de Waart's performance with the Rotterdam Orchestra is clear and accurate, but rather pale in character. The Suisse Romande Orchestra is not able to give enough weight to Weller's demands, who strives for a rich and powerful interpretation.
With a little bit of effort it should be possible to obtain Previn's recording, which is now part of an excellent complete edition (EMI 06302632).

PhilO/Ormandy, CBS 61991
OSR/Weller, Decca JB91
CO/Ashkenazy, Decca SXDL 7603
RPO/de Waart, Phil 9500 445

Symphony no. 2 in E minor, opus 27

Artistically, as well as technologically, Ashkenazy's CD recording now overshadows all rival versions of the work. This artist's instinctive feeling for the spirit of his compatriot was first demonstrated during Ashkenzay's piano-playing career, and is in no way diminished in his conducting. Yet he attempts nothing new; the symphony is allowed to speak for itself, its passages of greatness affirming their stature beside the composer's lapses into the pedestrian. Also available are a lively and somewhat florid account by Previn; and for those who prefer an understated performance of the symphony, there remain Weller's version and Maazel's recent recording with the Berlin Philharmonic.

LPO/Weller, Decca JB 92
CO/Ashkenazy, Decca SXDL 6554
LSO/Previn, EMI 063-02398

Symphony no. 3 in A minor, opus 44

Maazel clearly shows in this late, highly Romantic work of Rachmaninov what the symphonic attractions are of this late Russian master. He analyses the musical components, and reassembles them with a clear and convincing intelligence. This results in a performance that is not too sentimental and alertly played by the Berlin Philharmonic. Ashkenazy persuades the musicians of the Concertgebouw to respond to his warm, Russian approach. He is more provocative than Previn or Maazel, more extreme in changes of tempo and phrasing. He treats the fast parts quicker than his colleagues; the slow parts receive a broader approach, with shattering fermata.
Weller's recording is well done, with ample attention to atmosphere, but somewhat at the cost of detail.

BPO/Maazel, DG 2532065
LPO/Weller, Decca JB 93
LSO/Previn, EMi 063 02861
CO/Ashkenazy, Decca SXDL 7531

Symphonies 1–3

Rimsky-Korsakov's symphonic production is of uneven quality; the first and third symphonies scarcely bear comparison with the work of his contemporaries. Unfortunately his worthwhile second symphony has also suffered as a result and is rarely performed. Antar, the title of his symphony no. 2, opus 9, is the evocative musical portrayal of a fairy tale. It tells of the Arabian poet, Antar, who in a dream comes to the rescue of a gazelle; the gazelle is eventually revealed to be the good fairy Gulnazar who, out of gratitude, grants Antar's fondest wish. This ornate second symphony is given a performance of great alertness and beauty of sound by the Rotterdam Philharmonic Orchestra under the direction of David Zinman. Those hearing this work and desiring further acquaintance with Rimsky-Korsakov's symphonic art may investigate the 3-disc box from the Moscow Radio Orchestra and the USSR Symphony Orchestra, containing the three symphonies, Capriccio Espagnol, Sadko, Fantasia opus 6 **and** Sinfonietta opus 31.

RSOMoscow/USSRSO, HMV SLS 5150
RotPO/Zinman, Phil 9500 971

Symphony no. 3 in C minor, opus 78

The technical problem in this massive 'organ symphony' is to keep a good balance between organ and orchestra in surroundings which are optimal for both. Barenboim solved this, in 1976, by letting orchestra and organ play at different places: the orchestra in Chicago and the organ in the cathedral at Chartres. Karajan too adopted this principle. First Pierre Cochereau played the organ part in the Notre Dame in Paris. Later this was mixed with the orchestra's recording in Berlin. But Barenboim's sleight of hand succeeds better, with a clearer orchestral sound. In the duller-sounding Berlin orchestra, the strings have more poignancy than the wind instruments. Karajan takes the middle movement very slowly. (His version also appears on CD: DG CD400063-2.)

ORTF/Martinon, EMI 065-14070
CSO/Barenboim, DG 2530619
BPO/Karajan, DG 2532045
MontrealSO/Dutoit, Decca SXDL 7590
NYPO/Bernstein, CBS 76653

Salieri

Schubert

Symphonies

Antonio Salieri, variously suspected at times of having murdered Gluck, Mozart and Cimarosa, was a more than competent symphonist, as witness this anthology played by the London Symphony Orchestra under Zoltan Pesko. Three symphonic works are being presented: Sinfonia Veneziana 'La Scuola de Gelosi', Sinfonia 'Il Giorno Onomastico' and Variazioni sull aria 'La Follia di Spagna'. But it is important to note that all three works have been arranged by Pietro Spada. Spada didn't limit himself simply to getting the score ready for performance, but added resounding effects by multiplying brass and strings to a substantial degree. Richard Bonynge and the English Chamber Orchestra, on the other hand, give a clear and sweet account of some orchestral lollipops by this composer who was destined for obscurity by the overpowering genius of his youthful rival, Wolfgang Mozart.

LSO/Pesko, CBS 74088
ECO/Bonynge, Decca SA 24

Complete symphonies

In his account of all nine symphonies Sawallisch shows himself to be an extremely faithful conductor. Herein lies his strength but also his weakness. His reliable readings possess an ongoing neutrality which robs the earlier symphonies of their unhampered freshness and reduces the weightiness of the later ones. Where Sawallisch is impressive is in his attention to the smallest details; the pianissimo introductions could hardly be bettered. The Dresden State Orchestra play with great accuacy and control, but the Berlin Philharmonic is at once sharper and more refined. The big sound Karajan produces is inappropriate to the early symphonies but ideal for the later works. The Unfinished is the high point of Karajan's complete recording. In addition to the symphonies, both sets contain fill-ups, Karajan's, the theatre music D 797, Sawallisch's, the two Italian overtures.

BPO/Karajan, HMV 157 03285/89
BPO/Böhm, DG 2740127
DSO/Sawallisch, Phil 6747491

Symphony no. 3 in D major, D 200

For this early symphony Marriner, with his Academy of St Martin-in-the-Fields, has at his disposal an extremely appropriate ensemble. The group's perfect execution however lacks the necessary Viennese charm to bring out the music's warm naiveté. Marriner himself takes a superficial view, his fluent performance wanting detail. With equal precision and a much larger band of musicians, Karajan achieves far greater refinement. Carlos Kleiber is very imaginative, taking the slow movement unusually quickly to refreshing effect. Marriner's and Karajan's coupling is the fifth symphony; Kleiber's, the eighth.

VPO/Kleiber, DG 2531124
ASMF/Marriner, Phil 6514149
BPO/Karajan, EMI 065 03814

Symphony no. 4 in C minor, D 417 Tragic

Böhm's reliable performance of Schubert's fourth symphony holds no surprises. The opening allegro breathes an autumnal atmosphere with little of the forceful élan one would expect from a nineteen-year-old composer. Giulini's choice of tempo in the andante prevents its broadly melodic, inward-looking quality from singing out fully and provides insufficient contrast with the opening allegro, which is taken too slowly. Even the following scherzo is given a static profile. Böhm couples the Tragic with the third symphony; Giulini, with the eighth. Armin Jordan's fine recording also has the latter coupling. Maazel's disc contains the fourth and the eighth symphonies.

BPO/Böhm, DG 2530526
LSO/Giulini, DG 2531147
BPO/Maazel, DG 2535128
BaselSO/Jordan, Erato ECD 88008

Symphony no. 5 in B flat major, D 485

Böhm's three recordings of this symphony are still available, two with the Vienna Philharmonic, one with the Berlin forces. The latter received a Grand Prix du Disque in its day, but the performances with the Viennese have greater point and precision. All three share an engaging sense of energetic warmth. The discs listed below include the eighth symphony on the reverse side, the third couples Schumann's fourth symphony (DG 2531279). Marriner's approach to Schubert has been described in discussing the third symphony, with which the fifth is coupled. Contrary to most of his colleagues. he does take all the repeats, though the effect is more dutiful than convincing. The recording is also available on Compact Disc (Philips CD410045-2). The Berlin Philharmonic under Karajan play outstandingly.

ASMF/Marriner, Phil 6514149
CO/Haitink, Phil 9500099
BPO/Böhm, DG 139162
VPO/Böhm, DG 2531373
PO/Klemperer, EMI 037-00579

Schumann

Symphony no. 6 in C major, D 589

The discography of Schubert's sixth symphony is comparatively small. Böhm's coupling of the Rosamunde music is extremely attractive and his music-making has great rhythmic liveliness, although one could wish for a lighter touch from the Berlin Philharmonic. Marriner's recent digital recording is excellent and the Academy play with ideal alertness and exactitude, yet they seem incapable of producing a truly Viennese sound. The coupling is the second symphony. Maazel, with the same orchestra as Böhm, achieves greater exuberance.

BPO/Böhm, DG 2530422
BPO/Maazel, DG 2535128
ASMF/Marriner, Phil 6514208

Symphony no. 8 in B minor, D 759 – Unfinished

Maazel's recording was made in 1980 during a tour of Japan with the Vienna Philharmonic and this is taken from a live concert along with its uncommon coupling of Beethoven's fifth. Maazel's vision is extremely personal, even somewhat bizarre, taking the allegro moderato on the slow side, which produces moments of great dramatic tension but provides insufficient contrast with the following andante. The performance is also available on Compact Disc (CBS CD36711). Carlos Kleiber regards the work from almost exactly the opposite point of view, hurrying through the first movement and blurring the inner contrasts of the first and second themes. Karajan's sensible easy-going approach with the Berlin Philharmonic gives Schubert's music far greater naturalness. Toscanini's interpretation, coupled with Mozart's symphony no. 40, is of historical interest. A Compact Disc issue exists by Jordan and the Symphony Orchestra of Basel.

VPO/Kleiber, DG 2531124
BaselSO/Jordan, Erato ECD 88008
BPO/Karajan, EMI 065-03288
VPO/Maazel, CBS 36711
Toscanini, RCA VL 46003

Symphony no. 9 in C major, D.944 – Great

Loughran, in pursuit of a certain authenticity and integrity of interpretation, takes all the repeats, giving Schubert's ninth its true 'Heavenly length', an undertaking of considerable artistic merit; most of his illustrious colleagues omit the exposition repeats in the outer movements. The Hallé Orchestra however does not possess the refinement of orchestral sound available to Solti and Böhm. Böhm's performance with the Dresden State Orchestra, recorded at a concert in January 1979, furnishes a brilliant testimony to his deep admiration for Schubert, with well chosen tempos and great elasticity. Maazel's reading is also available on Compact Disc (Decca CD400082-2).

DSO/Böhm, DG 2531352
BPO/Furtwängler, DG 2535808
Hallé/Loughran, ASV ALH 905
VPO/Solti, Decca SXDL 7557
CO/Haitink, Phil 9500097

Complete symphonies

Muti gives affectionate and warm-blooded interpretations of all four symphonies, yet he sometimes inclines a little towards theatricality. His control of detail is excellent. The opening movement of the first symphony is definitely taken too fast, and loses out to lightness as a result. The remaining symphonies are faultlessly put over with great feeling for the music. Solti's reading of the first symphony is in the same class as his exemplary performances of the others. Not just the Florestan side, but also the Eusebius side, of Schumann's character is portrayed in all its fullness: turbulence and tenderness in incomparable balance. Levine, who shares with Solti a leaning towards the dramatic, comes less close to Schumann's gentle features. Kubelik, who has recorded all these symphonies once before for DG, is wise enough not to overreach himself in the new CBS version. The tone of the orchestra is sometimes rough. Karajan's perception is very sensitive.

BPO/Karajan, DG 2720104
PO/Muti, EMI 153-53704/6
SOBR/Kubelik, CBS 79324
PO/Levine, RCA RL 03907
VPO/Solti, Decca D 190 D3

Symphony no. 1 in B flat major, opus 38 – Spring

Muti's version, the last recorded in his survey of all Schumann's symphonies, is, oddly enough, the least convincing. He does deserve praise for presenting the work in its entirety, including all repeats, but this works to the advantage only of the outer movements; the overall symphonic structure loses something of its power, and the middle movements seem curiously underdeveloped. Muti is noticeably more successful in the coupling, Mendelssohn's Reformation Symphony. Kubelik's and Karajan's discs contain the first and the fourth symphonies. Karajan is the more energetic, but both performances are richly imaginative and both conductors draw from the same orchestra a sound of impressive substance and warmth.

BPO/Karajan, DG 2530169
BPO/Kubelik, DG 2535116
PO/Muti, EMI 063-03640

Scriabin

Shostako-vich

Symphony no. 3 in E flat major – Rhenish

Giulini's conception of the Rhenish brings out a distinct earthiness in the music but is not lacking in the necessary temperament. Clarity and exact definition are wanting from the LP version, but on Compact Disc this has been set to rights, the tuttis especially have far greater brilliance and transparency. The fill-up, the Manfred overture, is given a particularly sober reading, closer to Beethoven's Coriolanus than to Byron's Romantic hero. Kubelik performs this overture with greater openness and fire, and despite (or perhaps because of) the unmannered naturalness of his conducting, he gives to the third symphony a remarkably warm expression. The Rhenish is a lively work but with an underlying nobility of character, and Muti emphasizes this noble quality most eloquently. A work from Schumann's last years, the overture to Schiller's, play The Bride of Messina, forms an agreeable 'encore'. A recent recording by Mehta and the Vienna Philharmonic is also available.

LAPO/Giulini, DG 2532040
BPO/Kubelik, DG 2535118
PO/Muti, HMV ASD 3696
VPO/Mehta, Decca SXDL 7555

Symphony no. 4 in D minor, opus 120

Schumann's fourth symphony is usually coupled with his Spring Symphony or Mendelssohn's Italian. Böhm departs from tradition by combining it with Schubert's fifth symphony. He unfolds the symphony weightily by choosing broad tempos, but in so doing he loses tension. Tennstedt is definitely livelier; he raises the tension almost bar by bar. He gives a completely different view of this work than he does of Mendelssohn's Italian, which lacks flair. The digital recording has little brilliance but is sufficiently well defined to show up the fine playing of the Berliners. Furtwängler's historic recording of the same two works offers considerably more than Tennstedt's. Kubelik includes Schumann's first symphony with the fourth.

BPO/Karajan DG 2530169
BPO/Kubelik DG 2535116
BPO/Furtwängler DG 2535805
NPhO/Muti EMI 063-02876
BPO/Tennstedt EMI 067-03904

Symphonies 1–3

Symphonies no. 1 in E major, opus 26, no. 2 in C minor, opus 29; and no. 3 in the same key (with the title Le divin poème) have been added to Le poème de l'extase opus 54 and Prometheus opus 60 in a four-disc set, the only available recording of these works. Eliahu Inbal conducts a highly-polished performance, with the lovely-sounding choir of the Frankfurter Kantorei. Yet these elegant recordings are no match for the now-deleted performances of Yevgeny Svetlanov, notwithstanding the often rougher orchestral edge.

SO Frankfurt/Inbal Phil 676904

Symphonies nos. 1–3

On two digitally recorded discs, Haitink makes a sympathetic plea for the wider appreciation of Shostakovich's first three symphonies. Nos. 2 and 3 are on one record (SXDL 7535), while no. 1 appears on the other side of a recording of the ninth symphony. The performances have good, rich sound, clearly detailed throughout, though the first symphony seems to lack a little in excitement. The second and third symphonies are signally more successful, as Haitink allows himself a more idiomatic interpretation of the score.
LPO/Haitink Decca SXDL 7515
LPO/Haitink Decca SXDL 7535

Symphony no. 4 in C minor, opus 43

The fourth symphony, written in 1960, is one of the composer's most complicated works to perform. The problem is how to express wild, animal passion and still adhere to the compact, closely-structured score. Aided by some excellent engineering in the studio, Haitink does bring unexpected clarity to this difficulty piece, but what he gains in design he loses in intensity and characterisation. Previn achieves more expressive results through the brilliant playing of the Chicago Symphony Orchestra, but his thundering, apocalyptic vision suffers inevitably from a marked lack of clarity.

CSO/Previn, HMV ASD 3440
LPO/Haitink, Decca SXL 6927

Symphony no. 5 in D minor, opus 47

Bernstein's Romantic account of the fifth symphony was recorded at a public concert. It presents the work as a dramatic series of changes in mood: the first movement establishes a tension which remains brooding through the Mahlerian allegretto. In the slow movement, a sense of tragedy builds up inexorably, only to be dissolved in a brilliant finale.

Previn, while sticking closer to the published score, also manages to give a spontaneous and exciting account. There are also several Compact Disc recordings.

NYPO/Bernstein, CBS D35854
NSO/Rostropovich, DG 2532076
CO/Haitink, Phil. CD 410017-2
CSO/Previn, EMI 063-12957

Symphony no. 7 in C major, opus 60
Leningrad

This four-movement work, once described as an instrumental requiem for human suffering and violence, has its often overpowering and remorseless drive leavened with some passages of great lyrical beauty. It is of Mahlerian length (particularly the first and last movements), and receives in Haitink's performance an interpretation of deeply-felt sincerity. In this exemplary digital recording, he eschews any temptation to over-sensationalise the drama of the work. Even the notorious drum ostinato in the first movement, which is repeated 175 times, is shaped in a way that is nothing less than masterly.

LPO/Haitink, Decca D213 D2
Bournemouth/Berglund, EMi 163-05671/2
Moscow PO/Kondrashin, HMV SLS 5109

Symphony no. 9 in E flat major, opus 70

The ninth symphony of Shostakovich has sometimes been considered banal. Haitink shows that behind the lightness there is a sarcastic melancholy that lifts this short work above the level of superficiality. The London Philharmonic plays beautifully, and the digital recording is clear throughout. Neumann and the Czech Philharmonic Orchestra achieve a comparable liveliness in their version, but his interpretation of the Leningrad cannot compare with Haitink's.

LPO/Haitink, Decca SXDL 7515
CzPO/Neumann, Supr. 1101771-2

Symphony no. 13 in B flat minor – Babi Yar

This mighty work is a setting of poems by Yevtushenko, and brought its composer a lot of trouble. Its ill-concealed denunciation of the Soviet regime caused the symphony to be banned in Russia for several years after only three performances. Kondrashin's recording with the Bavarian Radio Symphony Orchestra was made at a public concert in 1981. it is a controlled and expressive account, in which the vocal and instrumental elements are carefully balanced. The bass Shirley-Quirk's performance is especially outstanding, and contributes enormously to increasing the symphony's dramatic power.

Previn concentrates more on the work's symphonic elements, often at the expense of the poetry's dark and lyrical beauty; but EMI give him a much better recording than Kondrashin receives from Philips.

LSO/Previn, EMI 063-3932
SOBR/Kondrashin, Phil 6514120

Symphony no. 14, opus 135

This grim and doom-laden work is a setting of eleven poems by, among others, Apollinaire, Lorca and Rilke. The importance of the words is paramount in this condemnation of tyranny, which is probably why Haitink chose to perform the poems in their original language rather than in the Russian translations that the composer used. It is a beautiful, moving and compelling performance, excellently recorded, that brings out all the passion, bitterness and despair of the poetry. Julia Varády and Dietrich Fischer-Dieskau are ideal soloists.

CO/Haitink, Decca SXDL 7 532
NYPO/Bernstein, CBS 7 4084

Sibelius

Symphony no. 15 in A major, opus 141

Haitink is already more than half-way to accomplishing his intention of recording all 15 symphonies of Shostakovich, and he will be the first non-Russian conductor to achieve this feat. He imbues this strange and idiosyncratic work with a cohesion that was all too often lacking in earlier accounts of it. The musical quotations, such as those from Wagner and Rossini, that Shostakovich used, are blended into the whole by Haitink not just with polish but with the most sensitive feeling for musical balance. As in previous symphonies, the playing of the London Philharmonic leaves nothing to be desired; and while the recording was made too early to be digital, the sound is very good.

LPO/Haitink, Decca SXL 6906

Symphony no. 1 in E minor, opus 39

Berglund with great munificence offers the first and seventh symphonies of Sibelius on one disc, enhancing the nobility of the composer's thought with a polished orchestral sound. The gloomy side of the composer receives greater attention in Tjeknavorian's version. The London Philharmonic Orchestra's playing, here as in 'The Swan of Tuonela', is reliable without being perfect. The same may also be said of the playing of the Helsinki ensemble. Karajan's excellent interpretation is followed by the Karelia Suite.

BPO/Karajan EMI 067-43050
RSOHelsinki/Kamu DG 2535457
LPO/Tjeknavorian RCA RL 25316
BournS/Berglund EMI ESD 7095

Symphony no. 2 in D major, opus 43

In both recordings by the Berlin Philharmonic, under the direction of Okko Kamu and Karajan alike, it is the precision and refinement of the orchestral playing that are striking. Thanks to digital recording, Karajan's reading has rather more clarity, with an excellent balance of dynamic contrasts between groups of instruments and varieties of timbre. In Askhenazy's interpretation too the great waywardness of the score in tempo and mood finds clear expression, but the broad tension sustained by Karajan and Kamu, especially in the slow movement, is lacking.

PO/Ashkenazy, Decca SXDL 7513
BPO/Karajan, EMI 067-43040
BPO/Kamu DG 2535458

Symphony no. 3 in C major, opus 52

Berglund offers a most generous coupling of the third and fifth symphonies at a reasonable price. His interpretation is good, carried out with an orchestra that plays accurately but without much sparkle. Kamu's sparkling reading excels in mood-painting and precision of tempo and dynamics. An excellent En Saga fills up the disc.

BournS/Berglund, EMI ESD 7094
RSOHelsinki/Kamu, DG 2535459

Symphony no. 4 in A minor, opus 63

Vladimir Ashkenazy gives a conscientious performance of this most audacious score, full of strange twists and turns. Fascinating moments of tone colour and instrumental technique come through as clearly as the contrasts in dynamics. This is impassioned music-making with a keen ear for freshness in orchestral sound. It is particularly interesting that Ashkenazy teams it with Finlandia and the song with orchestral accompaniment, by Elisabeth Söderström. Karajan draws a very rich sound from the Berlin Philharmonic, which does not seem an ideal means of penetrating the complex heart of the music, but the concentration of the reading produces great intensity. The disc is filled up with Valse Triste.

PO/Ashkenazy, Decca SXDL 7517
PO/Ashkenazy, Decca CD 40056-2
BPO/Karajan, DG 2535359

Tchaikovsky

Symphony no. 5 in E flat major, opus 82

Simon Rattle and Vladimir Ashkenazy have both recorded this most frequently played of Sibelius's later symphonies with the Philharmonia Orchestra. Both have found in it a very responsive ensemble, with which precision in technical finish, dynamics and distribution of tone colour can be achieved. Ashkenazy knows how to introduce a Romantic glow at the same time. The digital recording, which is also numbered in the CD series (Decca CD 410016-2), sounds very natural. Rattle's choice of tempo shown in the breadth of the first movement agrees with Karajan's reading, but differs from it in the less forced speed of the scherzo. The coupling with 'Night Ride and Sunrise', opus 55, makes Rattle's carefully proportioned performance extra attractive. Mention must be made of Berglund's attractively priced disc, which combines Sibelius's third and fifth.

PO/Ashkenazy, Decca SXDL 7541
PO/Rattle, EMI 067-07568
BPO/Karajan, EMI 065-02984
BournS/Berglund EMI ESD 7094

Symphonies

With the Berlin Philharmonic, Karajan has put the mature symphonies, from no. 4 up to and including no. 7, on to four discs, with richness of sound producing the maximum possible intensity of interpretation. A survey of all seven symphonies by Karajan is in preparation. Berglund has issued his complete recording of Sibelius's symphonies, including the Kullervo, which predates the first symphony, in singles. Scores are provided for all the symphonies (with some of the minor mistakes in the Hansen scores corrected); Berglund fails to put his own personal stamp on them. Davis, who displays similar integrity with regard to the scores, takes a very personal view, with great vitality and intensity. The playing of the Boston Symphony Orchestra is exemplary.

BPO/Karajan, DG 2740255
BSO/Davis, Phil 6709011
BournS/Berglund, EMI 151-06734/40
BournS/Berglund, EMI SLS 5129

Complete symphonies

After spending ten years in concentrating exclusively on the three later symphonies of Tchaikovsky, in 1979 Karajan turned his attention to the three earlier ones. However, in his complete version no break is detectable, although he had already committed the later symphonies to disc more than three times by 1979. The sharp rhythms which Karajan injects into the tone of the first three symphonies are of vital importance for a true understanding of these early, richly syncopated works. In contrast to Karajan, Haitink also includes the Manfred symphony in his complete set. Again in contrast to Karajan, Haitink respects all the markings on the scores, with regard alike to tempo changes, dynamics and colour.

BP/Karajan, DG 2720104
CO/Haitink, Phil 6768267

Symphony no. 1 in G minor, opus 13 – Winter Dreams

The recordings of Tchaikovsky's Winter Dreams symphony can compete on equal terms. Haitink and Karajan each develop a great richness of sound with their orchestras. It must also be mentioned that DG's tone-palate is sometimes rather unnaturally coloured, and the dynamic contrasts over-strongly marked, because of recording techniques. Karajan shows a fresher, more spontaneous inspiration than in his recordings of the later symphonies. Haitink's happy-go-lucky approach produces a reading free from exaggeration. Muti's interpretation is a good alternative.

BPO/Karajan, DG 2531285
CO/Haitink, Phil 9510777
NPhilO/Muti, EMI 063-02691

Symphony no. 2 in C minor, opus 17 – Little Russian

The comments made on Karajan's and Haitink's interpretations and recordings of the first symphony also hold good for the Little Russian. Moreover, it can even be said that Haitink chooses broader tempos for the slow introduction and the slow movement, thus achieving a relaxed and solemn expressiveness. An unusual bonus comes in the shape of Haitink's fill-up, the early work, The Storm. There are a number of excellent, low-priced other versions of the second symphony, which is well represented in discography, among which Previn's version deserves mention. He makes music with freshness and warmth. Liadov's eight Russian folksongs are also provided on the disc. Muti's exciting reading is complemented by an equally excellent Romeo and Juliet.

BPO/Karajan, DG 2531285
CO/Haitink, Phil 9500444
PO/Muti, EMI 063-02991
LSO/Previn, RCA GL 42960

Vaughan-Williams

Symphony no. 3 in D major, opus 29 – Polish

Muti, Karajan and Haitink have all produced model recordings, artistically as well as technically. The orchestral sound is in each case full of warmth and charm. Muti and Haitink have it in common that they indicate the ballet associations of the middle movements by their lightness of touch. Karajan's vision is symphonic in scale, with a tendency towards heavy-handedness, but always sparkling.

BPO/Karajan, DG 2531286
CO/Haitink, Phil 9500776
PO/Muti, EMI 063-2990

Symphony no. 4 in F minor, opus 36

This deservedly popular work has long been a great favourite with orchestral players as well as conductors and their audiences. Of the many recordings currently available, that by Igor Markevitch and the London Symphony Orchestra is particularly exciting, filled with power and energy.
Riccardo Muti and the Philharmonia give a performance that has great tension and a crackling pace, and the virtuoso playing of the orchestra in the fast movements is truly awe-inspiring. The version by Haitink and the Concertgebouw is also to be highly recommended, with the orchestral sound beautifully captured in the recording.

LSO/Markevitch, Phil Fest 6570 153
PO/Muti, HMV ASD 3816
CO/Haitink, Phil 9500 622

Symphony no. 5 in E minor, opus 64

The grandeur and scale of this thrilling work are well served by a recording made by Karl Böhm and the London Symphony Orchestra. Unlike many other conductors, he resists the temptation to let the music run away with him, and pays his customary attention to the finest details of the score.
The only account that would seem to rival it in the catalogues is one by the Philharmonia Orchestra with Vladimir Ashkenazy. It is a performance of great passion and urgency, with a third-movement waltz of irresistible charm. Seiji Ozawa and the Boston Symphony Orchestra have made a recording with very stylish playing and an overwhelming orchestral sound, lacking only the Russian ardour of Ashkenazy's version.

LSO/Böhm, DG 2532005
PO/Ashkenazy, Decca SXL 6884
BSO/Ozawa, DG 2530888

Symphony no. 6 in B minor – Pathétique

Tchaikovsky's last and – in the opinion of many – greatest symphony is notoriously vulnerable to widely differing interpretations. The most passionate and persuasive is that of Sir Georg Solti and the Chicago Symphony Orchestra, whose ardent approach to this profoundly human music is deeply moving.
Haitink's recording with the Concertgebouw is cooler than Solti's, but contains wonderful, long-spanned phrasing and sumptuous playing from the violins. Two Russian conductors have also made outstanding versions: Rostropovich with the London Philharmonic Orchestra, in a performance whose personality is deeply felt; and Ashkenazy, who steers the Philharmonia through this difficult work with a warm and invigorating spontaneity.

CSO/Solti, Decca SXL 6814
CO/Haitink, Phil 9500 610
LPO/Rostropovich, HMV ASD 3515
PO/Ashkenazy, Decca SXL 6941

Symphonies 1–9

Vaughan Williams's complete output of symphonies was committed to disc by André Previn in the years between 1968 and 1972. The set of nine is available in one box of seven discs, but the individual symphonies may also be bought separately. Those who find nine symphonies rather too much of a good thing would do well to choose Previn's very striking interpretation of the second (RCA GL 43557), the third (RCA GL 43580, also including the tuba concerto) and the fifth symphony (RCA GL 43578, coupled with the overture, The Wasps). Especially in these three works Previn achieves great depth of expression as well as of sheer musicianship. Apart from that, all nine symphonies receive very finished performances with excellent playing from the London Symphony Orchestra.

LSO/Previn, RCA RL 43371 (7)

A recording session in London under the direction of Sir Colin Davis.

Glossary

Technical terms have been avoided wherever possible throughout the book, but some words, phrases and Italian (the 'lingua franca' of music) terms are unavoidable. These are briefly explained in the following glossary, though for detailed, comprehensive information the reader is recommended to one of the numerous and inexpensive paperback dictionaries of music.

Accidentals: Sharps or flats attached to single notes, signifying they are not part of the same scale as the key of a piece.

Adagio: Slow. Also used to mean the movement of a symphony etc. marked with the speed direction Adagio.

Allegretto: At moderate speed; between allegro and andante.

Allegro: Lightly and quickly.

Allemande: German country dance, moderately lively and in quadruple time.

Andante: Literally, at walking pace. Fairly slow, between allegretto and adagio.

Andantino: A little less slow than andante.

Appoggiatura: An embellishment or 'grace note' using most often an adjacent note above or below the main note, and taking part of its time.

Arpeggio: The notes of a chord not sounded simultaneously, but one after another; literally, 'harp-like'.

Bar: A vertical line in musical notation which divides the written music into equal time spaces containing the same number of beats. The American term is 'measure'.

Bar, double: A vertical line embellished with two dots, which instructs the performer to go back and repeat the passage.

Bourrée: Fast French dance in duple time.

Cadence: Short passage signifying the end of a musical phrase, often consisting merely of two chords, like the 'Amen' at the end of a hymn for example.

Cadenza: A florid passage for the soloist, usually near the end of a concerto movement or aria, where the performer can show off his virtuosity. The music may be written by the composer, or there may just be a 'general pause' in which the performer supplies his own cadenza.

Canon: A contrapuntal composition in which parts (or voices) take up the same melody one after another. 'Three Blind Mice' is an example.

Cantabile:	Literally, in singing style; signifying the music is to be performed smoothly and lyrically.
Cantata:	Literally, a work that is sung rather than played ('sonata'); this is an extended work for voice(s) usually with orchestral accompaniment.
Capo, da:	A sign instructing the performer to repeat a passage.
Chaconne:	A slow French dance in triple time, but may also be a set of variations over a bass (see also Passacaglia).
Chorale:	A hymn-tune, generally from the German Protestant Church.
Chord:	Group of three or more notes sounded together.
Coda:	The 'tailpiece' of a section or musical movement which rounds it off.
Concerto:	A work, generally in three movements, for solo instrument(s) and orchestra.
Concerto Grosso:	Orchestral work in several movements, of the Baroque period, in which a small group of instruments is contrasted with the larger orchestral forces.
Courante:	A rapid French or Italian dance in triple time.
Counterpoint:	The art of combining melodies, above and below each other in such a way as to make harmonic sense.
Divertimento:	Light orchestral work, which may contain a number of contrasting dance movements.
Dominant:	The fifth note of the scale; and, by extension, the key of the fifth note. E major therefore is said to be 'dominant' in the key of A major.
Dotted:	A dot after a note increases its time value by one half. Dotted rhythm therefore consists of many adjacent notes of unequal length, and sounds 'jerky'.
Forte:	Loudly.
Fortissimo:	Very loudly.
Fugato:	In the style of a fugue (q.v.).
Fugue:	A polyphonic composition in which a short melody, known as the theme or subject, is introduced and taken up in turn by the other parts. Not as strict as canon (q.v.), it contains numerous restatements of the subject, interspersed with free episodes.
Galliard:	A lively dance in triple time.
Gavotte:	Originally a slow dance from the Alps; now a dance movement in quadruple time, beginning on the third beat of the bar.
Gigue:	Jig. A lively dance in dotted rhythm.
Harmony:	Simultaneous sounding of notes, and the art of doing this to make musical sense.
Key:	Term referring to the particular scale in which the music is set. There are twelve different major keys, from A to G including sharps and flats, and twelve minor, making twenty-four in all.
Ländler:	A rustic Austrian dance in triple time, from which the waltz developed.
Larghetto:	Not quite as slow as Largo.
Largo:	Slow, stately and solemn, often tragic in character.
Legato:	Notes played smoothly one after another, as in a single movement of a bow. The opposite of Staccato (q.v.).
Maestoso:	Majestically.
Major:	One of the two modes, together with Minor, in which diatonic music is set.
Malizia, con:	Slyly.
Marcia:	March, in march-time.
Minor:	see Major.
Minuet:	Originally a French country dance in triple time, the minuet was gradually refined into a stately and formal dance. In this form it

	is used as one of the movements in a symphony or sonata, though later replaced by the scherzo.
Moderato:	At moderate speed.
Modulation:	Moving from one key to another.
Octave:	The interval composed of the first and eighth notes of the scale, e.g. the note C and the next C above or below it.
Opera buffa:	Comic opera, often containing spoken dialogue.
Opera, grand:	Opera without spoken dialogue.
Oratorio:	An opera for soloists, choir and orchestra, but without staging, and often on a sacred subject.
Overture:	An orchestral prelude or introductory musical piece. A concert overture, however, is generally self-contained and more extended, such as Mendelssohn's **Hebrides.**
Passacaglia:	A slow and stately dance in triple time; see Chaconne.
Pavane:	A slow, elegant dance in duple time.
Pentatonic scale:	Scale of five notes, equivalent to the black keys on the piano. It is often used in folk-music: the well-known 'Auld Lang Syne' employs it.
Pianissimo:	Very softly.
Piano:	Softly.
Pizzicato:	Plucked; strings plucked with the fingers instead of played with the bow.
Ponticello, sul:	Literally, on the little bridge. Method of playing a string instrument with the bow close to the bridge, thus modifying the sound.
Prestissimo:	Very quickly.
Presto:	Fast.
Quadruple:	Four beats in the bar.
Quaver:	(Amer: eighth-note). Note equal in length to half a crotchet (Amer: quarter-note).
Recitative:	Free, declamatory sung speech, providing narrative between arias etc. in opera and oratorio.
Rhapsody:	Romantic orchestral or instrumental piece, in no set form.
Romanze:	Song-like short instrumental or orchestral piece.
Rondo:	Piece in which the principal melody returns repeatedly, interspersed with other themes and episodes.
Ruhig:	(Ger.) Quietly, gently.
Saltarello:	Lively, skipping dance in triple time.
Sarabande:	Slow dance in triple time, with the accent on the second beat.
Scherzo:	A light and lively movement which replaced the minuet in symphonies, sonatas etc. Generally the third movement.
Semibreve:	(Amer: Whole-note). The longest note in current musical usage, equal to four crotchets (quarter-notes).
Serenade:	Light instrumental work in several movements.
Sinfonia:	In the baroque period this was an overture (q.v.) or instrumental interlude in a vocal work.
Singspiel:	A light theatrical opera, sung and partly spoken. An English example is the ballad opera, **The Beggar's Opera.**
Sonata:	Originally music played as opposed to sung (cantata); it has come to mean an instrumental work from the Classical period and later in three or (more usually) four movements. A symphony is a sonata for orchestra.
Sonata form:	See p 15.
Sostenuto:	Sustained.
Staccato:	Opposite of staccato (q.v.). Notes or chords to be played in a sharply divided manner.

Syncopation:	A displacing of the rhythmic accent or stress on to the weak beats of the bar.
Tarantella:	A rapid dance in 6/8 (dotted) time.
Tempo:	Time indication – allegro, andante etc. – in which a piece is to be played.
Time:	Quite simply, the number of beats in a bar.
Timpani:	Kettledrums. These are tuned to required pitches, whereas the bass drum simply booms.
Tonic:	The keynote. In the key of C, C (the first note of the scale) is the tonic.
Tremolo:	Quavering effect, usually on strings, in instrumental music, produced by rapid alternations of the bow on the same note.
Tutti:	All the orchestral forces playing together.
Vibrato:	Alternating of a note, as in a trill, rapidly with one slightly above or below it. Often confused with Tremolo (q.v.).
Vivace:	Lively.

Index

The editor and publishers would like to express their thanks to the following for their help with THE GREAT SYMPHONIES: Jane Deam, Ferdie McDonald, Bruce Bernard, Jan van Bart and the Paul Stokes Society. Also to Bob Bouma and Wim Huslage of Phonogram International for their assistance with the illustrations, in particular the photographs of Seiji Ozawa (by Michael Evans), of Leonard Bernstein (bij Werner Neumeister) and of The Concertgebouw Orchestra by A3-Studio (on pp 182/183).